Lecture Notes in Computer Science   8897

Commenced Publication in 1973
Founding and Former Series Editors:
Gerhard Goos, Juris Hartmanis, and Jan van Leeuwen

Virginio Cantoni · Dimo Dimov
Massimo Tistarelli (Eds.)

Biometric Authentication

First International Workshop, BIOMET 2014
Sofia, Bulgaria, June 23–24, 2014
Revised Selected Papers

Editors

Virginio Cantoni
University of Pavia
Pavia
Italy

Dimo Dimov
Bulgarian Academy of Sciences
Sofia
Bulgaria

Massimo Tistarelli
University of Sassari
Alghero
Sassari
Italy

ISSN 0302-9743   ISSN 1611-3349   (electronic)
Lecture Notes in Computer Science
ISBN 978-3-319-13385-0   ISBN 978-3-319-13386-7   (eBook)
DOI 10.1007/978-3-319-13386-7

Library of Congress Control Number: 2014957391

LNCS Sublibrary: SL6 – Image Processing, Computer Vision, Pattern Recognition, and Graphics

Springer Cham Heidelberg New York Dordrecht London

Printed on acid-free paper

Springer International Publishing AG Switzerland is part of Springer Science+Business Media
(www.springer.com)

Preface

The following are the Proceedings of the First International Workshop on Biometrics (BIOMET 2014), held in Sofia, Bulgaria, during June 23–24, 2014. This initiative is part of the FP7 Capacity Programme project AComIn (Advanced Computing for Innovation) of the Institute of Information and Communication Technologies at Bulgarian Academy of Sciences (IICT-BAS). Besides, the Workshop was organized with the active participation of key members of the European COST Action IC1106 (Integrating Biometrics and Forensics for the Digital Age). Another scientific community that cooperated in the organization of the Workshop is the Technical Committee on Biometrics of the GIRPR (Group of Italian Researchers in Pattern Recognition) as well as the Computer Vision and Multimedia Laboratory (CVML) of the University of Pavia (Italy).

BIOMET 2014 is intended to provide a forum to present the current work and new ideas in this challenging field. It renovates and continues the Biometrics tradition (2007–2010) of the CompSysTech International Conferences, one of the longest running international conferences in computer science in Bulgaria that started in 2000. At the same time, BIOMET 2014 is primarily connected with the goals of the IICT-BAS's AComIn project (http://www.iict.bas.bg/acomin) to disseminate recent advances in Biometrics among the research groups and companies in Bulgaria and Balkan countries as well.

The Workshop consisted of a pilot phase of four invited lectures, from renowned world experts, on the state of the art of the Workshop's main thematics, and suggesting possible synergies between different modalities and strategies, stressing links and outlining open questions. In detail, the four basic thematics were given by Mark Nixon ("On Semantic Soft-Biometric Labels"), Andrzej Drygajlo ("From Speaker Recognition to Forensic Speaker Recognition"), Massimo Tistarelli ("Biometrics in Forensic Science: Challenges, Lessons and New Technologies"), and Chang-Tsun Li ("People Identification and Tracking Through Fusion of Face and Gait Features"). Besides these advances, seven special sessions were organized in conjunction with the workshop submissions in order to fathom a few selected topics of current interest: Gait and behavior analysis; Iris analysis and eye tracking; Voice recognition and speech analysis; 3D ear recognition; Face and facial attributes analysis; Handwriting and signature recognition; Multimodal and soft biometrics. The volume's Table of Contents varies somewhat from the scheduled Workshop program, to accommodate the various positions that emerged as significant contributions in the paper discussions and from the debates.

The Workshop raised considerable interest among researchers from different fields, and this volume has emerged from an intense and careful reviewing process which perfected the highly qualified papers submitted. The good number of contributions concerning real-world applications attests to the field's maturity.

Besides the four invited papers, further 17 papers were presented at the Workshop, and the number of participants and listeners topped 30, half of them from Bulgaria, as well as from Italy, the UK, Cyprus, Finland, Saudi Arabia, etc. A paper from Iran was also presented *in absentia*. For young participants in the Workshop, the GIRPR offered a best student paper award to promote their contributions, give them opportunities to interact with senior colleagues, and sustain our initiative. In recognition of the originality of his research, the quality of his presentation and contribution to the development of biometrics, the award was conferred on Atanas Nikolov, a PhD student in the Institute for Information and Communication Technology of the Bulgarian Academy of Sciences.

Face, voice, fingerprint, and signature recognition were the main inspiration and driving forces behind the practical application of authentication and identification processes. Presently, new challenges are arising from areas like the iris but also gait and the ear considered with both 2D and 3D data are increasingly being investigated. But very often, it is the merging of a subset of these sources that comes to be considered even in practical applications, naturally paying careful attention to meeting computational demands. Multimodal approaches may improve authentication and identification through more effectiveness, provided that the different modes are combined synergistically. Nevertheless, how to integrate the different modes is still a subject for research. We expect that research regarding these topics will increase rapidly. On the whole, these proceedings represent the latest results from both academia and industry and address challenging topics in the field.

Acknowledgments

The Workshop, and thus indirectly these proceedings, have been made possible through the generous financial support of the AComIn project of IICT-BAS, and the organizational backing of the CVML of the University of Pavia (Italy). The Signal Processing and Pattern Recognition Department of IICT-BAS has also well contributed to the Workshop's organization. Their support is gratefully acknowledged.

The editors would also like to express their appreciation to the Program Committee members for reviewing the submitted papers as well as to the invited lecturers for their suggestions during the Workshop. Thanks must also go to the Bulgarian Academy of Sciences, and especially to Prof. Svetozar Margenov, the Director of IICT-BAS, and to the administration of IICT-BAS as well as all those who helped in the organization and gave hospitality to the Workshop.

Special thanks must go to Prof. Galia Angelova, coordinator of the AComIn project, for her precious help and patience in organizing the Workshop. Particular appreciation goes to Alessandra Setti from the University of Pavia, our scientific secretary, for her precision in managing the process of communication (information, papers, reviews, etc.) as well as for her skill in keeping up the workshop site (http://vision.unipv.it/SOFIA-2014/).

July 2014   Virginio Cantoni
                                                      Dimo Dimov
                                                 Massimo Tistarelli

Organization

Committees

General Chair

Virginio Cantoni   University of Pavia, Italy

Workshop Chair

Dimo Dimov   Bulgarian Academy of Sciences, Sofia, Bulgaria

Program Chair

Massimo Tistarelli   University of Sassari, Italy

Organization Chair

Alessandra Setti   University of Pavia, Italy

Program Committee

Gennady Agre   Bulgarian Academy of Sciences, Sofia, Bulgaria
Kiril Alexiev   Bulgarian Academy of Sciences, Sofia, Bulgaria
Ognian Boumbarov   Technical University of Sofia, Bulgaria
Maria De Marsico   University of Rome "Sapienza", Italy
Jana Dittmann   Magdeburg University, Germany
Michael Fairhurst   University of Kent, UK
Georgi Gluhchev   Bulgarian Academy of Sciences, Sofia, Bulgaria
Stefan Hadjitodorov   Bulgarian Academy of Sciences, Sofia, Bulgaria
Svetozar Margenov   Bulgarian Academy of Sciences, Sofia, Bulgaria
Michele Nappi   University of Salerno, Italy
Stavri Nikolov   Attentive Displays Ltd., Sofia, BG
Javier Ortega-Garcia   Autonomous University of Madrid, Spain
Marco Porta   University of Pavia, Italy
Slobodan Ribarić   University of Zagreb, Croatia
Pencho Venkov   Technical University of Sofia, Bulgaria

Contents

Gait and Behaviour Analysis

On Semantic Soft-Biometric Labels

Sina Samangooei and Mark S. Nixon[✉]

School of Electronics and Computer Science, University of Southampton,
Southampton, UK
msn@ecs.soton.ac.uk

Abstract. A new approach to soft biometrics aims to use human labelling as part of the process. This is consistent with analysis of surveillance video where people might be imaged at too low resolution or quality for conventional biometrics to be deployed. In this manner, people use anatomical descriptions of subjects to achieve recognition, rather than the usual measurements of personal characteristics used in biometrics. As such the labels need careful consideration in their construction, and should demonstrate correlation consistent with known human physiology. We describe our original process for generating these labels and analyse relationships between them. This gives insight into the perspicacity of using a human labelling system for biometric purposes.

Keywords: Soft Biometrics · Human Descriptions · Retrieval · Semantic Labels

1   Introduction

Descriptions of humans based on their physical features has been explored for several purposes including medicine, eyewitness analysis [1] and human identification [2]. Descriptions gathered vary in levels of visual granularity and include features that can be measured visibly and those that are only measurable using specialised tools. To understand the recent use of labels for recognition [3, 4], we must explore the semantic terms people use to describe one another. Once these terms are outlined, the second task becomes the collection of a set of manually ascribed annotations against these terms. In isolation these terms allow the exploration of semantic descriptions as a tool for identification. To explore their capabilities in biometric fusion and automatic retrieval, these annotations must be collected against a set of individuals in an existing biometric dataset.

We developed [3] a set of key semantic terms people use to describe one another at a distance. We start with an overview of human description, from early anthropometry, to modern usage in police evidence forms and in soft biometrics. We then outline a set of key physiological traits observable at a distance and explore a set of semantic terms used for their description. The contents of the semantic annotation datasets are examined and we perform correlation analysis, exploring the underlying structures and other facets of the gathered data. We describe a study of the labels and their properties, concerning in particular information content and utility.

© Springer International Publishing Switzerland 2014
V. Cantoni et al. (Eds.): BIOMET 2014, LNCS 8897, pp. 3–15, 2014.
DOI: 10.1007/978-3-319-13386-7_1

2   Bertillonage

One of the first attempts to systematically describe people for identification based on their physiological traits was the anthropometric system developed by Bertillon [5] in 1879. By 1809 France had abandoned early methods of criminal identification such as branding. However, no systematic method of identification was outlined as an alternative, which meant the verification of repeat offenders or confirmation of criminals' identity of was nearly impossible. Long descriptions, including semantic terms such as "Large" or "Average" to describe height and limbs, proved inadequate due to subjectivity as well as to disproportionate numbers of individuals of "Average" height and "Brown" haired. This, coupled with an uncontrolled lexicon, resulted in many descriptions which added nothing to identification process. By 1840, the photography of criminals was introduced. However, the photographic techniques themselves were not standardised and, though useful for confirmation of identity, a photograph is of little use in discovery of identity when relying on manual search. Bertillon noted the failings of the police identification and cataloguing system and developed his father's anthropological work to a more systematic method of identifying people. His system of anthropometrics, eponymously Bertillonage, outlined the tools and techniques for the careful measurement of:
- physiological features including length/width of head, lengths of certain fingers and the dimensions of the feet, arm, right ear and standing height;
- descriptions of the dimensions of the nose, eye and hair colour; and
- the description and location of notable scars, tattoos and other marks

FIGURE 11. 2D.
LEFT MIDDLE FINGER.

FIGURE 14.
LEFT FORE-ARM.

Fig. 1. Examples of Bertillon's gathering of measurements [5]

The method for gathering these features was outlined in Bertillon's manual [5] along with a set of diagrams (see Fig. 1). The measurements for a given individual were held on separate slides along with standardised photographs of the individual. The metrics of the system were chosen primarily to be simple so that they could be gathered accurately. As such measurements were taken by a trained individual, though not necessarily a skilled individual. To this end, features were chosen to allow easy identification of points to begin and to end measurement. The success of Bertillonage came from its ability to geometrically reduce the probability of type 1 errors. Though two individuals may have very similar height, the chance of the same two having similar measurements for the other features is unlikely. Furthermore, Bertillonage inherently allowed for efficient discovery of an individual's existing measurement card and therefore their identity. Cards were stored according to specific range combinations of each metric in a given order. As such that once new measurements of an unidentified individual were taken the identity of the individual could be easily ascertained.

Achieving great success and popularity in France, Bertillonage progressed to the United States as well as Great Britain in the late 19th century. Difficulties in cases such as West vs. West [6] (where Bertillonage could not reconcile differences between identical twins, though this was later disputed) led it being superseded by forms of identification such as fingerprint analysis (since the fingerprints of identical twins differ) and more recently biometric analysis. In spirit, all these systems attempt to reduce the identity of an individual to a representative and measurable set of classification metrics, though not using descriptions of the human body as a whole.

3   Data Acquisition

3.1   Traits

To match the advantages of automatic surveillance media, a primary concern is to choose traits that are discernible by humans at a distance. To do so, it is needed to determine which traits humans are able to consistently and accurately notice in each other and describe at a distance. The traits can be grouped by similar levels of meaning, namely:

- global traits (sex, ethnicity etc.)
- build features that describe the target's perceived somatotype (height, weight etc.); and
- head features, an area of the body humans pay great attention to if it is visible (hair colour, beards etc.).

With regards to global attributes, three independent traits - Age, Race and Sex – are agreed to be of primary significance in cognitive psychology with respect to human description. For gait, humans have been shown to successfully perceive such categories using generated point light experiments and in other adverse viewing conditions involving limited visual cues.

In eyewitness testimony research there is a relatively well formed notion of which features witnesses are most likely to recall when describing individuals. Koppen and Lochun [1] provide an investigation into witness descriptions in archival crime reports. Unsurprisingly, the most accurate and highly mentioned traits were Sex (95% of the respondents mentioned this and achieved 100% accuracy), Height (70% mention 52% accuracy), Race (64% mention 60% accuracy) and Skin Colour (56% mention, accuracy not discussed). Detailed head and face traits such as Eye Shape and Nose Shape are not mentioned as often and when they are mentioned, they appear to be inaccurate. More prominent head traits such as Hair Colour and Length are mentioned more consistently. Descriptive features which are visually prominent yet less permanent (e.g. clothing) often vary with time and are of less interest than other more permanent physical traits.

Traits regarding build are of particular interest in our investigation having a clear relationship with gait while still being reliably recalled by eyewitnesses at a distance. Few studies thus far have attempted to explore build in any amount of detail beyond passing mention of Height and Weight. MacLeod et al. [7] performed a unique analysis on whole body descriptions using bipolar scales to define traits. There were two phases in their approach towards developing a set of descriptive build traits.

Firstly a broad range of useful descriptive traits was outlined with a series of experiments where a mixture of moving and stationary subjects were presented to a group of annotators who were given unlimited time to describe the individuals. A total of 1238 descriptors were extracted, of which 1041 were descriptions of overall physique and the others were descriptions of motion. These descriptors were grouped together (where synonymous) and a set of 23 traits generated, each formulated as a bipolar five-point scale.

Secondly the reliability and descriptive capability of these traits was gauged. Annotators were asked to watch video footage of subjects walking at a regular pace around a room and rate them using the 23 traits identified. The annotators were then split into two groups randomly from which two mean values were extracted for each subject for each trait. Pearson's product-moment correlation coefficient (Pearson's r) was calculated between the sets of means and was used as an estimate of the reliability for each trait. Principal Components Analysis (PCA) was also used to group traits which represented similar underlying concepts. The 13 most reliable terms, the most representative of the principal components, have been incorporated into the final trait set described later.

3.2   Terms

Having outlined the considerations made in choosing the physical traits which should be collected, the next question is how these traits should be represented. One option for their representation is a free text description for each trait. The analysis of such data would require lexical analysis to correlate words used by different annotators. Following the example of existing soft biometric techniques, a mixture of semantic categorical metrics (e.g. Ethnicity) and value metrics (e.g. Height) could be used to represent the traits. Humans are generally less accurate when making value judgements when compared to category judgements. Therefore a compromise is to formulate all traits with sets of mutually exclusive semantic terms. This approach avoids the inaccuracies of value judgments, being more representative of the categorical nature of human cognition. Simultaneously this approach avoids the complex synonymic analysis that would be required to correlate two descriptions if free text descriptions were gathered. With categorical metrics there is an inherent risk that none of the categories fit, either because the information is unclear or due to the presence of a boundary case where any annotation whatsoever may feel disingenuous. For this purpose each trait is given the extra term "Unsure", allowing the user to make the ambiguity known. For reasons covered in Section 4 the "Unsure" annotation is also the default option for any given trait on the annotation user interface. What remains is the selection of semantic terms that best represent the many words that could be used to describe a particular trait. This task can be logically separated by considering those traits which are intuitively describable using discrete metrics and those intuitively requiring value metrics.

4   Semantic Annotation

In this section we describe the process undertaken to gather a novel dataset of semantic annotations of individuals in an existing biometric dataset. We outline the design of the data entry system created to allow the assignment of manual annotations of physical attributes to individuals. Using this system, individuals in the Southampton Large (A) HumanID Database (HIDDB) and the new Southampton Multibiometric Tunnel Database (TunnelDB) datasets [8] were annotated against recordings taken of the individuals in lab conditions. The original purpose of these recordings was the analysis of subject gait biometrics and, in the case of TunnelDB, their face and ear biometrics. We discuss the composition of these datasets in greater detail in Section 5, here we concentrate on the procedure undertaken to assign annotations. Two systems were developed to gather annotations: The PHP based Gait Annotation system (GAnn), and later, the Python/Pylons based Python Gait Annotation system (Py-GAnn).

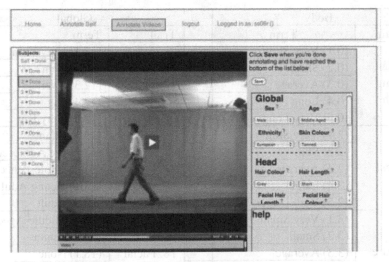

Fig. 2. GAnn interface

Both systems were used to collect semantic annotations using the web interface initially designed for the GAnn web application (Fig. 2). This interface allows annotators to view all samples of an arbitrary biometric gathered from a subject as many times as they require. Annotators were asked to describe subjects by selecting semantic terms for each physical trait. They were instructed to label every trait for every subject and that each trait should be completed with the annotator's own notions of what the trait meant. Guidelines were provided to avoid common confusions, for example that rough overlapping boundaries for different age terms and height of an individual should be assigned absolutely compared to perceived global "Average", while traits such as Arm Length could be annotated in comparison to the subject's overall physique.

To attain an upper limit for the capabilities of semantic data we strive to assure our data is of optimal quality. The annotation gathering process was designed carefully to avoid (and allow the future study of) inherent weaknesses and inaccuracies present in human generated descriptions. The error factors that the system was designed to deal with include:

- **Memory** - Passage of time may affect a witness' recall of a subject's traits.
- **Defaulting** - Features may be left out of descriptions in free recall, often not because a witness failed to remember a feature, but rather that it has a default value.
- **Observer Variables** [9] - A person's own physical features, namely their self perception and mental state, may affect recall of physical variables.
- **Anchoring** - When a person is asked a question and is initially presented with some default value or even seemingly unrelated information, replies given are often weighted around those initial values.

Table 1. Some Semantic Traits and Labels

Body			Global	
Trait	Term		Trait	Term
0. Arm Length	(0.1) Very Short		12. Figure	(12.1) Very Thin
	(0.2) Short			(12.2) Thin
	(0.3) Average			(12.3) Average
	(0.4) Long			(12.4) Big
	(0.5) Very Long			(12.5) Very Big
2. Chest	(2.1) Very Slim		13. Age	(13.1) Infant
	(2.2) Slim			(13.2) Pre Adolescence
	(2.3) Average			(13.3) Adolescence
	(2.4) Large			(13.4) Young Adult
	(2.5) Very Large			(13.5) Adult
3. Figure	(3.1) Very Small			(13.6) Middle Aged
	(3.2) Small			(13.7) Senior
	(3.3) Average		18. Facial Hair Length	(18.1) None
	(3.4) Large			(18.2) Stubble
	(3.5) Very Large			(18.3) Moustache

The semantic data gathering procedure was designed to accommodate these factors. Memory issues were addressed by allowing annotators to view videos of subjects as many times as required, allowing repeat of a particular video if necessary. Defaulting was avoided by explicitly asking individuals for each trait outlined in Table 1, this means that even values for apparently obvious traits are filled in and captured. This style of interrogative description, where constrained responses are explicitly requested, is more complete than free-form narrative recall but may suffer from inaccuracy, though not to a significant degree. Observer variables can never be completely removed so instead we allowed the study of differing physical traits across various annotators. Users were asked to self-annotate based on self-perception, also certain subjects being annotated themselves provided annotations of other individuals. This allows for some concept of the annotator's own appearance to be taken into consideration when studying their descriptions of other subjects. Anchoring can occur at various points of the data capture process. Anchoring of terms gathered for individual traits was avoided by setting the default term of a trait to a neutral "Unsure" rather than any concept of "Average". Another potential source of anchoring is that attributed by the order subjects are presented to an annotator. A sequence of relatively tall individuals may unfairly weight the perception of an averaged sized individual as short. We aimed to account for this by randomising the order of subjects presented to different annotators. In order to use the annotations in future analysis, they were represented numerically.

5   Dataset Statistics

The Southampton Large (A) HumanID Database (HIDDB) contains between 6 and 20 sample videos of 115 individual subjects each taken from side-on; the later Southampton Multibiometric Tunnel Database (TunnelDB) contains samples of subjects for which 10 gait sample videos from between 8 to 12 viewpoints are taken simultaneously and stored to extract 3D gait information [8]. TunnelDB also contains high resolution frontal videos to extract face information and high resolution still images taken to extract ear biometrics. There are roughly 10 such sets of information gathered for each subject in TunnelDB The GAnn annotation system used to collect data against the HIDDB was designed to allow annotation by anonymous annotators across the internet, though in reality the primary source of annotations came from two separate sessions involving a class of psychology students. In the first session, all the students were asked to annotate the same group of subjects, while in the second session 4 equally sized groups of subjects were allocated between the students.

The PyGAnn annotation system used to collect data against the TunnelDB was designed to gather annotations after recording biometric signatures when annotators were asked to annotate themselves and a group of 15 subjects. Due to time constraints some annotators annotated fewer subjects but all annotators captured provided a self-annotation. We selected 4 groups of 15 subjects to be annotated by progressively few annotators, aiming to maximise the number of annotators describing the same subjects

while simultaneously annotating the maximum spread of subjects. Table 2 shows a summary of the data collected. The annotations gathered are discussed in three ways:
- **Self Annotations** - Annotations an individual gave to themselves;
- **Subject Annotations** - Annotations given by an individual to a subject; and
- **Ascribed Annotations** – derived from subjects in TunnelDB who were also annotators.

Table 2. Summarising composition of the annotations gathered in 2 biometric datasets

		HIDDB	TunnelDB	Totals
Terms	Observed	20976	58023	78999
	Self	1659	4957	6616
	Of Annotators	0	31874	31874
Partial Descriptions	Observed	334	956	1290
	Self	10	77	87
	Of Annotators	0	544	544
Complete Descriptions	Observed	625	1685	2310
	Self	63	149	212
	Of Annotators	0	904	904
Individuals Described	Observed	115	71	186
	Self	73	226	299
	Of Annotators	0	43	43

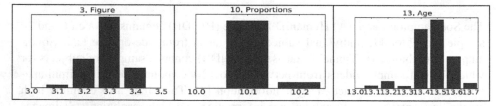

Fig. 3. Example distributions of self-annotations of the TunnelDB

6   Dataset Distributions

Trait Distribution Comparison. In the datasets a total of 414 individuals were described. For the normalised distribution of self and subject annotations for all traits in both datasets. An aspect of note is the distribution of measures of physical length including Height, Leg Length and Arm Length. For both datasets ascribed lengths tend towards long and average annotations meaning annotators avoid the use of the term short. This is in contrast to measurements of thickness or bulk such as Figure, Weight, Chest and Arm/Leg Thickness which display a more normal distribution. From these graphs, Fig.3, we can also see different terms for traits such as Proportions were not used. It is possible that such traits were not perceived or the trait itself was not understood by either group of annotators, with most subjects described as having normal Proportions. Alternatively, the subjects collected may indeed portray inherently "Normal" proportions. Leg Direction seemed to enjoy similar term patterns in both datasets, a relatively unexpected result as the HIDDB did not provide the viewpoints one would expect to be necessary to make such judgements. The results for the major global features seem weighted towards Young Adult as Age; White as Ethnicity and Male as Sex. This distribution is to be expected from the datasets as both contain many subjects from the Engineering departments of the University of Southampton, UK. Overall, we note that self-annotations taken in both systems used semantic terms in ratios comparable to those used in the ascribed annotations, as well as ratios comparable to each other. This is evidence towards the idea that individuals do not wholly believe themselves to be an average; rather individuals can reasonably describe themselves as others might see them, using the full set of semantic terms others might use. Despite this, later use of relative measurements was demonstrated to relieve problems associated with categorical labels, especially height [3].

Table 3. Lowest p-values of the difference in annotations between the TunnelDB and HIDDB dataset

Trait	p-value
Ethnicity	0.62
Hair Colour	0.7
Hair Length	0.84
Facial Hair Length	0.84
Age	0.9
Shoulder Shape	0.91
Sex	0.92
Leg Direcation	0.92

(a) ascribed annotations

Trait	p-value
Hair Colour 0.66	0.66
Facial Hair Length	0.66
Skin Colour	0.79
Sex	0.80
Facial Hair Colour	0.86
Ethnicity	0.87
Hair Length	0.92
Figure	0.93

(b) self-annotations

Cross-Dataset Distribution Comparison. In Table 3 we explore the differences in the distribution from self-annotations and ascribed annotations of the two datasets. There are small disparities between the self- annotations of HIDDB when compared to those of TunnelDB, though these are mostly insignificant differences with large p-values. The p-values in these tables represent the probability of a shared distribution having created the annotation distributions across the HIDDB and TunnelDB datasets. Two extremely similar distributions will produce p-values close to 1.0 while completely dissimilar distributions will produce p-values close to 0.

The individuals annotated were overall similarly distributed in appearance. More precisely, disparate groups of annotators described the different individuals in the different datasets using similar annotations. Some traits enjoy higher disparity between the datasets and therefore lower p-values; namely Ethnicity and associated attributes of Hair Colour. A special effort was made in the collection of TunnelDB to include individuals of different ethnic backgrounds in order to analyse ethnicity as a covariate of gait; this may explain the apparent higher degree of ethnic disparity reported by annotators of the TunnelDB. Individuals with beards were specifically chosen to be annotated in the TunnelDB due to a lack of such individuals in the HIDDB. This was performed to test the ability of the facial hair related traits to some degree. With regards to self-annotations across the two datasets, both from the graphs and the relatively lower p-values in Table 3, we note a disparity in the ratio of self-annotation of Sex. However, the graphs and p-values show comparatively similar distributions in other traits.

6.1   Internal Correlations

Having outlined the overall content and distributions of the gathered datasets in the previous sections, it is appropriate to explore notable correlations found between the various semantic annotations gathered. The goal of this section is to highlight internal structures inherent in the datasets gathered, some of which are supported by previous studies, therefore confirming the data's validity. In this section the correlation between relevant pairings of self, subject and ascribed annotations (see Section 5) are ex[lored. Though interesting for its own merits, these correlations could also have some useful practical applications. For example, by knowing the correlation between traits, estimated terms for missing traits could be inferred. This would result in more accurate results for a given incomplete semantic query, though such query competition could also be achieved through related techniques. In this section we also explore in greater detail the correlation between especially notable traits, such as Sex and Ethnicity when compared to other physical characteristics.

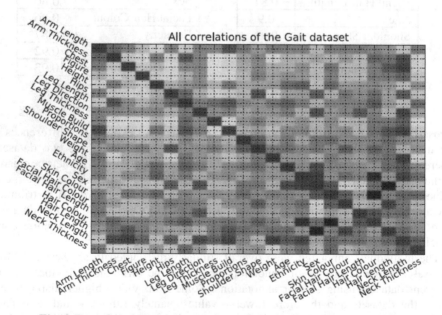

Fig. 4. Term Correlations of annotations ascribed by individuals in HIDDB

The correlation matrices containing the Pearson's r between each term are represented graphically. Colours closer to red represent correlation coefficients closer to 1.0 and thus a positive correlation, while colours closer to blue represent correlation coefficients closer to -1.0 and thus a negative correlation. Pale green represents positive correlation.

We calculate the correlation coefficient between two terms using individual annotator responses of individual subjects. Pearson's r is calculated as:

$$r = \frac{\sum_{i=1}^{n}(X_i - \overline{X})(Y_i - \overline{Y})}{\sqrt{\sum_{i=1}^{n}(X_i - \overline{X})^2}\sqrt{\sum_{i=1}^{n}(Y_i - \overline{Y})^2}} \qquad 2.1$$

where X and Y represent two semantic terms. Each semantic term was set to 1 if the annotation contains the term and 0 if the annotation did not. X_i and Y_i are the value ascribed to an individual in a single annotation, where there exist n annotations. Note that if $(X_i - \overline{X})(Y_i - \overline{Y}) > 0$ then X_i and Y_i lie on the same side of their respective means. In the binary case, where X and Y can only take the values 0 or 1, this denotes simultaneous annotation. Therefore, Pearson's r when applied to these semantic annotations is positive if X_i and Y_i are simultaneously present in an annotation. Furthermore, a higher correlation simultaneously represents how far an appearance of X or Y is from the mean, as well as the frequency of simultaneous appearances of X and Y across all n annotations.

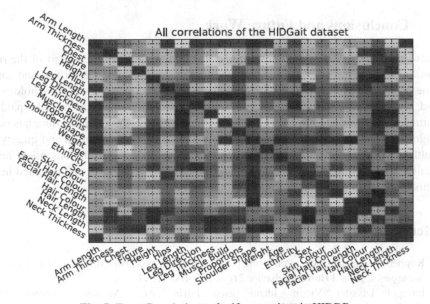

Fig. 5. Term Correlations of self annotations in HIDDB

In Fig. 4 we explore the correlations between subject annotation autocorrelation, representing how often individual trait and term pairings were used by annotators. Due to its nature, in the identity of the graph we achieve a perfect correlation. This is a trivial result meaning simply that a term appeared with itself every time it was used in an annotation. More informative correlations can be seen firstly between traits 0 to 12. These are build traits whose terms describe overall thickness and length of the body, as well as extremities. We note that Figure and Weight are highly correlated. In turn they are both correlated with Arm Thickness, Leg Thickness and Chest annotations. Correlation can also be noted between Height and Leg Length, each also portraying correlations with Arm Length. We also notice some inverse correlations.

In Neck Length against Neck Thickness we see signs of thinner necks being correlated with longer necks, bulky necks with shorter necks and so on. This inverse correlation can also be noted in both Neck Length and Neck Thickness compared to other traits of bulk and length respectively, though it should be noted that these inverse relationships are not as significant. There seems to exist two groups of traits whose terms correlate in ascending order. Namely traits denoting some notion of bulk or girth (represented by Weight, Figure etc.) and those denoting some notion of length (represented by Height and appendage lengths).

In Fig. 5 we see the auto-correlations of self-annotations. The correlations in self annotations are very similar to those found between ascribed annotations and many of the same statements with regards to build and global features can be made as above. This shows that in describing themselves that annotators are as consistent as they are when describing other people. This corresponds well with the similarity in annotations distributions noticed.

7   Conclusions and Future Work

A new approach to soft biometrics aims to use human description as part of the recognition/ retrieval process. A semantic labelling system has been described and some of the properties explored. The semantic labels have been chosen with psychology in mind: the labels are those derived from human vision and attention must be paid to minimise bias introduced by the (human labelling) process. As the procedure has been design for use with surveillance video, with necessarily low resolution and quality, it would prove interesting to study the effect of these on the correlations noted here. Equally, a fruitful avenue of research might be to explore the structure revealed here, as this might enable recovery of occluded labels.

References

1. Koppen, V., Lochun, S.K.: Portraying perpetrators; the validity of offender descriptions by witnesses. Law and Human Behavior **21**(6), 662–685 (1997)
2. Interpol Disaster Victim Identification Form (Ante Mortem, Yellow) 2008. http://www.interpol.int/INTERPOL-expertise/Forensics/DVI-Pages/Forms
3. Samangooei, S., Guo, B., Nixon, M.S.: The use of semantic human description as a soft biometric. In: Proc. IEEE BTAS 2008
4. Reid, D., Nixon, M.S., Stevenage, S.: Soft biometrics; human identification using comparative descriptions. IEEE Trans. PAMI **36**(6), 1216–1228 (2014)

5. Bertillon, A.: Instructions for taking descriptions for the identification of criminals and others, by means of anthropometric indications. American Bertillon Prison Bureau (1889)
6. Cole, S.A.: Twins, Twain, Galton, and Gilman: Fingerprinting, Individualization, Brotherhood, and Race in Pudd'nhead Wilson. Configurations 15(3), 227–265 (2007)
7. MacLeod, M.D., Frowley, J.N., Shepherd, J.W.: Whole body information: its relevance to eyewitnesses. Adult Eyewitness Testimony CUP, Chapter 6, 125–142 (1994)
8. Seely, R.D., Samangooei, S., et al.: The University of Southampton multi-biometric tunnel and introducing a novel 3D gait dataset. In: Proc. IEEE BTAS 2008 (2008)
9. Flin, R.H., Shepherd, J.W.: Tall stories: Eyewitnesses' ability to estimate height and weight characteristics. Human Learning 5(1), 29–38 (1986)
10. Samangooei, S., Nixon, M.S.: Performing content-based retrieval of humans using gait biometrics. Multimedia Tools and Applications 49, 195–212 (2010)

Human Classification Using Gait Features

Elena Gianaria[✉], Marco Grangetto, Maurizio Lucenteforte,
and Nello Balossino

Dipartimento di Informatica, Università degli Studi di Torino,
Corso Svizzera 185, 10149 Torino, Italy
elena.gianaria@unito.it

Abstract. Gait exhibits several advantages with respect to other biometrics features: acquisition can be performed through cheap technology, at a distance and without people collaboration. In this paper we perform gait analysis using skeletal data provided by the Microsoft Kinect sensor. We defined a rich set of physical and behavioral features aiming at identifying the more relevant parameters for gait description. Using SVM we showed that a limited set of behavioral features related to the movements of head, elbows and knees is a very effective tool for gait characterization and people recognition. In particular, our experimental results shows that it is possible to achieve 96% classification accuracy when discriminating a group of 20 people.

Keywords: Gait characterization · Gait analysis · Kinect · Support Vector Machine

1 Introduction and Related Work

Biometrics is the science that studies the human characteristics for anthropometry research, people identification, access control and many more. Biometric features are measurable data classified as physical or behavioral [1]. The former are related to the body and its shape. Some examples are face, hand, iris, retina and fingerprint. Behavioral characteristics are associated to particular human action, for instance handwriting and walking. Automatic recognition systems are often expensive, intrusive and require the cooperation of the subject during the acquisition. The latter cannot be always guaranteed, for instance in a video surveillance context. In this case, it is useful to recognize people through biometric parameters that can be captured at a distance and without the collaboration of the person, such as gait [2].

Gait analysis finds interest in video surveillance systems [3,4] and forensics science [5,6]. Furthermore, many applications analyze the gait in order to discover pathologies of the body movement [7], rehabilitation therapy [8], identify the fall risk in elderly population in order to assess the frailty syndrome [9,10]. All these applications are based on the analysis of video and 2D images. Images and videos are processed in order to collect gait parameters applying both model-based approaches, using the definition of a 3D model of the body in movement [11–13], or by model-free approaches, that process the silhouette of a walking person [14].

© Springer International Publishing Switzerland 2014
V. Cantoni et al. (Eds.): BIOMET 2014, LNCS 8897, pp. 16–27, 2014.
DOI: 10.1007/978-3-319-13386-7_2

In this paper we implemented a model-based approach using the Microsoft Kinect sensor. Kinect is more that a simple RGB camera, since it is equipped with a depth sensor providing 3D information related to the movements of body joints. The 3D data are more precise compared to the 2D information extracted from images but, on the contrary, the depth sensor, based on the infrared rays, does not work in outside environment and the depth range is quite limited. In literature exists some applications that exploit Kinect 3D data for people recognition and classification. Preis *et al.* [15] used only anthropometric features, such as height, length of limbs, stride length and speed, for gait characterization. They tested few combination of features using three different classifiers: 1R, a C4.5 decision tree and a Naive Bayes classier. Borras *et al.* [16] extracted 2D and 3D gait features based on the body silhouettes, to achieve gender identication using a Kernel SVM. Satta *et al.* [17] combined the body silhouette, colors clothing and 3D skeleton data (torso and legs length) aiming at tracking people for video-surveillance application. Ball *et al.* [18] proposed several angular features related to the leg articulations and used K-means algorithm, with an Euclidean distance metric, for classification.

A preliminary work has been already presented in [19], where we only shown that dynamic gait features extracted from Kinect allow one to discriminate between two subjects with similar biometric features, a much simpler scenario as opposed to the classification task studied in this paper.

The major contributions of this paper are:

- exploitation of cheap and widespread Kinect sensor for joint acquisition of static biometric features, e.g. height, leg length, etc.., and dynamic parameters related to gait, e.g. knees movement, head oscillation;
- analysis and selection of the biometric and gait features that are the most effective for people identification;
- experimental campaign worked out on a set of 20 subjects showing that the proposed set of features can be profitably exploited to classify people using SVM.

The paper is organized as follows. In Sect. 2 is explained our method to extract gait features while the clustering approach is presented in Sect. 3. The experiments done are shown in Sect. 4 together with the discussion of achieved results. Conclusion and future work are outlined in Sect. 5.

2   Proposed Method

In this work we propose a model-based approach for gait characterization using dynamic skeleton acquisition. In particular, we have used the widespread diffuse Microsoft Kinect sensor for acquisition of gait parameters. Kinect is a popular gaming device, that is able to capture body motion and gestures based on camera and depth sensor. Kinect is able to track in real-time a skeleton model, composed of 20 body joints J_i shown in Fig. 1. The skeleton can be used to describe body movements in real-time and in 3D space [20].

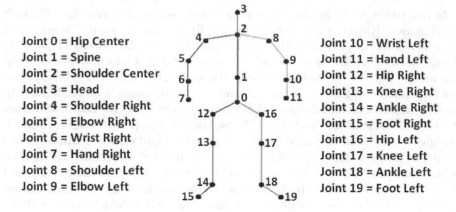

Joint 0 = Hip Center
Joint 1 = Spine
Joint 2 = Shoulder Center
Joint 3 = Head
Joint 4 = Shoulder Right
Joint 5 = Elbow Right
Joint 6 = Wrist Right
Joint 7 = Hand Right
Joint 8 = Shoulder Left
Joint 9 = Elbow Left

Joint 10 = Wrist Left
Joint 11 = Hand Left
Joint 12 = Hip Right
Joint 13 = Knee Right
Joint 14 = Ankle Right
Joint 15 = Foot Right
Joint 16 = Hip Left
Joint 17 = Knee Left
Joint 18 = Ankle Left
Joint 19 = Foot Left

Fig. 1. Kinect skeleton model

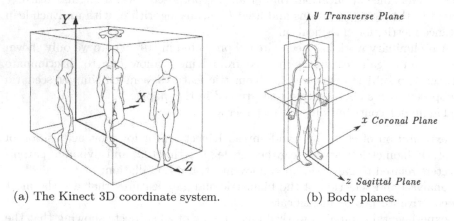

(a) The Kinect 3D coordinate system.   (b) Body planes.

Fig. 2. Kinect reference system and coordinate system according to the walking direction

The skeleton data provided by Kinect consist in the coordinates of the 20 joints in its local reference system as shown in Fig. 2-(a) where (X, Y, Z) are the horizontal, vertical and depth direction, respectively. Joint coordinates are provided at a rate of 30 Hz along with the estimated floor clipping plane, that is the plane where the user is walking. The floor plane equation is derived as $AX + BY + CZ + D = 0$, where (A, B, C) is the normal vector to the plane and D is the height of the camera center with respect to the floor. As opposed to the Kinect reference system, human biometric parameters are usually measured with respect to the body planes shown in Fig. 2-(b), where coronal, sagittal and transverse plane are represented. The latter is clearly parallel to the floor clipping plane provide by Kinect, whereas the sagittal plane can be determined if we infer the walking direction. Since the Kinect depth range is between 80 centimeters and 4 meters, we can easily assume that the observed subject follows a straight path within a single gait acquisition. As a consequence, we have estimated the walking direction as the line connecting the initial and final coordinates of the center of mass (Joint 0). To make the estimation more robust, the initial and final coordinates of the center of mass are averaged at the beginning and at the end of the acquisition. Finally, the novel reference system (x, y, z) is constructed as shown in Fig. 2-(b), considering the floor clipping plane, its normal and the walking direction as the novel z axis. In the following all the joints coordinates will be expressed according to (x, y, z).

Since Kinect depth sensor exhibits limited resolution and precision, all joint estimates can be considered as noisy acquisitions. To limit this effect we propose to use median filter on all acquired data before performing any further processing. Such refined estimates are then exploited to define our gaits feature vector that comprises both physical and behavioral parameters, as detailed in the following. All the collected features are summarized in Table 1.

Table 1. Gait features list

Label	Features
α	arms length
β	legs length
γ	height
δ	stride length
υ	walking speed
ϵ	elbows distance
κ	knees distance
η	hands distance
λ	ankles distance
$\mu_{J_3,x} - \sigma^2_{J_3,x}$	mean/variance of head (along x)
$\mu_{J_3,y} - \sigma^2_{J_3,y}$	mean/variance of head (along y)
$\mu_{J_4,x} - \sigma^2_{J_4,x}$	mean/variance of left shoulder (along x)
$\mu_{J_8,x} - \sigma^2_{J_8,x}$	mean/variance of right shoulder (along x)
$\mu_{J_{13},y} - \sigma^2_{J_{13},y}$	mean/variance of left knee (along y)
$\mu_{J_{17},y} - \sigma^2_{J_{17},y}$	mean/variance of right knee (along y)

2.1 Physical Features

Using joint coordinates we have estimated some physical biometric features that are almost constant during the walk, namely the height and the length of arms and legs, respectively. The height is defined as:

$$\gamma = \sum_{i \in \tau} \sqrt{(J_{i,x} - J_{i+1,x})^2 + (J_{i,y} - J_{i+1,y})^2 + (J_{i,z} - J_{i+1,z})^2}$$

where $\tau = [3, 2, 1, 0, 12, 13, 14, 15]$ or $\tau = [3, 2, 1, 0, 16, 17, 18, 19]$, i.e. the joints going from the head to the right (or left) foot. All the estimates of γ acquired during a given gait acquisition are averaged to get a single average value. Similarly, we compute the length of the left (and right) arm as the overall length of the skeleton segments from the shoulder to the hand. A single parameter α is obtained by averaging both left and right arm lengths along all the acquisition period. The same approach is used to get a single feature β by averaging the lengths of the skeleton segments from the hip to the feet.

2.2 Behavioral Features

A clear advantage of using Kinect is the possibility to devise a rich set of behavioral gait features derived by the continuous monitoring of joint positions. Usually gait behavior is characterized in terms of stride length and walking speed. The former is the distance between two stationary position of the same foot while walking. The stride is detected using the same technique we already presented in [19]. The latter is the ratio between the distance covered by the center of mass and its duration in a single stride. In this study we estimate such features in real time and all their measurements are averaged to get the gait parameters δ and v shown in Table 1. We complement these standard gait parameters with other behavioral features that are related to the gait dynamic, in particular the movement of head, shoulders, elbows, hands, knees and ankles. To this end, we track the movement of the corresponding joints along the x and y axes, i.e. we measure the vertical and lateral oscillations of the corresponding skeleton joints. Then the dynamic of their trajectory during the acquisition is represented in terms of mean value μ and variance σ^2. These features are denoted as $\mu_{J_{i,x}}$, $\mu_{J_{i,y}}$, $\sigma^2_{J_{i,x}}$, $\sigma^2_{J_{i,y}}$ where i indexes the relevant joint and x (or y) refers to the considered coordinate component (see Table 1).

Finally, our experiments showed that other important gait features are the distance between the left and right elbows ϵ, hands η, knees κ and ankles λ. Also in this case we average all the estimates during the acquired walking period. All the collected features are summarized in Table 1.

3 Classification

In this paper we used Support Vector Machine (SVM), a widely-used and robust clustering algorithm, to classify people based on both physical and behavioral gait biometric feature. SVM is a supervised learning method for data classification. The main idea is to find the pair of parallel hyperplane that separates between a set of features having different class memberships. Each pair of parallel hyperplanes is characterized by specific sets of feature points, the so-called support vector. In a $2D$ feature space the planes are fully defined by three support vectors, so in ND the support vector examples should have $N + 1$ points, in order to avoid overfitting. Since SVM is a supervised algorithm, the classification task involves separating data into training and testing sets. Each instance in the training set contains one "target value" (i.e. the class labels) and several "attributes" (i.e. the features or observed variables). The goal of SVM is to produce a model (based on the training data) which predicts the target values of the test data.

The hyperplane algorithm proposed by Vapnik in 1963 was a linear classifier. The nonlinear classification, proposed in 1992 [21], is possible by applying the so-called kernel trick, originally proposed by Aizerman *et al.* [22]: the dimensional space of the function is mapped into an higher (maybe infinite) dimensional space, so that it is possible to find a linear separating hyperplane with the maximal margin in that higher dimensional space. The advantage of the kernel function is that it does not require explicit calculation of the data coordinates in the new space. It is done by simply computing the inner products between the images of all pairs of data in the feature space: this is a computationally cheaper operation respect to the explicit computation of the coordinates. To construct an optimal hyperplane, SVM employs an iterative training algorithm, which is used to minimize an error function. According to the form of the error function, in multi-class classification, SVM models can be classified into two distinct groups: classification SVM Type 1 (also known as C-SVM classification) and classification SVM Type 2 (also known as ν-SVM classification).

The C-SVM training involves the minimization of the error function:

$$\frac{1}{2} w^T w + C \sum_{i=1}^{N} \xi_i, \quad C > 0$$

subject to the constraints:

$$y_i(w^T \phi(x_i) + b) \geq 1 - \xi_i \quad and \quad \xi_i \geq 0, \quad i = 1, \ldots, N$$

where C is the capacity constant, w is the vector of coefficients and ξ represents parameters for handling nonseparable data (input). x_i is the training vector, so the index i labels the N training samples, that are mapped into an higher dimensional space by the function ϕ. b is a constant. C should be chosen with care to avoid overfitting.

The ν-SVM model minimizes the error function:

$$\frac{1}{2} w^T w - \nu\rho + \frac{1}{N} \sum_{i=1}^{N} \xi_i, \quad 0 \leq \nu \leq 1$$

subject to the constraints:

$$y_i(w^T \phi(x_i) + b) \geq \rho - \xi_i, \quad \xi_i \geq 0, \quad i = 1, \ldots, N \quad and \quad \rho \geq 0$$

The kernel functions that can be used in SVM are:

- Linear: $K(x_i, x_j) = x_i^T x_j$.
- Polynomial: $K(x_i, x_j) = (\gamma x_i^T x_j + r)^d, \gamma > 0$.
- Radial Basis Function (RBF): $K(x_i, x_j) = exp(-\gamma \|x_i - x_j\|^2), \gamma > 0$.
- Sigmoid: $K(x_i, x_j) = tanh(\gamma x_i^T x_J + r)$.

where γ, r and d are kernel parameters.

The effectiveness of SVM depends on the selection of kernel and the kernel's parameters.

4   Experimental Results

The goal of our experimentation is, first to find out which features collected in Sect. 2 are more relevant for gait characterization, and then to evaluate the achievable classification accuracy.

Since a standard gait dataset acquired with the Kinect sensor is not available, we have collected a set of gait samples. To this end we acquired gait samples with Kinect for Windows, recording 20 subjects that were asked to walk naturally along a corridor; each subject is acquired 10 times for a total of 200 gait samples. The software model to estimate the features proposed in Sect. 2 has been developed using SDK 1.7.

Finally, for classification, we resort to the LIBSVM tool [23], an SVM free library. We used both the C-SVM type and the ν-SVM type, with linear and RBF kernel function. The dataset is divided in two subset: 60% of samples are used for training and the remaining for testing. Before applying SVM we normalized our features matrix to the range $[0, 1]$. Scaling data is very important in order to avoid attributes in greater numeric ranges dominating those in smaller numeric ranges. Another advantage is to simplify the calculations of the kernel function. As said in Sect. 3 the parameters C and ν should be chosen with care. The C parameter is computed using the K-fold cross-validation procedure [23]. The training set is divided into K subsets of equal size. A single subset is tested using the classifier trained on the remaining $K - 1$ subsets. The process is repeated K times for each of the K subset. The K results are then averaged to produce a single estimation. The ν parameter is calculated as suggested in [24]:

$$\nu = 2 * min(|SVs^+|, |SVs^-|)/|SVs|$$

where SVs is the vector containing the support vector elements (the feature points of each hyperplane), while SVs^+ and SVs^- are the vectors containing the positive and negative support vectors, respectively.

As an objective metric for performance evaluation we used the classification accuracy, defined as:

$$accuracy = \frac{\psi}{\Omega} * 100\%$$

where ψ is the number of correctly classified samples and Ω is the total number of samples.

4.1   Discussion

To investigate the effectiveness of the different features that we proposed, we analyze the classification accuracy obtained with several sets of gait parameters.

Table 2. Classification accuracy of different features sets.

Set	Features	C-SVM Linear	C-SVM RBF	ν-SVM Linear	ν-SVM RBF
S_1	α, β, γ	37.50	25.00	62.50	58.75
S_2	δ, υ	23.75	23.75	13.75	17.50
S_3	$\alpha, \beta, \gamma, \delta, \upsilon$	46.25	41.25	48.75	37.50
S_4	$\epsilon, \kappa,$	37.50	38.75	52.50	46.25
S_5	$\epsilon, \kappa, \lambda$	42.50	37.50	55.00	53.75
S_6	ϵ, κ, η	41.25	38.75	32.50	35.00
S_7	$\epsilon, \kappa, \lambda, \eta$	45.00	43.75	56.25	55.00
S_8	λ, η	18.75	17.50	15.00	10.00
S_9	$\alpha, \beta, \gamma, \epsilon, \kappa$	72.50	55.00	75.00	76.25
S_{10}	$S_1, S_4, \sigma^2_{J_3,x}, \sigma^2_{J_3,y}$	70.00	56.25	61.25	46.25
S_{11}	$S_1, S_4, \mu_{J_3,x}, \mu_{J_3,y}$	86.25	85.00	86.25	85.00
S_{12}	$S_1, S_4, \sigma^2_{J_{13},y}, \sigma^2_{J_{17},y}$	75.00	52.50	63.75	51.25
S_{13}	$S_1, S_4, \mu_{J_{13},y}, \mu_{J_{17},y}$	81.25	65.00	81.25	81.25
S_{14}	$S_1, S_4, \sigma^2_{J_4,x}, \sigma^2_{J_8,x}$	66.25	55.00	55.00	45.00
S_{15}	$S_1, S_4, \mu_{J_4,x}, \mu_{J_8,x}$	77.50	71.25	77.50	77.50
S_{16}	$S_1, S_4, \sigma^2_{J_3,x}, \sigma^2_{J_3,y}, \sigma^2_{J_4,x}, \sigma^2_{J_8,x}$	65.00	57.50	57.50	41.25
S_{17}	$S_1, S_4, \mu_{J_3,x}, \mu_{J_3,y}, \mu_{J_4,x}, \mu_{J_8,x}$	83.75	82.50	86.25	83.75
S_{18}	$S_1, S_4, \sigma^2_{J_3,x}, \sigma^2_{J_3,y}, \sigma^2_{J_{13},y}, \sigma^2_{J_{17},y}$	70.00	53.75	55.00	46.25
S_{19}	**$S_1, S_4, \mu_{J_3,x}, \mu_{J_3,y}, \mu_{J_{13},y}, \mu_{J_{17},y}$**	**88.75**	**82.50**	**90.00**	**90.00**
S_{20}	$S_1, S_4, \sigma^2_{J_3,x}, \sigma^2_{J_3,y}, \sigma^2_{J_4,x}, \sigma^2_{J_8,x}, \sigma^2_{J_{13},y}, \sigma^2_{J_{17},y}$	66.25	55.00	58.75	42.50
S_{21}	$S_1, S_4, \mu_{J_3,x}, \mu_{J_3,y}, \mu_{J_4,x}, \mu_{J_8,x}, \mu_{J_{13},y}, \mu_{J_{17},y}$	87.50	82.50	90.00	88.75
S_{22}	$S_4, \sigma^2_{J_3,x}, \sigma^2_{J_3,y}$	48.75	41.25	46.25	43.75
S_{23}	$S_4, \mu_{J_3,x}, \mu_{J_3,y}$	90.00	80.00	92.50	91.25
S_{24}	$S_4, \sigma^2_{J_{13},y}, \sigma^2_{J_{17},y}$	36.25	35.00	46.25	48.75
S_{25}	$S_4, \mu_{J_{13},y}, \mu_{J_{17},y}$	58.75	57.50	57.50	45.00
S_{26}	$S_4, \sigma^2_{J_4,x}, \sigma^2_{J_8,x}$	47.50	38.75	55.00	51.25
S_{27}	$S_4, \mu_{J_4,x}, \mu_{J_8,x}$	61.25	50.00	57.50	57.50
S_{28}	$S_4, \sigma^2_{J_3,x}, \sigma^2_{J_3,y}, \sigma^2_{J_4,x}, \sigma^2_{J_8,x}$	48.75	37.50	45.00	35.00
S_{29}	$S_4, \mu_{J_3,x}, \mu_{J_3,y}, \mu_{J_4,x}, \mu_{J_8,x}$	86.25	76.25	87.50	88.75
S_{30}	$S_4, \sigma^2_{J_3,x}, \sigma^2_{J_3,y}, \sigma^2_{J_{13},y}, \sigma^2_{J_{17},y}$	45.00	32.50	32.50	32.50
S_{31}	**$S_4, \mu_{J_3,x}, \mu_{J_3,y}, \mu_{J_{13},y}, \mu_{J_{17},y}$**	**92.50**	**81.25**	**96.25**	**96.25**
S_{32}	$S_4, \sigma^2_{J_3,x}, \sigma^2_{J_3,y}, \sigma^2_{J_4,x}, \sigma^2_{J_8,x}, \sigma^2_{J_{13},y}, \sigma^2_{J_{17},y}$	48.75	32.50	41.25	30.00
S_{33}	$S_4, \mu_{J_3,x}, \mu_{J_3,y}, \mu_{J_4,x}, \mu_{J_8,x}, \mu_{J_{13},y}, \mu_{J_{17},y}$	92.50	78.75	76.25	65.00
S_{34}	$S_1, \sigma^2_{J_3,x}, \sigma^2_{J_3,y}$	45.00	42.50	43.75	37.50
S_{35}	$S_1, \mu_{J_3,x}, \mu_{J_3,y}$	71.25	65.00	73.75	73.75
S_{36}	$S_1, \sigma^2_{J_{13},y}, \sigma^2_{J_{17},y}$	40.00	27.50	46.25	33.75
S_{37}	$S_1, \mu_{J_{13},y}, \mu_{J_{17},y}$	61.25	45.00	67.50	70.00
S_{38}	$S_1, \sigma^2_{J_4,x}, \sigma^2_{J_8,x}$	45.00	43.75	37.50	31.25
S_{39}	$S_1, \mu_{J_4,x}, \mu_{J_8,x}$	55.00	43.75	62.50	62.50
S_{40}	$S_1, \sigma^2_{J_3,x}, \sigma^2_{J_3,y}, \sigma^2_{J_4,x}, \sigma^2_{J_8,x}$	48.75	51.25	47.50	36.25
S_{41}	$S_1, \mu_{J_3,x}, \mu_{J_3,y}, \mu_{J_4,x}, \mu_{J_8,x}$	68.75	58.75	75.00	76.25
S_{42}	$S_1, \sigma^2_{J_3,x}, \sigma^2_{J_3,y}, \sigma^2_{J_{13},y}, \sigma^2_{J_{17},y}$	46.25	46.25	41.25	33.75
S_{43}	**$S_1, \mu_{J_3,x}, \mu_{J_3,y}, \mu_{J_{13},y}, \mu_{J_{17},y}$**	**77.50**	**60.00**	**75.00**	**78.75**
S_{44}	$S_1, \sigma^2_{J_3,x}, \sigma^2_{J_3,y}, \sigma^2_{J_4,x}, \sigma^2_{J_8,x}, \sigma^2_{J_{13},y}, \sigma^2_{J_{17},y}$	50.00	51.25	42.50	35.00
S_{45}	$S_1, \mu_{J_3,x}, \mu_{J_3,y}, \mu_{J_4,x}, \mu_{J_8,x}, \mu_{J_{13},y}, \mu_{J_{17},y}$	78.75	58.75	77.50	80.00

As a benchmark for classification accuracy, we run a first experiment where we discriminate subjects considering only physical features, in particular their height (γ) and arms (α) and legs (β) lengths; this is representative of usual classification based only on simple anthropometric parameters. The classification results using this set of features (S_1) are shown in Table 2, where it can be noted that ν-SVM yields an accuracy of about 60%. As a second trial we used the set S_2 that includes two standard gait parameters, namely stride length (δ) and walking speed (v) but, as shown in Table 2, the achieved classification accuracy turns to be rather poor. Also, jointly using sets S_1 and S_2 (set S_3 in Table 2) we cannot improve performance, significantly. The limited performance obtained using gait parameters in S_2 can be explained by considering the limited depth range of the Kinect, that allows one to acquire only three/four strides, leading to poor estimates of δ and v.

As a consequence, we move our investigation towards other gait features that can be estimated more reliably by Kinect, i.e. the inter-distance between corresponding left and right body joints. A subset of the obtained classification results is reported in Table 2 (see sets S_4-S_9). Inspecting these results one can notice that, using physical features and the distance between elbows and knees (set S_9) we achieve about 75% accuracy, with an improvement of about 15% with respect to the S_1 benchmark.

Then, we try to further improve the classification accuracy including in the features vector the remaining dynamic parameters defined in Sect. 2, namely the mean and variance of the position of head, shoulders, elbow and knees. In sets S_{10}-S_{21} these latter are used along with S_1 and S_4. It can be noted that a few parameter sets yield accuracy larger than 80%. In particular, the best classification is obtained by S_{19} that yields 90% accuracy with ν-SVM. In sets S_{22}-S_{33} we perform the same experiments removing S_1 from the feature vector, i.e. without using the standard physical features. In this case a few combinations reach an accuracy around 90%. In particular, the features set S_{31} exhibits an accuracy of 96%, that represents the best result we obtained. Finally, the remaining experiments S_{34}-S_{45} use S_1 along with the proposed dynamic gait parameters, but the obtained accuracy does not achieves 80%.

To better appreciate all our experimental results in Fig. 3 we plot the accuracy as a function of the features sets for C-SVM (a) and ν-SVM (b), respectively. To improve the readability of the graph the last three groups of parameters sets, are highlighted by boxes labeled by A, B and C respectively.

In conclusion, our experiments show that gait parameters extracted using Kinect, can be used as a powerful biometric feature. In particular, we can argue that simple statistics estimated from a set of skeletal joints are very effective for people classification based on SVM.

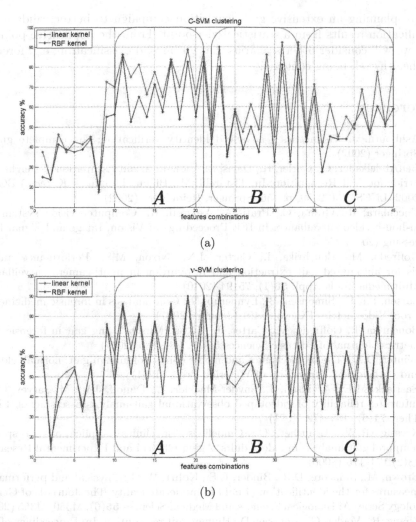

(a)

(b)

Fig. 3. Classification accuracy of C-SVM (a) and ν-SVM (b) for different combinations of gait features

5   Conclusions and Future Work

Relying on the information provided by the Kinect sensor, an analysis system able to classify people based on their gait has been proposed. We have especially pointed out that the movement of elbows, knees and head are of great importance for diversifying gait. The achieved results obtained by using the robust SVM clustering algorithm show an accuracy classification equal to 96.25% when a suitable parameter set is chosen. Future works include the exploitation of other statistical procedures, such as the principal component analysis, to better rank the importance of gait parameters in terms of classification accuracy. Moreover, we are planning an extensive gait acquisition campaign to better validate the classification results from a statistical viewpoint. From the applicative point of view we will consider other scenarios that go beyond classification, e.g. forensic and health/well-being contexts.

References

1. Ashbourn, J.: Biometrics - advanced identity verification: the complete guide. Springer (2002)
2. BenAbdelkader, C., Cutler, R., Davis, L.: View-invariant Estimation of Height and Stride for Gait Recognition. In: Tistarelli, M., Bigun, J., Jain, A.K. (eds.) ECCV 2002. LNCS, vol. 2359, p. 155. Springer, Heidelberg (2002)
3. Cucchiara, R., Grana, C., Prati, A., Vezzani, R.: Computer vision system for in-house video surveillance. In IEE Proceedings of Vision, Image and Signal Processing (2005)
4. Goffredo, M., Bouchrika, I., Carter, J.N., Nixon, M.S.: Performance analysis for automated gait extraction and recognition in multi-camera surveillance. Multimedia Tools Appl. **50**(1), 75–94 (2010)
5. Larsen, P.K.E., Simonsen, B., Lynnerup, N.: Gait analysis in forensic medicine. In Proc. Videometrics IX., vol. 6491 (January 2007)
6. Bouchrika, I., Goffredo, M., Carter, J., Nixon, M.: On using gait in forensic biometrics. Journal of Forensic Sciences **56**(4), 882–889 (2011)
7. Winter, D.A.: The biomechanics and motor control of human gait: normal, elderly and pathological. University of Waterloo Press (1991)
8. Eastlack, M.E., Arvidson, J., Snyder-Mackler, L., Danoff, J.V., McGarvey, C.L.: Interrater reliability of videotaped observational gait-analysis assessments. Phys. Ther. **71**(6), 465–472 (1991)
9. Kressig, R.W., Beauchet, O.: Guidelines for clinical applications of spatio-temporal gait analysis in older adults. Aging Clinical and Experimental Research, 18(2):174–176 (2006)
10. Brown, M., Sinacore, D.R., Binder, E.F., Kohrt, W.M.: Physical and performance measures for the identification of mild to moderate frailty. The Journals of Gerontology Series A: Biological Sciences and Medical Sciences **55**(6), M350–M355 (2000)
11. Zhang, R., Vogler, C., Metaxas, D.: Human gait recognition. In: Proceedings of the 2004 Conference on Computer Vision and Pattern Recognition Workshop (CVPRW 2004) Volume 1 - Volume 01, CVPRW 2004, IEEE Computer Society. pp. 18–25, Washington, DC (2004)
12. Urtasun, R., Fua, P.: 3d tracking for gait characterization and recognition. In: Proc. IEEE Automatic Face and Gesture Recognition, Seoul, Korea, pp. 17–22 (2004)
13. Yoo, J.-H., Nixon, M.: Automated markerless analysis of human gait motion for recognition and classification. ETRI Journal **33**(3), 259–266 (2011)
14. Wang, L., Tan, T., Ning, H.: Silhouette analysis-based gait recognition for human identification. IEEE Trans. Pattern Anal. Mach. Intell. **25**(12), 1505–1518 (2003)
15. Preis, J., Kessel, M., Werner, M., Linnhoff-Popien, C.: Gait recognition with kinect. In: Proceedings of the First Workshop on Kinect in Pervasive Computing (2012)
16. Borràs, R., Lapedriza, À., Igual, L.: Depth Information in Human Gait Analysis: An Experimental Study on Gender Recognition. In: Campilho, A., Kamel, M. (eds.) ICIAR 2012, Part II. LNCS, vol. 7325, pp. 98–105. Springer, Heidelberg (2012)

17. Satta, R., Pala, F., Fumera, G., Roli, F.: Real-time appearance-based person re-identification over multiple kinect cameras. In: 8th International Conference on Computer Vision Theory and Applications (VISAPP 2013), Barcelona, Spain, 21/02/2013 (2013)
18. Ball, A., Rye, D., Ramos, F., Velonaki, M.: Unsupervised clustering of people from 'skeleton' data. In: Proceedings of the Seventh Annual ACM/IEEE International Conference on Human-Robot Interaction, HRI 2012, ACM. pp. 225–226, New York (2012)
19. Gianaria, E., Balossino, N., Grangetto, M., Lucenteforte, M.: Gait characterization using dynamic skeleton acquisition. In: IEEE 15th International Workshop on Multimedia Signal Processing (MMSP), pp. 440–445 (September 2013)
20. Shotton, J., Sharp, T., Kipman, A., Fitzgibbon, A., Finocchio, M., Blake, A., Cook, M., Moore, R.: Real-time human pose recognition in parts from single depth images. Commun. ACM **56**(1), 116–124 (2013)
21. Boser, B.E., Guyon, I.M., Vapnik, V.N.: A training algorithm for optimal margin classifiers. In: Proceedings of the Fifth Annual Workshop on Computational Learning Theory, COLT 1992, ACM. pp. 144–152, New York (1992)
22. Aizerman, M.A., Braverman, E.A., Rozonoer, L.: Theoretical foundations of the potential function method in pattern recognition learning. Automation and Remote Control **25**, 821–837 (1964)
23. Chang, C.-C., Lin, C.-J.: LIBSVM: A library for support vector machines. ACM Transactions on Intelligent Systems and Technology, 2:27:1–27:27 (2011)
24. Crisp, D.J., Burges, C.J.C.: A geometric interpretation of v-svm classifiers. In: Solla, S.A., Leen, T.K., Müller, K. (eds.) Advances in Neural Information Processing Systems 12, MIT Press. pp. 244–250 (2000)

Using Mutual Information for Multi-Anchor Tracking of Human Beings

Silvio Barra[1], Maria De Marsico[2(✉)], Virginio Cantoni[3], and Daniel Riccio[4]

[1] Università di Cagliari, Cagliari, Italy
silvio.barra@unica.it
[2] Sapienza Università di Roma, Roma, Italy
demarsico@di.uniroma1.it
[3] Università di Pavia, Pavia, Italy
virginio.cantoni@unipv.it
[4] Università di Napoli Federico II, Napoli, Italy
daniel.riccio@unina.it

Abstract. Tracking of human beings represents a hot research topic in the field of video analysis. It is attracting an increasing attention among researchers thanks to its possible application in many challenging tasks. Among these, action recognition, human/human and human/computer interaction require body-part tracking. Most of the existing techniques in literature are model-based approaches, so despite their effectiveness, they are often unfit for the specific requirements of a body-part tracker. In this case it is very hard if not impossible to define a formal model of the target. This paper proposes a multi-anchor tracking system, which works on 8 bits color images and exploits the mutual information to track human body parts (head, hands, ...) without performing any foreground/background segmentation. The proposed method has been designed as a component of a more general system aimed at human interaction analysis. It has been tested on a wide set of color video sequences and the very promising results show its high potential.

1   Introduction

Tracking human beings in video sequences represents a challenging problem that is increasingly attracting the researchers attention, as it is essential for many applications in video analytics. Significant progresses have been achieved in many recent works in literature along this research line [1][5][12]. Most approaches from the present state of the art focus their attention on the estimation of the human body configuration, since they are aimed at recognizing human actions and activities. The first step of the tracking process consists in segmenting the human shape from the background. It represents a very complicated problem, as real-world applications work with complex and possibly moving backgrounds, large changes in illumination conditions and self-occlusions. In order to address these issues, several approaches have been proposed, which are based on background subtraction [10], optical flow [8] or statistical modeling of the human appearance [13][4]. All those methods try to segment video frames to extract edges, silhouettes or blobs. Blobs are often preferred with respect to

© Springer International Publishing Switzerland 2014
V. Cantoni et al. (Eds.): BIOMET 2014, LNCS 8897, pp. 28–39, 2014.
DOI: 10.1007/978-3-319-13386-7_3

other features, as they are more suited to the task of detecting human body parts. As a matter of fact, in connection with a suitable model of the body structure, tracking single body parts allows to compensate for partial occlusions due to mutual people overlapping during interaction, or caused by objects in the scene that may partially hide a person for a few frames. Blobs are also more suitable than other descriptors, like 2D contour, for modeling the articulated motion of human body parts. Models for approximating the articulated motion generally rely on a stick figure, which was first defined by Johansson [6] as the union of segments linked by joints [9]. Thus, detection methods can either locate blobs composing the human shape or simply the joints and end points of a stick figure (elbows, knees, head, hands, feet).

Yilmaz et al. categorized all detection methods in four main classes: i) background subtraction, ii) segmentation, iii) supervised learning, iv) point detector. Approaches based on background subtraction suffer from illumination changes and partial occlusions, since precisely separating the human silhouette from a cluttered background with several moving objects may turn in a very difficult task. Similarly, segmentation methods also encounter problems with complex scenes, even if they further rely on additional features like color or gradient direction. Supervised learning overcomes all these limitations, but it requires a training phase, which binds the tracker to a specific application context. A point based method detects interest points that are considered representative in terms of a specific feature, like contour, intensity or color. Interest points have been largely used in computer vision to solve a wide range of problems like image registration, image retrieval or tracking systems. Due to the higher robustness of this kind of approach, we adopt it here. We track interest points defined as *anchors*, without requiring a prior separation of foreground from background. As a matter of fact, this latter task is often very complex and its precision strongly influences tracking results. In our case, anchor tracking is performed by locally processing information right in the color frame, without any kind of foreground detection. To this aim, we exploit concepts borrowed from Information Theory. The core idea of the algorithm, named MIMA (Mutual Information Multi-Anchor), is to use mutual information [10] for multi-anchor tracking of human figures.

Mutual information (MI) finds several uses in the context of computer vision, such as the detection of cut/fade in video sequences [1]. Dame and Marchand used it with good results, for the tracking of feature points in the context of augmented reality [3]. Probabilistic measures are used in [7] to track multiple faces in scenes with a simplified setting with respect to the one addressed here, and tracking cues are provided by mutual information.

The above works suggest that MI can be a valuable tool, even for multi-anchor tracking of people. As a matter of fact, MIMA uses MI to track relevant interest points tied to the human body (head, hands , ...). Compared to classical methods , it has the additional advantage of working on color images. This is crucial to assure greater precision also on regions, such as the hands, which in a video with a limited resolution have a structure not easily distinguishable and, therefore, difficult to track in grayscale images. Furthermore, the lack of a geometric reference model, difficult to formalize as in the case of the hands, makes it difficult to apply techniques such as that described in [3], which is strongly model-based.

2   Mutual Information

Shannon theory is a mathematical abstract one that has very important applications in many concrete fields, such as physics (thermodynamics), economics (Stock Market), computer science (data compression and transmission). Entropy is a key measure of information, which quantifies the uncertainty involved in predicting the value of a random variable. Starting from it, the joint entropy, the conditional entropy and the mutual information can be derived. Given a random variable X defined over a set of values $\mathcal{X}$ with distribution function $p_X(x)$, entropy is defined as:

$$H(X) = -\sum_{x \in \mathcal{X}} p_X(x) \cdot \log p_X(x). \tag{1}$$

Given two random variables X and Y defined over two alphabets $\mathcal{X}$ and $\mathcal{Y}$, with respective marginal distribution function $p_X(x)$ and $p_Y(y)$, and with joint distribution function $p_{XY}(x, y)$, mutual information is defined as:

$$MI(X; Y) = \sum_{x \in \mathcal{X}} \sum_{y \in \mathcal{Y}} p_{XY}(x, y) \cdot \log \frac{p_{XY}(x, y)}{p_X(x) \cdot p_Y(y)}. \tag{2}$$

The above formulation for mutual information (MI) is the generic one applied to the communication theory. In the following we will rely on a more specific definition better bound to the problem at hand. In the context of image processing, the random variables I and J refer to the intensity values of the pixels in two images, denoted as I^1 and I^2. These intensity values are respectively denoted as i and j. For instance, if I^1 and I^2 are two grey-level images, i and j can take values in the interval $\Omega_{I^1} = \Omega_{I^2} = [0,255] \subset \mathbb{N}$. The probability $p_{I^1}(i)$ is related to the frequency with which the intensity value i appears in image I^1. In general, such probability is estimated through histograms:

$$p_{I^1} = \frac{1}{W \cdot H} \sum_{x,y} \delta(i - I^1(x, y)) \tag{3}$$

Where (x, y) will denote from now on the position within the image, $M = W \cdot H$ (W and H represents the image width and height, respectively) is the total number of pixels in the image and $\delta(k)$ is the Kronecker function defined as:

$$\delta(k) = \begin{cases} 1 & \text{if } k = 0 \\ 0 & \text{otherwise} \end{cases} \tag{4}$$

In histogram computation, every time $I^1(x, y) = i$ the value of the i-th bin of the histogram is incremented by 1. Likewise, the joint probability $p_{I^1 I^2}(i, j)$ of the pair (i, j) indicates the frequency of joint occurrence of (i,j) in the pair of images (I^1, I^2), in the sense that when i appear in I^1, j appears in I^2 in the same position. Its value is obtained by computing the joint histogram of the two images normalized to the same number M of pixels:

$$p_{I^1 I^2(i,j)} = \frac{1}{W \cdot H} \sum_{x,y} \delta(i - I^1(x, y)) \cdot \delta(j - I^2(x, y)) \tag{5}$$

As a consequence, the MI for a pair of images can be expressed as:

$$MI(I^1, I^2) = \sum_{i \in \Omega_{I^1}} \sum_{j \in \Omega_{I^2}} p_{I^1 I^2}(i,j) \cdot \log \left(\frac{\log p_{I^1 I^2}(i,j)}{p_{I^1}(i) \cdot p_{I^2}(j)} \right). \tag{6}$$

3 MIMA System

MIMA is a multi-anchor tracking system which exploits the mutual information to follow the movement of the anchors in a video sequence. The system pre-processes the single frames so that the individual channels of the color image undergo a process of quantization, and the resulting bits are interleaved. In this way, though converting an image, originally represented in an RGB color space, into one with 8 bits depth, part of the information concerning the color is still preserved. The MI is the base of the tracking process, which has also been made more robust through further expedients such as the use of a weight matrix to discard outliers from the selection of the current position for an anchor, and the integration of a skin detection algorithm to increase the accuracy of hands tracking.

3.1 Image Preprocessing

The first step in the MIMA operations pipeline is the transformation of a 24-bit RGB image into a new 8-bit representation. The conversion is meant to preserve part of the information given by the color, which would be irretrievably lost with a trivial conversion of the image in grayscale. MIMA divides the image into the three fundamental channels R, G and B and for each of them considers only the most significant bits: namely three for red, three for green and two for blue. The bits selected for the individual channels are interleaved in order to form a string of 8 bits of the form <R_1 G_1 B_1 R_2 G_2 B_2 R_3 G_3>. The resulting image has the same aspect of a grayscale image, but carries information related to both luminance and chrominance. An example is provided in Figure 1.

Fig. 1. An example of a frame before and after reduction to 8 bits

3.2 Anchor Selection and Tracking

A correct initial selection of each anchor is an important condition for the general performance of tracking. Actually, this is a key problem in any tracking algorithm, because a wrong selection leads to a faster loss of the anchor. In a real application, the anchor would be selected automatically and in the shortest possible time, so as not to delay the start of the tracking process. Since the focus of our present work is on tracking rather than detection, in its current state MIMA provides manual selection for the initialization of the anchors. However, it is possible to adopt any algorithm in literature for automatic detection of head and hands, and use its results for automatic initialization of the anchors. MIMA represents each anchor A_k with a data structure, which contains the first and last frame in which the anchor has been detected, and the list of the coordinates of the upper left corner of its bounding box B_k, in the consecutive frames in this interval.

MIMA works on pairs of consecutive frames (F_{i-1}, F_i). Given the position of each anchor A_k in F_{i-1}, it looks for its position in the following frame F_i. The search process assumes that, although an anchor changes its position in two consecutive frames, the movement is limited within a neighborhood of the original position. Therefore, MIMA calculates the MI between the region of F_{i-1} contained within the bounding box B_k, starting from the upper left corner (x, y), and with width w and height h, and all its possible homologous ones contained in the rectangular region of F_i delimited by the vertices $(x-w, y-h)$ and $(x+2w, y+2h)$, as shown in Figure 2. Of course a containment test is performed for each possible homologous, to check if it is inside the image.

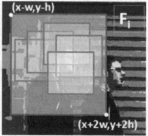

Fig. 2. Searching the position of an anchor in a frame, given its position in the preceding one

The values for *MI* computed for homologous bounding boxes are included in a matrix M, with dimension $2w \times 2h$. In particular, position $M(l, m)$ contains the value of *MI* computed between B_k in F_{i-1} at position (x, y) and the homologous in F_i at position $(x-w+l, y-h+m)$ with l in [0,2w] and m in [0, 2h]. The more similar the two homologous bounding boxes, the higher the *MI*. As a consequence, to determine the position of the anchor in the frame F_i it is sufficient to find the cell (l^*, m^*) in M corresponding to the maximum value of *MI*. The upper left corner of B_k in F_i will be therefore fixed at $(x-w+l^*, y-h+m^*)$.

3.3   Outlier Discarding and Error Correction

In the calculation of the matrix M, we might observe the possible presence of more maxima, some of which would possibly be relatively far away from the actual position of the anchor. The selection of one of these maxima, in place of the correct one, causes the bounding box to move to an incorrect position. Since the latter is considered afterwards for the search of a further new position for the anchor, the error would propagate frame by frame leading to a completely wrong position of the anchor (drift problem, see Figure 3).

Fig. 3. Propagation of an anchor location error

We can notice that, while the correct maximum of matrix M is usually in the centre of a cloud of relatively high values, maxima different (and relatively far) from the correct one are isolated and can be therefore considered as outliers. MIMA weights the values in matrix M with respect to the distance of the new candidate point in frame F_i from the anchor position in frame F_{i-1}. Each weight is computed as:

$$\gamma(l,m) = 1 - \frac{\sqrt{(w-l)^2 + (h-m)^2}}{\sqrt{w^2 + h^2}} \tag{7}$$

Therefore, the new weighted matrix M_γ is in the form:

$$M_\gamma(l,m) = \gamma(l,m) \cdot M(l,m) \tag{8}$$

where $0 \leq l \leq 2w$ and $0 \leq m \leq 2h$. A further increase in the precision of the tracker can be obtained by considering the specific context in which the MIMA system operates, namely, the tracking of human body parts. In fact, both the hands and the face (frontal and side pose) are usually characterized by a high content of skin. MIMA integrates a skin detector to increase the tracking accuracy of anchors attached to hands and face. The method adopted by MIMA for skin detection is the Explicitly Defined Skin Region, i.e., it defines the threshold values for the region of skin in the YCbCr colorspace. During the search for the new position of the bounding box B_k associated to the anchor A_k, MIMA does not select the absolute maximum in the weighted matrix M_γ, but considers the n highest values (in the present implementation, $n=5$). In this phase, the original color frames are considered. For each of the corresponding positions, MIMA measures the amount of skin present in the bounding box and selects the one with more skin. In practice, each out of the n candidate bounding boxes is transformed from the RGB color space to the YCbCr color space and a skin map is computed for it, i.e., a binary image where white pixels (value 1) represent skin and black pixels (value 0) represent a no-skin regions (Figure 4), according to the following equation:

$$skinmap(l,m) = \begin{cases} 1 & \begin{array}{l} if\ Cb(l,m) \in [77,127] \\ and\ Cr(l,m) \in [137,155] \end{array} \\ 0 & x \geq 0 \end{cases} \tag{9}$$

The amount of skin for the bounding box B_k is computed by counting the number of pixels set to one inside it.

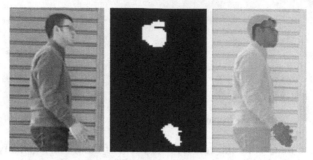

Fig. 4. Skin map for the anchors of hand and face

3.4   Anchors Overlapping and Algorithm for Conflict Solution

Occlusion and self-occlusion represent an important critical element for all tracking systems, since the overlap of two anchors may cause that when they separate the system continues to track only one of the two. MIMA solves this problem by using an algorithm to resolve conflicts between anchors. Even for this specific procedure, color frames are considered. The process of conflict resolution is limited to the analysis of only the portion of the image occupied by the bounding boxes involved in the collision (Figure 5) and is divided into two steps: i) recognition of the frame in which two disjoint bounding boxes merge/collide, ii) reallocation of the right anchors to the two bounding boxes detected. To this aim, when MIMA detects the collision between two anchors, it starts storing the centroid c_k of each bounding box involved in the collision. In addition, MIMA calculates and stores for the same bounding boxes the corresponding color histogram H_k. Specifically, the histogram H_k on the three channels R, G, and B is obtained by concatenating the three histograms calculated on individual channels. MIMA needs this information to be able to reassign correctly the anchors when they separate again. In the following we provide a more detailed description of the two steps of the algorithm for conflict resolution.

Fig. 5. Collision between two hands shaking

3.4.1   Detection of the Separation Between Two Overlapping Bounding Boxes

To better understand conflict resolution, assume to track two bounding boxes B_1 and B_2, associated respectively to anchors A_1 and A_2, and with centroids c_1 and c_2. The algorithm which determines the moment when the two anchors separate again works as follows:

1. determine the segment joining the two centroids and computes its midpoint $c_m(x_m, y_m)$;
2. using the method described in Section 3.3, compute the skin map for the portion of image delimited by the vertices $(x_m\text{-}s, y_m\text{-}t)$ e $(x_m\text{+}s, y_m\text{+}t)$, where s and t are the dimensions of the smaller bounding box between the two conflicting ones; then apply to the skin map the cascade of morphological operators opening, closing and hole filling.
3. identify the set of connected components C in the skin map obtained (regions with only 1s); the result of this step is the starting point to identify a possible anchor separation (i.e., the separation of a formerly merged region);
4. if at the previous point two connected components at least, say C_A and C_B, have been identified with a number of pixels higher than a threshold δ (in present implementation, δ=100 pixels and depends on image resolution), then execute the procedure to reassign anchors; in case of more candidates, the biggest ones are chosen.

3.4.2   Reassignment of Anchors to the Corresponding Bounding Boxes
The procedure to reassign anchors to the corresponding bounding boxes computes the Pearson correlation coefficient. The procedure uses the two histograms H_1 and H_2, that MIMA stored for the two bounding boxes B_1 and B_2, when it detected the collision, and the two histograms H_A e H_B computed for the two connected components identified when the bounding boxes separated. MIMA computes the four correlation coefficients, one for each possible coupling $H_{1,2}/H_{A,B}$, and selects the greatest one to determine the first final coupling; the second one is a mere consequence.

4   Experiments and Results

The test set [14] includes 24 videos (720×480) with different length and presenting different challenges. It was necessary to create a new dataset, since publicly available ones are not suited to carry out tests on the specific problem of body-part tracking, and in particular on the detection and recognition of interactive actions, which will be the object of our future work. As an example, the dataset described and made available at http://www-prima.inrialpes.fr/FGnet/data/03-Pointing/index.html#Scene%20setup is limited to video sequences of hand gestures, while we address a more complex setting were gestures are immersed in a real scenario involving full-body images of more subjects. Human Activity Video Datasets (https://www.cs.utexas.edu/~chaoyeh/web_ action_data/dataset_list. html) includes either datasets with higher "resolution" actions, like running, walking, etc., or with finer action classes which are out of the scope of our study. The whole dataset created for this work was partitioned into two groups, characterized by different kinds of problems. The first group includes videos where anchors do not undergo occlusions; the second group includes videos with partial or total occlusions of the anchors to track. Figure 6 shows an example of the first group (subjects exchanging a document) while Figure 7 shows a further example of the second group (see also Figure 5).

Videos were manually annotated to build a ground truth that is used to compare the anchor positions determined by MIMA. For each frame F_i, the coordinates of each anchor A_k in the ground truth are denoted with $GT_{i,k}(x_{i,k}^{GT}, y_{i,k}^{GT})$, while those determined by MIMA are denoted as $B_{i,k}(x_{i,k}^{B}, y_{i,k}^{B})$. Similarly, rectangular regions corresponding to the anchors from the ground truth and MIMA are denoted by $R_{i,k}^{GT}$ and $R_{i,k}^{B}$, respectively.

Fig. 6. Example frame with no anchor collision

Fig. 7. Example frame with anchor collision

Performance were measured according to the *Pascal index*, which offers an assessment of the validity of the determined anchor position. It is defined as:

$$P_{i,k} = \frac{Area\left(R_{i,k}^{GT} \cap R_{i,k}^{B}\right)}{Area\left(R_{i,k}^{GT} \cup R_{i,k}^{B}\right)}, \tag{10}$$

An anchor tracking is considered incorrect when the corresponding Pascal index falls below a threshold set to 1/3. A frame where all anchors are tracked correctly is considered as valid, while if for one anchor at least the index falls below the threshold, the frame is considered invalid. Though useful to determine the correctness of an estimated anchor position, Pascal index provides no information about the amount of error. For this reason we use a further indicator which evaluates the error between the positions of the bounding boxes estimated by the algorithm with respect to the ground truth of each anchor. The position error is given by the Euclidean distance between the coordinates $B_{i,k}$ estimated by MIMA for the anchor and the corresponding ones contained in ground truth $GT_{i,k}$:

$$E_{i,k} = \|B_{i,k} - GT_{i,k}\|^2. \tag{11}$$

In Table 1 we report the results for videos in the first group, where anchors are never occluded:

Table 1. Results for videos without anchor occlusion (Group I)

Video	Frames	Anchors	Valid Frames	Position Error
Video_01	65	4	(87,7 %)	0.56%
Video_02	45	4	(100 %)	0.34%
Video_03	180	4	(98,3 %)	0.46%
Video_04	100	4	(95 %)	0.46%
Video_05	100	4	(100 %)	0.23%
Video_06	125	4	(100 %)	0.34%
Video_07	120	4	(100 %)	0.46%
Video_08	75	4	(89,3 %)	0.46%
Video_09	70	4	(98,6 %)	0.34%
Video_10	85	4	(100 %)	0.34%
Video_11	130	4	(100 %)	0.34%
Video_12	40	4	(100 %)	0.34%
Video_13	55	4	(100 %)	0.46%

Table 2. Results for videos with anchor occlusion (Group II)

Video	Frames	Anchors	Valid Frames	Position Error
Video_15	82	4	(98,8 %)	0.23%
Video_16	50	2	(88 %)	0.46%
Video_17	95	2	(87,4 %)	0.56%
Video_18	180	4	(98,3 %)	0.23%
Video_19	130	4	(94,4 %)	0.56%
Video_20	95	4	(92,6 %)	0.46%
Video_21	110	4	(92,7 %)	0.46%
Video_22	100	4	(83 %)	0.56%
Video_23	92	4	(86,9 %)	0.46%
Video_24	90	4	(93,3 %)	0.46%
Video_15	82	4	(98,8 %)	0.23%

Table 3. Summary of results

Video	Frames	Valid Frames	Position Error
Group I	1280	(98 %)	0.46%
Group II	1024	(92,3 %)	0.34%

From Table 1, Table 2 and Table 3 we can see that the percentage of valid frames is firmly around 98% for videos without occlusion, and 92% for videos with partial or total anchor occlusion. Therefore, MIMA is able to achieve good results even with problematic anchor tracking. A slightly lower percentage of valid frames is obtained for videos in the second group, because the positioning of bounding boxes on the respective anchors during overlap is not optimal; this is due to the fact that the bounding boxes are located on the area pertaining to the anchor appearing in the foreground in the video. However, for such videos the position error is lower on the average, because after overlap the bounding boxes are positioned precisely from the conflict resolution procedure.

5   Conclusions

We proposed MIMA, a new multi-anchor approach for tracking human body parts. The system pre-processes the original RGB frame to obtain a new 8 bits grayscale image carrying on most color information. Mutual information allows MIMA to track anchors without performing any foreground/background segmentation. Several experiments have been carried out on 24 color video sequences. Results are encouraging: all targets were precisely tracked, as demonstrated by the low error rate. Anchor overlapping also does not represent a critical issue, since MIMA implements a collision detection/resolving protocol. Our current research along this line aims at integrating MIMA in a more general system for human interaction analysis. To this aim, a new dataset has been created and is publicly available, which better supports experiments related to the detection of specific interactive actions. In the future such dataset will be further extended and enlarged.

References

1. Bregler, C., Malik, J.: Tracking people with twists and exponential maps. In: IEEE Computer Vision and Pattern Recognition, pp. 8–15 (1998)
2. Cernekova, Z., Pitas, I., Nikou, C.: Information theory-based shot cut/fade detection and video summarization. IEEE Transactions on Circuits and Systems for Video Technology **16**(1), 82–91 (2006)
3. Dame, A., Marchand, E.: Accurate real-time tracking using mutual information. In: 9th IEEE International Symposium on Mixed and Augmented Reality, pp. 47–56 (2010)
4. Haritaoglu, I., Harwood, D., Davis, L.S.: W^4: real-time surveillance of people and their activities. IEEE Trans. on Pattern Analysis and Machine Intelligence **22**(8), pp. 809–830 (2000)

5. Hogg, D.: Model based vision: A program to see a walking person. Image and Vision Computing **1**(1), 5–20 (1983)
6. Johansson, G.: Visual motion perception. Science American **232**(6), 76–88 (1975)
7. Loutas, E., Pitas, I., Nikou, C.: Probabilistic multiple face detection and tracking using entropy measures. IEEE Transactions on Circuits and Systems for Video Technology **14**(1), 128–135 (2004)
8. Okada, R., Shirai, Y., Miura, J.: Tracking a person with 3D motion by integrating optical flow and depth. In: 4th IEEE International Conference on Automatic Face and Gesture Recognition, France, pp. 336–341 (2000)
9. Qian, R.J., Huang, T.S.: Estimating articulated motion by decomposition, Time-Varying Image Processing and Moving Object Recognition, 3-V. Cappellini (Ed.), pp. 275–286 (1994)
10. Sato, K., Aggarwal, J.K.: Tracking and recognizing two-person interactions in outdoor image sequences. In: IEEE Workshop on Multi-Object Tracking, Canada, pp. 87–94 (2001)
11. Shannon, C.: A mathematical theory of communication. Bell System Technical Journal **27**(3), 379–423 (1948)
12. Sidenbladh, H., Black, M.J., Fleet, D.J.: Stochastic Tracking of 3D Human Figures Using 2D Image Motion. In: Vernon, D. (ed.) ECCV 2000. LNCS, vol. 1843, pp. 702–718. Springer, Heidelberg (2000)
13. Wren, C., Azarbayejani, A., Darrell, T., Pentland, A.: Pfinder: real-time tracking of the human body. IEEE Trans. on Pattern Analysis and Machine Intelligence **19**(7), 780–785 (1997)
14. http://biplab.unisa.it/InterActions.zip

A Framework for Fast Low-Power Multi-sensor 3D Scene Capture and Reconstruction

Aleksandra Chuchvara, Mihail Georgiev, and Atanas Gotchev[✉]

Tampere University of Technology, Tampere, Finland
{aleksandra.chuchvara,mihail.georgiev,atanas.gotchev}@tut.fi

Abstract. We present a computational framework, which combines depth and colour (texture) modalities for 3D scene reconstruction. The scene depth is captured by a low-power photon mixture device (PMD) employing the time-of-flight principle while the colour (2D) data is captured by a high-resolution RGB sensor. Such 3D capture setting is instrumental in 3D face recognition tasks and more specifically in depth-guided image segmentation, 3D face reconstruction, pose modification and normalization, which are important pre-processing steps prior to feature extraction and recognition. The two captured modalities come with different spatial resolution and need to be aligned and fused so to form what is known as view-plus-depth or RGB-Z 3D scene representation. We discuss specifically the low-power operation mode of the system, where the depth data appears very noisy and needs to be effectively denoised before fusing with colour data. We propose using a modification of the non-local means (NLM) denoising approach, which in our framework operates on complex-valued data thus providing certain robustness against low-light capture conditions and adaptivity to the scene content. Further in our approach, we implement a bilateral filter on the range point-cloud data, ensuring very good starting point for the data fusion step. The latter is based on the iterative Richardson method, which is applied for efficient non-uniform to uniform resampling of the depth data using structural information from the colour data. We demonstrate a real-time implementation of the framework based on GPU, which yields a high-quality 3D scene reconstruction suitable for face normalization and recognition.

Keywords: ToF · 2D/3D · Depth · Fusion · Denoising · NLM · Face · ICP

1   Introduction

In the fields of pattern recognition, computer vision and biometrics, 2D and 3D scene capture and understanding are active areas of research due to the variety of practical applications such as biometric identification/authentication for security and access control purposes, behavioral and psychological analysis for various commercial applications, object tracking, and many others. Among visual scenes, scenes containing human faces are of particular interest and the task of face recognition has been thoroughly studied mainly by using two-dimensional (2D) imagery. One particular advantage of conventional face recognition systems based on 2D images is a fast and low-cost data acquisition. However, 2D facial images can vary strongly depending on

© Springer International Publishing Switzerland 2014
V. Cantoni et al. (Eds.): BIOMET 2014, LNCS 8897, pp. 40–53, 2014.
DOI: 10.1007/978-3-319-13386-7_4

many factors such as viewpoint, head orientation, illumination, different facial expressions, even aging and makeup, which can significantly decrease the system performance. Thus, in most cases, it is necessary to maintain a canonical frontal facial pose and consistent illumination in order to achieve good recognition performance.

In order to overcome the above-mentioned limitations and improve face recognition accuracy, more and more approaches suggest utilizing 3D facial data, which can be acquired by dedicated range sensors. Systems utilizing structural information of the facial surface are less dependent to the pose and/or illumination changes, which mostly affecting 2D image based systems. Accurate depth sensing is a challenging task especially in presence of a real-time constraint. Recent advances in Time-of-Flight (ToF) depth sensing technologies made fast acquisition of 3D information about facial structure and motion a feasible task. ToF sensors are much less expensive and more compact than other traditional 3D imaging systems used for 3D model acquisition. ToF sensors can deliver range data at high frame rates enabling real-time interactive applications. ToF depth sensors acquire depth information in a form of perspective-fixed range images often referred to as 2.5D models, which provides valuable information for object detection and recognition and can greatly assist tasks of face segmentation, i.e. removal of non-facial data such as neck, torso and hair, and face normalization, i.e. alignment of the face data in a canonical position. These tasks are usually performed before the actual feature extraction and recognition take place.

A number of ToF imaging applications has been proposed in the fields of face detection and recognition [1–4], gesture recognition [5], and real-time segmentation and tracking [6, 7]. A survey on face recognition and 3D face recognition using depth sensors has been presented in [1]. A face recognition system based on ToF depth images has been proposed in [2]: as the performance of 3D face recognition is highly dependent upon the distance noise, the problem of low quality of the ToF data has been specifically addressed. A ToF face detection approach has been presented in [3], where range data yields a significant robustness and accuracy improvement of the face detector. Other systems tend to utilize multimodal approaches combining 2D and 3D features. A face recognition system using a combination of color, depth and thermal-IR data has been proposed in [4]. The system is calibrated and tested in order to select optimal sensor combination for various environmental conditions. In [5], a real-time 3D hand gesture interaction system based on ToF and RGB cameras has been presented: an improved hand detection algorithm utilizing ToF depth allows for recognition of complex 3D gestures. A framework for real-time segmentation and tracking fusing depth and color data has been proposed in [6], aimed at solving some common problems, such as fast motion, occlusions and tackling objects with similar color. In [7], a low-complexity real-time segmentation algorithm utilizing color and ToF depth information has been presented. The robust performance for the approach is based on simultaneous analysis of depth, color and motion information.

The major advantage of a ToF sensor compared to other depth estimation techniques is its ability to deliver entire depth map at a high frame rate and independently of textured surfaces and scene illumination. However, current ToF devices have certain technology limitations associated with their working principle, such as low sensor resolution (e.g. 200×200 pixels) compared to Full High-Definition (HD) (1920×1080) of color cameras, inaccuracies in depth measurements, and limited ability to capture color information [8]. A solution is to combine a depth sensor with one or multiple 2D cameras responsible for color capture into a single multisensor system.

In this paper, we propose an end-to-end multi-sensor system combining a conventional RGB camera and a ToF range sensor with the purpose to perform real-time 3D scene sensing and reconstruction, which is instrumental for face recognition tasks, e.g. 3D face reconstruction, depth-guided segmentation, pose modification and normalization. Different combinations of high-resolution video cameras and low-resolution ToF sensors have been studied. The setups most related to our work, which utilize configuration with a single color view and a single ToF sensor, are described in [9–12]. A rather straightforward data fusion scheme has been implemented in [9]. The data fusion is implemented by mapping the ToF data as 3D point clouds and projecting them onto the color camera sensor plane, resulting in pixel-to-pixel projection alignment of color and depth maps. Subsequently, the color image is back-projected as a texture onto ToF sensor plane. Approaches described in [11] up-sample low-resolution depth maps by means of adaptive multi-lateral filtering (proposed in [13]) in a way that it prevents edge blurring in geometry data while smoothing it over continuous regions. With GPU implementation, this approach is shown to be feasible for real-time applications. An efficient method for the ToF and color data fusion, which generates the 3D scene on-the-fly utilizing FPGA hardware, has been presented in [10]. In [12] an efficient spatio-temporal filtering approach has been proposed that simultaneously denoises the depth video and increases its spatial resolution to match the color video.

2   System Overview

In this section, an end-to-end 3D video system for real-time 3D scene sensing and reconstruction is presented (Fig. 1). The input data is generated by a multisensor setup combining a ToF depth sensor and a color camera. The two sensors are displaced and have different field of view and spatial resolution. Therefore, the distance data acquired from the low-resolution ToF sensor needs to be projectively aligned and fused with color data; a process, referred to as 2D/ToF data fusion. Computationally, this requires reprojection of the depth data from the low-resolution grid to world coordinates and then back on the higher-resolution grid of the color sensor followed by resampling to get the depth values at the grid points.

An accurate fusion of distance and color information requires reliable estimation of the relative positions of the cameras and their internal calibration parameters. A number of approaches have been published aimed at calibrating multiple color cameras with range sensors [14–16]. Calibration between depth and color sensors by a

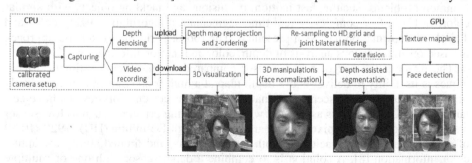

Fig. 1. Capturing, streaming and data processing pipeline

maximum likelihood solution utilizing a checkerboard similar to a stereo system calibration has been proposed in [14, 15]. Range-specific calibration techniques have been proposed in [14, 16]. First, the cameras are calibrated separately for the internal parameters, such as focal length and principal point coordinates, resulting in the camera calibration matrices K_{RGB} and K_{TOF}. Second, the stereo calibration step provides the external camera parameters: a rotation matrix - R_{3x3} and a translation vector – t_{3x1}, which form the relative transformation $RT_{TOF \rightarrow RGB}=[R|t]$ between optical centers of the ToF camera and the RGB camera. Due to the fixed setup, these parameters have to be determined only once during the preliminary initialization stage in offline mode.

In our setup, a ToF camera based on the Photonic Mixer Device (PMD) principle is used [17]. To get distance data, a PMD sensor measures the phase-delay between an emitted wave and its reflected replica. A typical PMD consists of a beamer, an electronic light modulator and a sensor chip (e.g. CMOS or CCD). The beamer is made of an array of light-emitting diodes (LED) operating in near-infrared wavelengths (e.g. 850 nm). It radiates a point-source light of a continuously-modulated harmonic signal which illuminates the scene. The light reflected from object surfaces is sensed back by pixels of the sensor chip, which collects pixel charges for some interval denoted as *integration time*. For each pixel, the range data is estimated in relation to phase-delay between the sensed signal and the one of the light modulator. The phase-delay estimation is performed as a discrete cross-correlation of several successively captured samples taken between equal intervals during same modulation periods of fixed frequency. Denote the sample data as R_n (n=1, 2,..., N-1, $N \geq 4$). The amplitude A and phase φ of the signal are estimated from the sampled data, while the sensed distance D is proportional to the phase φ:

$$A = \frac{2}{N} \left| \sum_{n=0}^{N-1} R_n e^{-j2\pi\frac{n}{N}} \right|, \varphi = \arg\left(\sum_{n=0}^{N-1} R_n e^{-j2\pi\frac{n}{N}} \right), D \propto \frac{\varphi}{4\pi f} c_L, \quad (1)$$

where j is the imaginary unit, f is the frequency of the emitted signal and c_L is the speed of light through dry air (~298.109km/h).

Due to the operational principles of the ToF range sensor, significant amount of noise is present in the captured range data. The depth measurement noise is amplified during the fusion process and degrades the quality of the fused data. Thus, prior to the data fusion step, denoising of depth data should be performed in order to reduce the noise and remove outliers. The problem of denoising of ToF data has been addressed in a number of works [18-21]. Modern denoising approaches, such as edge-preserving bilateral filtering [22] and non-local filtering [23], have been modified to deal with ToF data [19, 21]. In [18], a range-adaptive bilateral filter has been proposed, by adjusting its size according to ToF amplitude measurements, since the noise level in distance measurements varies depending on the amplitude of the recorded signal [19]. In our work, we specifically consider the 2D/ToF fusion in the so-called low-sensing mode. In such a mode, the ToF sensor is restricted, e.g. by technological limitations, to operate in poor imaging conditions. These include low number of emitting diodes, or low power or short integration time. In such conditions, the noise becomes a dominant problem, which should be addressed by dedicated denoising methods [20, 21].

2.1   ToF Denoising

Measurement accuracy of a ToF sensor is limited by the power of the emitted signal and depends on many factors, such as light intensity, different reflectivity of surfaces, distances to objects in a scene, etc. Erroneous range measurements [21] can be caused e.g. by multiple reflections to the sensed signals, sensing objects having low-reflectivity materials and colors, or small incident angle.

When in low-powered sensing mode, the ToF sensor is usually also with low spatial resolution, meeting technological limitations such as requirements for miniaturization of the beamer size and reducing the number of LED elements for cost-efficient hardware and embedding into portable devices. This leads to very noisy range images of a very low resolution. Degradations in the range data impede the projective mapping function in the 2D/3D fusion process. The case is illustrated in Fig. 2: one can observe that while the original noisy range data represents some scene structure, the fused output is fully degraded and useless. The process of surface based z-ordering becomes extremely unstable and no confidence of occluded and hidden data can be estimated (Fig. 2 3rd row). Due to the noise influence on the projected position, some areas of the rendered surface get artificially expanded and shadow some true areas. The effect impedes the non-uniform resampling at the stage of data fusion and also illustrates the importance of proper care of the range noise prior to fusion procedure.

We specifically address the noise reduction as a post-capture stage applied to low-sensed range data with the aim to achieve a 2D/ToF data fusion result with quality as if the ToF sensor was working in normal operating mode (Fig. 2). We have proposed a three-stage denoising technique: a raw data (system) denoising, point-cloud projection and denoising, and non-uniform resampling combined with depth refinement.

For the system denoising stage, we propose a technique based on the state-of-the art *non-local means* (NLM) denoising approach [24]. The general idea of NLM filtering is to find blocks (patches) similar to a reference block and to calculate a noise-free estimate of the central pixel of that reference block based on weighted average of the corresponding pixels in the similar blocks, where weights are proportional to the measured similarities.

In our approach, the signal components of the phase-delay and the amplitude of the sensed signal are regarded as components of a complex-valued random variable and processed together in a single step. The map for similarity search, denoted by U in our approach is chosen to be the pre-computed maps of $(A, \varphi) - (A_U, \varphi_U)$ given in Eq.(1) and pixel-wise combined into a complex-valued map, denoted by Z, while the modified NLM filter (NLM_{CLX}) is given by:

$$(\varphi_U, A_U) \rightarrow Z = A_U \left(e^{j\varphi_U} \right), \ Z \rightarrow A_U = |Z|, \ Z \rightarrow \varphi_U = \arg(Z)$$

$$NLM_{CLX}[x] = \frac{1}{C_N(x)} \int_\Omega \exp\left(-\frac{G \times |Z(x+.) - Z(y+.)|(0)}{h^2} \right) Z(y) dy . \tag{2}$$

In the equation C_N denotes a normalization factor, G is a Gaussian kernel, Ω is the search range, U is the pixel map, x is the index of filtered pixel, y is the running index of center pixels in similarity patches, h is a tuning filter parameter, and $\times \cdot (0)$ denotes a centered convolution operator, while $(+.)$ denotes the range of pixel indices of spatial neighborhood.

Fig. 2. Role of denoising. Left, (clockwise): ToF range image; detected face region; noisy (I_T=50μs) face region; GT face region. Right, in rows: fusion, segmentation and z-ordering; using (in columns) GT, noisy, denoised depth.

The complex-valued representation of the sensed signal facilitates the block search stage and leads to better filter adaptivity and similarity weighting with reduced computational complexity. The complex-domain filtering implies simultaneous filtering of all signal components in a single step, thus it provides additional feedback in the form of improved (noise-reduced) confidence parameter given by A, which can be utilized in iterative de-noising schemes. Such NLM_{CLX} filter can be easily extended to similarity search in temporal neighborhood of successively-captured frames, where temporal similarity is beneficial [28]. Such spatio-temporal filtering provides significant boost in denoising for small number of frames (e.g. 3) and for decreased size of the searched spatial neighborhood. The spatio-temporal search allows additional trade-off for using shorter integration times, and thus increases the number of frames which can be used. This provides an effective over-complete observation structure instrumental for effective denoising. Further modification is focused on speed. We have proposed a real-time version of NLM_{CLX} denoising filter – $S(implified)NLM_{CLX}$. It is only slightly inferior in terms of quality, however achieves an $O(1)$ complexity. The idea is to first apply a global pre-filtering in order to simplify the patch similarity search by utilizing summed area tables (SATs) and smart look-up table data fetching [28].

In contrast to other 2D/ToF fusion approaches, which suggest working in planar coordinates, our approach includes a second-stage denoising refinement data projected in the 3D world coordinate system (i.e. data point cloud). It makes use of the surface information presented in the point cloud of range measurements [20]. The property that surf mesh data could exist on the unique optical ray formed by corresponding range pixel and camera center can be used for a surface mesh denoising in the flavor of the techniques given in [13].

2.2 Resampling and Data Fusion

Depth and color data fusion refers to a process of depth data reprojection and color-aided resampling. As the two cameras in the setup cannot be placed at the same position, their viewpoints are shifted relative to each other and also viewing directions may be slightly different. Thus, to align the depth information with the color image, every pixel of the depth image needs to be reprojected in the coordinate system of the color image. This transformation is usually performed in two steps, often referred to as 3D warping. First, each pixel of the ToF image $d(u, v)$ is converted into a corresponding 3D point in terms of a homogeneous coordinate – $(x, y, z, w)^T$:

$$x = u \cdot z / f_{TOF}, y = v \cdot z / f_{TOF}, z = f_{TOF} \cdot d(u,v) / \sqrt{f_{TOF}^2 + u^2 + v^2}, \ w = 1, \tag{3}$$

where f_{TOF} is the focal length of the ToF sensor. The second step is to project every 3D point on the image plane of the color camera:

$$(x, y, w)_{RGB} = K_{RGB} \cdot RT_{TOF \to RGB} \cdot (x, y, z, w)^T, \ (u, v)_{RGB} = (x, y)_{RGB} / w_{RGB}, \tag{4}$$

where $RT_{TOF \to RGB}$ and K_{RGB} are calibration parameters of the system and $(u, v)_{RGB}$ are the image coordinates for a global point $(x, y, z, w)^T$ within the RGB image grid.

In order to obtain a dense depth map, the depth data should be upscaled to match the resolution of the color image. One particular problem is that the points projected to the color camera image grid do not fall to the integer positions and also are very sparse due to the low resolution of depth data. The unknown values at the regular positions of color image grid need to be estimated from sparsely scattered irregular data, imposing a non-uniform resampling problem. An accurate non-uniform to uniform resampling in real time is a challenging task and still an open research problem [24]. It is important to utilize structural information presented in the high-resolution color data in the depth resampling process to properly align the multisensory data.

A non-uniform to uniform iterative resampling method has been proposed in [20]. The proposed method makes use of the color information by applying color-driven bilateral filter to the result of interpolated depth at each iteration (referred to as joint- or cross-bilateral filter [13]). The depth-refining resampling starts from an initial depth approximation on the high definition grid obtained by fitting Voronoi cells (V) around projected irregular depth samples followed by nearest-neighbor interpolation in the flavor of [25]. So-interpolated depth map d undergoes a joint-bilateral filtering (JBF) as defined in [13]. The role of the JBF is to smooth any blocky artifacts arising from the preceeding interpolation while aligning it with object edges of the color image. In order to estimate the error between the interpolated and the initial depth values, the values at the starting irregular locations are calculated by bilinear interpolation (L) of the refined depth d. The obtained error values are then interpolated again with V and added to d, and the procedure is repeated. By defining the depth map

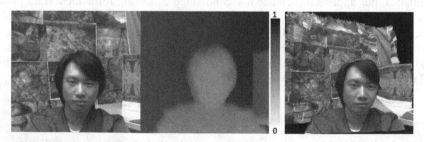

Fig. 3. Data fusion: view-plus-depth frame and 3D textured surface

obtained after i-th iteration as d_i, initial depth values at irregular positions as z, and a relaxation parameter by λ, the whole iterative procedure can be formalized as follows:

$$d_{i+1} = JBF(d_i + \lambda V(z - L(d_i))). \tag{5}$$

The use of bilinear interpolation for depth values calculation at the irregular locations is motivated by the observation that depth maps can be modeled as piecewise-linear functions at local neighborhood and interpolators of higher degree are not beneficial.

The point-based depth reprojection comes along with one particular problem, namely z-ordering of projected points for detecting possible dis-occlusions. This requires an additional pre-processing of the projected data: ToF samples which are not visible from the color camera position are considered as "hidden points" and have to be filtered out before interpolation, in order to prevent the liking of hidden background information. A solution to the z-ordering problem is provided by our GPU-based rendering approach [26]. In order to generate a depth map corresponding to the viewpoint of the color camera, the algorithm makes use of a 3D mesh representation of the scene obtained using the ToF depth data. The depth data is represented as a triangulated surface mesh and then rendered as if observed from the point of view of the color camera. This constructs a depth map projectively aligned with the color image. During the rendering process, some depth testing is performed automatically and only the minimum per-pixel z-distance is stored in the depth buffer. Modern GPUs provide hardware support for triangulated non-uniform bi-linear resampling, which can be used for the fast resampling of the obtained depth map. However, the depth map obtained with bilinear interpolation needs to be further refined by a color-controlled filtering, e.g. *JBF*, so that color edges and depth discontinuities get aligned. The color image can be applied as a texture to the refined 3D depth surface. The textured surface can be then rotated, scaled and translated as needed to generate any arbitrary view (Fig. 3).

2.3   Depth-Assisted Segmentation

In a color plus depth imagery, a region containing a face can be detected by a cascade classifier mechanism, as in [27]. Then, the associated depth can be utilized for efficient face segmentation. An example of fast depth-assisted segmentation approach utilizing 2D color and depth information as well as motion information has been proposed in [7], where motion between two consecutive color and range frames is analyzed to locate preliminary region of interest within the scene. Then, a refinement algorithm delineates the segmented area. Object motion in a scene is detected by tracking pixel-wise color and depth changes between two consecutive frames. The temporal differences between both color and depth are mutually thresholded with certain value resulting in a region mask of detected motion. Initial foreground mask is estimated by applying a region growing algorithm, which uses so called "pixel seeds", which in our case are the ones detected in motion mask. The idea of the region growing algorithm is the following: a chosen seeding pixel is compared for similarity with the neighboring ones, and then added to the seeding region, thus growing it.

The foreground mask obtained with the growing algorithm can contain false inclusion of background areas due to errors in the depth map. This kind of errors can be tackled by using more precise edge information from the color data, which results in improved foreground mask. To reduce boundary errors, so-called 'tri-map' is generated as follows: pixels inside the foreground mask are marked as 'certain foreground', the ones outside – as 'certain background', and pixels near the edges are marked as 'uncertain'. Then a *K-nn* search of the nearest pixels is performed in order to decide whether an uncertain pixel belongs to foreground or background by comparing its color to the certain foreground and certain background neighbors. The segmentation results, obtained using the described method, are illustrated in Fig. 2 Right.

2.4   Face Normalization by Iterative Closest Point Methods

A proper face alignment is viable for biometric applications involving facial data such as facial feature extraction, expression estimation, motion tracking and recognition. Usually such applications heavily rely on the use of trained classified data where certain face pose of limited misalignment variation was utilized for training. The process of face alignment to certain pose is referred in the state of the art literature to as face normalization [3, 4, 32, 33]. A rigid alignment for face normalization utilizing degrees of freedom (DoF) such as: angle rotations, translation shifts, and scaling can be obtained by utilizing so called Iterative Closest Points (ICP) algorithm [31].

Basically, the ICP algorithm is data registration applied on 3D data point clouds [30]. First, the algorithm takes a source of point cloud data as reference and targets one as template. Then, for each point in the template, it locates the closest point in the source, and aims at minimizing the error between these points by applying a rigid transformation between the two meshes. This process is repeated until a threshold error is reached. The ICP solution may vary according to data selection [34], outlier filtering [31, 34], minimization constraints [29], or "closeness" metrics [34].

3   Performance Validation on Biometric Pre-processing Tasks

We illustrate the performance of our 3D capture and processing framework by experiments characteristic for typical biometric tasks such as face detection, tracking and recognition [2, 3, 4]. The first experiment demonstrates face projection alignment and fusion of color and depth data in the presence of noise. The second experiment demonstrates the performance of the system for ICP-based face normalization. The experimental equipment consists of custom designed 2D/ToF camera setup consisting of a Prosilica GE-1900C high-definition color camera and a PMDTech CamCube 2.0 ToF device mounted on a rig, where both cameras are vertically aligned with a baseline $B = 6$ cm. The scene represents a person frontally facing the cameras at a distance of 1.2 meters and sitting in front of a flat background situated in 2.5 meters.

3.1   2D/ToF Fusion of Face Images

The face is detected utilizing a real-time modification of the Viola and Jones algorithm [27], [35] (Fig. 2). The detected face region U_F in the range map is used to quantify the denoising performance. The effect of noise in low-powered sensing environment was simulated by changing the integration times of the ToF sensor for range $I_T \in [2000 \div 50] \mu s$, where the normal operating mode corresponds to $I_T = 2000 \mu s$. To get ground truth data (GT), we have averaged 200 consecutively captured frames in normal operating mode. The low-sensing case is characterized by measured amplitude of the reflected signal A<250 units [21]. For such amplitudes, it is expected that the error of the measured depth exceeds the one specified for normal operating mode [17]. The corresponding input low-sensed (and potentially wrong) depth pixels are counted as percentage of all available depth pixels and denoted as "BAD" (Table 1). Pixels having measurement error twice exceeding the corresponding GT range value after processing are considered uninformative and marked as "IMP". The noisy data has been processed by our $SNLM_{CLX}$ approach, working in real time. The denoising results are given in Table 1 and depicted in Fig. 4, where the comparison metrics are calculated as follows:

$$PSNR[dB] = 20\log_{10}\left(\frac{D_{MAX}}{\sqrt{MSE}}\right), \; MSE = \frac{1}{S_U}\sum_{j=0}^{S_U-1}(U_F(j) - U_F'(j))^2, \tag{6}$$

where U_F and U_F' correspond to noise-free input and noisy (or denoised) range output of face regions, S_U is number of pixels, and D_{MAX}=7.5m. The results demonstrate a robust denoising performance as the processed output is quite close to the ground truth data. Facial features such as filtrum, nose, and eyelids are apparently visible (c.f. Fig. 4). The denoising improvement is substantial and higher than 14 dB. As commented in [2], a denoising improvement of 12-14 dB ensures some 50-70 percent improvement in recognition when PCA or M(LDA) classifiers are used (see Table 1 in [2]).

Table 1. Denoising performance of proposed algorithms

$I_T[\mu s]$	2000	1000	800	500	400	200	100	80	50
BAD pixels, [%]	1	20	26	44	51	100	100	100	100
IMP pixels[%]	0	0	0	0	0	0.1	1.7	6.5	11.8
Noisy,[dB]	40.18	36.29	35.43	31.64	29.82	23.41	14.92	12.29	14.32
$SNLM_{CLX}$,[dB]	47.23	38.15	39.62	37.89	37.73	36.01	32.75	30.21	30.02

3.2   Face Normalization

For the face normalization experiment we have implemented the classical ICP approach as presented in [29]. The following test was performed. A face with given GT

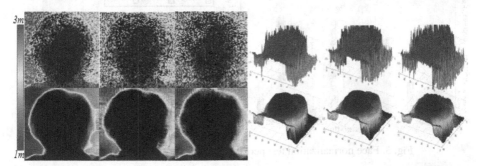

Fig. 4. Image and surface plots. Rows: noisy input and denoised output for I_T= 200, 100, 50 μs.

geometry was transformed in 6 degrees of freedom (DoF) consisting of 3D axial angles Pitch(φ), Yaw (θ), Roll(ψ) and vector of translation shifts $T = (x, y, z)$. The angles got arbitrary values in the (extreme) range [-30°, 30°] and the translation was fixed to a rather big shift of 40 cm. For the face normalization purposes, the proper estimation of T is considered insignificant [4], what is important in our case is to acquire data "*en face*". The results of face normalization by ICP are given in Table 2 and depicted in Fig. 5. Two metrics were utilized: the mean and the variance of misalignment error denoted as E_{MEAN} and E_{VAR} respectively. The results demonstrate the benefit of denoising pre-processing of low-sensed data. The results of E_{MEAN} and E_{VAR} show a substantial decrease of misalignment error (i.e. low E_{MEAN}) and improvement of robustness (i.e. low E_{VAR}). There is an interesting anomaly in the result. The face normalization performance of denoised results for less noisy input data (e.g. I_T=1000μs) is inferior to the ones for shorter integration times (e.g. I_T=50μs), thus noisier. This is explained by the adaptive mechanism of our filter. For the sensed data that is *expected* to have relatively small amount of noise according to higher values of A, our technique does not apply heavy filtering. However, in the case of facial data, low-sensing artifacts caused by multi-reflectivity paths are observed in the areas of eye pupils and hair [21]. They are presented in the depth modality but not in the amplitude one. Still, the obtained results for less noisy data show good robust performance for E_{MEAN}= ~1° and E_{VAR} = ~0°. An additional demonstration of ICP performance for face normalization is given in Fig. 6, where misaligned angle error is visually depicted for the extreme angle misalignments of 30°.

Table 2. Face normalization by ICP

	$I_T[\mu s]$	1000			200			100			50		
	DoF	φ	Θ	Ψ	Φ	θ	ψ	Φ	θ	ψ	φ	θ	Ψ
Noisy	$E_{MEAN},$ [°]	0.4	1.1	1.2	1.9	3.3	2.5	4.1	4.1	4.2	4.4	4.3	4.5
	$E_{VAR},$ [°]	0.1	1.3	0.1	2.2	7.4	5	9.5	13	10	14	19	12
Denoised	$E_{MEAN},$ [°]	0.5	0.5	1.5	0.3	0.4	0.9	0.2	0.3	0.3	0.5	0.8	0.2
	$E_{VAR},$ [°]	0.1	0.4	0	0	0.5	0	0	0.3	0	0	0.7	0

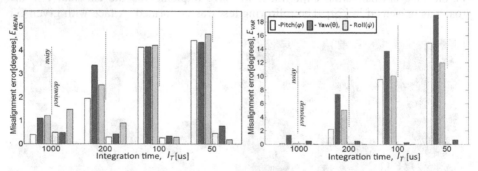

Fig. 5. Face normalization test performance for E_{MEAN} and E_{VAR} metrics

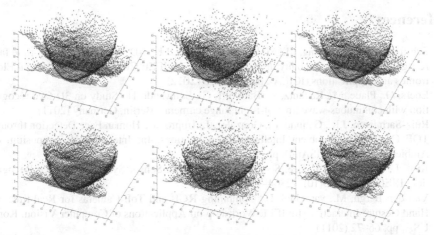

Fig. 6. Demonstration of ICP misalignment performance (columns): a) GT, b) noisy data – I_T=50μs, and c) denoised output; (rows): d) initial displacement – (φ, θ, ψ) = 30°, e) face normalized output by ICP

4   Conclusion

In this paper, we have presented a framework for 3D scene capture and reconstruction. It includes hardware and software systems aimed at efficient sensing and computing in real time. The hardware module includes an RGB color camera of high definition and a ToF active range sensor of rather low resolution. The two sensors are vertically aligned and properly jointly calibrated. The main aim of the computing system is to support the work of the sensors in low-sensing mode. Thus, it contains specific solutions for range data denoising, upscaling and 2D/ToF data fusion. Three-stage denoising approach has been proposed. The first stage employs a version of the NLM method, modified to work with complex-valued spatio-temporal data. The second stage performs denoising in the point cloud by making use of the specific nature of depth data. The third stage utilizes structural information from the aligned color sensor and refines the upscaled depth at the stage of non-uniform resampling. As a result, the 2D+depth data provides 3D scene reconstruction with quality as high as if the range sensor was working in normal sensing mode. The performance of the system has been validated by experiments aimed at preprocessing for typical biometric tasks such as face detection, segmentation, surface mapping and normalization. The denoising improves the signal to noise ratio by more than 14 dB thus providing 2.5 D face data good enough for the subsequent stage of feature extraction and recognition. ICP-based face normalization works also fine on the denoised depth maps. In this case, it turns out that noisier data can lead to even better denoising results due to the amplitude component, which implicitly controls the distances between similar patches in the complex-valued modification of the NLM method. While demonstrated for face recognition tasks, the 3D capture and reconstruction framework is perfectly applicable to other biometric tasks where the availability of dynamic 3D scene is required. Such tasks may include body segmentation and tracking for e.g. human behavioral analysis.

References

1. Schimbinschi, F., Wiering, M., Mohan, R.E., Sheba, J.K.: 4D unconstrained real-time face recognition using a commodity depth camera. In: 7th IEEE Conference on Industrial Electronics and Applications (ICIEA), pp. 166–173 (2012)
2. Ebers, O., Plaue, M., Raduntz, T., Barwolff, G., Schwandt, H.: Study on 3D face recognition with continuous-wave time-of-flight range cameras, Berlin, Germany (2011)
3. Ruiz-Sarmiento, J.R., Galindo, C., Gonzalez, J.: Improving Human Face Detection through TOF Cameras for Ambient Intelligence Applications. In: International Symposium on Ambient Intelligence (ISAmI), pp. 125–132 (2011)
4. Kim, J., Yu, S., Kim, I., Lee, S.: 3D Multi-Spectrum Sensor System with Face Recognition. IEEE Sensros **13**(10), 12804–12827 (2013)
5. Van den Bergh, M., van Gool, L.: Combining RGB and ToF Cameras for Real-time 3D Hand Gesture Interaction. In: IEEE Workshop on Applications of Computer Vision, Kona, USA, pp. 66–72 (2011)
6. Bleiweiss, A., Werman, M.: Fusing Time-of-Flight Depth and Color for Real-Time Segmentation and Tracking. In: DAGM Workshop on Dyn. 3D Imaging, Germany (2009)
7. Mirante, E., Georgiev, M., Gotchev, A.: A fast image segmentation algorithm using color and depth map. In: 3DTV (2011)
8. Kolb, A., Barth, E., Koch, R., Larsen, R.: Time-of-flight cameras in computer graphics. Computer Graphics Forum **29**(1), 141–159 (2010)
9. Lindner, M., Kolb, A., Hartmann, K.: Data-fusion of PMD-based distance-information and high-resolution RGB-images. In: Symposium on Signals Circuits and Systems (ISSCS), pp. 121–124 (2007)
10. Linarth, A., Penne, J., Liu, B., Jesorsky, O., Kompe, R.: Fast fusion of range and video sensordata. In: Advanced Microsystems for Automotive Applications, pp. 119–134 (2007)
11. Chan, D., Buisman, H., Theobalt, C., Thrun, S.: A noise-aware filter for real-time depth upsampling. In: Workshop on Multi-camera and Multi-modal Sensor Fusion Algorithms and Applications, European Conference on Computer Vision (ECCV) (2008)
12. Richardt, C., Stoll, C., Dodgson, N., Seidel, H., Theobalt, C.: Coherent Spatiotemporal Filtering, Upsampling and Rendering of RGBZ Videos. In: Computer Graphics Forum (Proceedings of Eurographics), vol. 31 (2012)
13. Kopf, J., Cohen, M., Lischinski, D., Uyttendaele, M.: Joint Bilateral Upsampling. In: Special Interest Group on Comp. Graphics and Int. Techniques (SIGGRAPH) (2007)
14. Kim, Y.M., Chan, D., Theobalt, C., Thrun, S.: Design and calibration of a multi-view ToF sensor fusion system. In: CVPR W. on Time-of-flight Computer Vision (2008)
15. Zhang, C., Zhang, Z.: Calibration between depth and color sensors for commodity depth cameras. In: Multimedia Expo (ICME), Barcelona, Spain, pp. 1–6 (2011)
16. Herrera, C., Kannala, J.: Joint depth and color camera calibration with distortion correction. IEEE Trans. on Patt. Anal. and Machine Intell. **34**, 2058–2064 (2012)
17. PMDTechnologies GmbH, PMD[Vision] CamCube 2.0., in Siegen, Germany (2010)
18. Lenzen, F., Kim, K.I., Schäfer, H., Nair, R., Meister, S., Becker, F., Garbe, C.S., Theobalt, C.: Denoising Strategies for Time-of-Flight Data. In: Grzegorzek, M., Theobalt, C., Koch, R., Kolb, A. (eds.) Time-of-Flight and Depth Imaging. LNCS, vol. 8200, pp. 25–45. Springer, Heidelberg (2013)
19. Frank, M., Plaue, M., Hamprecht, F.: Denoising of Continuous-wave Time-of-flight Depth Images Using Confidence Measures. J. of Optical Engineering 48(7) (2009)
20. Georgiev, M., Gotchev, A., Hannuksela, M.: Joint denoising and fusion of 2D video and depth map sequences sensed by low-powered ToF range sensor. In: ICME(2013)

21. Georgiev, M., Gotchev, A., Hannuksela, M.: Denoising of distance maps sensed by Time-of-Flight devices in poor sensing environment. In: ICASSP(2013)
22. Tomasi, C., Manduchi, R.: Bilateral filtering for gray and color images. In: International Conference on Computer Vision (ICCV), pp. 839--847 (1998)
23. Buades, A., Morel, J.: A non-local algorithm for image denoising. Computer Vision and Pattern Recognition (CVPR) 2, 60–65 (2005)
24. Sankaran, H., Georgiev, M., Gotchev, A., Egiazarian, K.: Non-uniform to uniform image resampling utilizing a 2D farrow structure. In: SMMSP (2007)
25. Strohmer, T.: Efficient methods for digital signal and image reconstruction from nonuniform samples. PhD thesis, University of Vienna (1993)
26. Chuchvara, A., Georgiev, M., Gotchev, A.: A speed-optimized RGB-Z capture system with improved denoising capabilities, In: (SPIE), vol. 9019 (2014)
27. Viola, P., Jones, M.: Robust real-time face detection. Int. J. of Comp. Vision 57(2) (2004)
28. Georgiev, M. Gotchev, A., Hannuksela, M.: Real-Time Denoising of ToF Measurements by Spatio-Temporal Non-Local Mean Filtering. In: Hot3D Workshop, pp. 1--6 (2013)
29. Rusinkiewicz, S., Levoy, M.: Efficient variants of the ICP algorithm. In: IEEE on 3-D Digital Imaging and Modeling, pp. 145–152 (2001)
30. Besl, P., McKay, N.: A method for registration of 3-D shapes. IEEE Trans. Pattern Anal. Mach. Intell., 239–256 (1992)
31. Murphy-Chutorian, E., Trivedi, M.M.: Head pose estimation in computer vision: A Survey. Pattern Anal. Mach. Intell. 31, 607–626 (2009)
32. Yin, L., Wei, X., Longo, P., Bhuvanesh, A.: Analyzing facial expressions using intensity-variant 3D data for human computer interaction. In: ICPR, vol. 1, pp. 1248–1251 (2006)
33. Mpiperis, I., Malassiotis, S., Strintzis, M.: Bilinear models for 3-D face and facial expression recognition. IEEE Trans. Inf. Forensics Secur. 3(3), 498–511 (2008)
34. Pomerleau, F., Colas, F., Ferland, F., Michaud, F.: Relative Motion Threshold for Rejection in ICP Registration. In: Field and Service Robots, pp. 229–238 (2009)
35. Boev, A., Georgiev, M., Gotchev, A., Daskalov, N., Egiazarian, K.: Optimized visualization of stereo images on an OMAP platform with integrated parallax barrier autostereoscopic display. In: European Signal Conference EUSIPCO (2009)

Iris Analysis

Iris Detection Through Watershed Segmentation

Alessio Ferone[1], Maria Frucci[2(✉)], Alfredo Petrosino[1], and Gabriella Sanniti di Baja[3]

[1] Università degli Studi di Napoli Parthenope, Napoli, Italy
{alessio.ferone,petrosino}@uniparthenope.it
[2] Istituto di Calcolo e Reti ad Alte Prestazioni, CNR, Napoli, Italy
maria.frucci@cnr.it
[3] Istituto di Cibernetica "E. Caianiello", CNR, Napoli, Italy
gabriella.sannitidibaja@cnr.it

Abstract. In this paper, we present a new iris detection method based on the use of watershed segmentation. The watershed transform is used for both pupil and iris detection, in combination with image quantization, aimed at reducing the number of gray levels, and image thresholding, aimed at obtaining a tentative discrimination between foreground and background. The method has been tested on the CASIA-Iris-Interval Image database.

Keywords: Biometrics · Iris detection · Watershed transformation

1 Introduction

Biometric systems, based on a single biometric or on the combination of different biometrics, are of interest for many applications, such as physical access control, employee identification, and information systems security. In this context, iris recognition is frequently employed for the identification of individuals by means of pattern recognition techniques applied to video images of their eyes. Indeed the iris of a human being is characterized by complex patterns that are peculiar and remain stable during her/his entire life. Moreover, the iris can be scanned at different distances, from a few centimeters up to a few meters, and acquisition does not cause troubles to the subject due to the use of iris cameras that operate in the near infrared spectrum, [1,2], or with visible light technology, [3].

The whole iris recognition process includes acquisition of the eye image, iris segmentation with the purpose of separating both iris and pupil from the rest of the image, features extraction to associate a template to the detected iris, and recognition accomplished by using mathematical and statistical algorithms to compare the current template with those stored in a suitable database. Accuracy is extremely important as regards iris segmentation, since the outcome of the whole recognition process is highly conditioned by the quality of the detected iris. See the two recent special issues [4,5] devoted to iris segmentation and iris recognition, respectively.

In this paper, we focus on iris segmentation. We refer to the CASIA-Iris-Interval Image database Version 4.0, [6] and introduce a new method based on watershed transformation that allows us to obtain precise iris segmentation. The paper is

© Springer International Publishing Switzerland 2014
V. Cantoni et al. (Eds.): BIOMET 2014, LNCS 8897, pp. 57–65, 2014.
DOI: 10.1007/978-3-319-13386-7_5

organized as follows. In Section 2, the watershed based iris segmentation method is described. Section 3 is devoted to iris and pupil detection. A brief conclusion is given in Section 4.

2   Segmentation

We refer to the CASIA-Iris-Interval Image database Version 4.0 [6], which consists of 2639 gray level images with size 320×280. To reduce the computation time, all images in the database are preliminarily resized to 160×140. See Fig. 1 left, where a 160×140 resized image I is shown that will be used as running example throughout the paper. Size reduction is achieved by using a linear interpolation scaling down method with reduction factor set to 0.5. Noise removal and smoothing of sharp gray level differences is then obtained by using a median filter with window size 7×7 (see Fig. 1 middle). Finally, the gradient image is computed by using the Sobel operator (see Fig. 1 right). Size reduction, noise removal, smoothing, and gradient image extraction have been implemented by using standard OpenCV libraries.

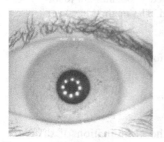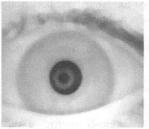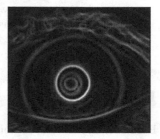

Fig. 1. From left to right, a 160×140 resized image, image resulting after median filter application, and gradient image

For iris segmentation we use the watershed transformation, introduced in [7], which originates a partition of the image by applying region growing to a suitable set of seeds. The seeds are generally detected as the regional minima in the gradient image. Region growing is accomplished by taking into account a specific homogeneity criterion so that each region of the partition will be homogeneous, while the union of any two adjacent regions will not.

Different approaches can be followed to compute the watershed transform. In this paper, we use the topographical distance watershed transformation suggested in [8] and explain how the partition of the image is obtained by resorting to the paradigm of the landscape drenched with rain.

The 2D gray level gradient image is seen as a topographic relief, where the gray level of a pixel is interpreted as its altitude in the relief. If rain floods the landscape, raindrops falling on the topographic relief flow from the areas of high altitude (regions with high gray level in the 2D image), along paths of steepest descent until they reach regional minima (regions with low gray level in the 2D image). The catchment basins are the drainage areas of regional minima and are separated by dams (watershed lines). The watershed lines surround the basins and are located on the outer ridges of each catchment basin. For any pixel p of a watershed line, there are at least two paths of steepest descent starting from p, which lead to different regional minima. To simulate flooding along the paths of steepest descent, any non-minimum *plateau* (i.e., any region with constant altitude) should be eliminated so that raindrops do not stop and flow down along areas with lower altitude. This goal is reached by applying to the gradient image the Lower Completion process [8] that originates an image (*lower complete*) in which any non-minimum plateau is transformed into a slope. Precisely, any pixel of the lower complete image that doesn't belong to any regional minimum has at least one neighbor with smaller value. The effect of Lower Completion as regards plateau removal can be seen in the synthetic example in Fig. 2 left, where a section of a landscape is shown before and after the application of the process. Each non-minimum plateau, visible along the profile (a), is replaced by a slope in the profile (b). The result of applying Lower Completion to the gradient image of the running example is the lower complete image shown in Fig. 2 right.

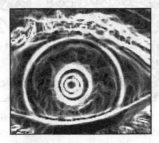

Fig. 2. Left, section of a landscape where each plateau in the profile (a) is replaced by a slope in the profile (b). Right, lower complete image of the gradient image for the running example.

Once the lower complete image of the gradient image is available, we flood it according to the Hill-Climbing algorithm [8] to obtain the desired watershed partition into a number of disjoint regions R_i. If all regional minima in the lower complete image are taken as seeds, the watershed partitioned image results to be over-segmented (see Fig. 3 left, where for visualization purpose the watershed lines are shown superimposed on a white background). To reduce over-segmentation, some regional minima of the lower complete image have to be removed. To this purpose, before flooding the lower complete image, we apply the faster version [9] of the Multi Otsu Threshold Algorithm [10], so as to group pixels according to three increasing thresholds into four different classes, each of which including pixels lighter than the pixels in the previous class. Then, we set to zero in the lower complete image the very dark pixels, i.e., those belonging to the first class, which mainly correspond to quasi-uniform regions of the input image. This process reduces the number of regional minima by merging some scattered regional minima in a single connected component. The effect can be seen in Fig. 3 middle, where the watershed transform computed starting from the reduced set of seeds is shown. The pixels in the remaining classes of the lower complete image are left unchanged. In fact, some pixels of the iris boundary may be not characterized by very dark gray level. They would become regional minima by setting their value to zero, so causing the loss of parts of the iris boundary. In turn, light pixels are mainly contour pixels, which should definitely be kept.

We observe that the reduction of the number of seeds significantly reduces over-segmentation, by originating wide regions in correspondence of the main quasi-uniform areas (sclera, iris and eyelids) in the image. We are aware that our seed reduction does not totally eliminate over-segmentation. In principle, the number of regions of the watershed partitioned image might be furthermore reduced by setting to zero also some of the pixels not belonging to the first class, or by applying a merging process based on some features of adjacent regions. However, for the database used in this work, the contrast among iris, sclera and eyelids is generally rather low, and texture changes are not particularly relevant. Thus, we argue that the use of a larger tolerance when setting to zero pixels in the lower complete image, or a further merging process to be done once the watershed partition is obtained could cause the loss of some parts of the iris boundary.

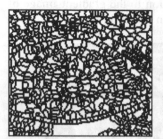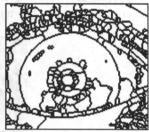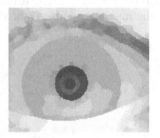

Fig. 3. Watershed lines obtained by using all regional minima in the lower complete image of the gradient image, left, watershed lines obtained after thresholding the lower complete image, middle, quantized image, right

3 Iris and Pupil Detection

Let W be the watershed transform computed so far. First, W is used for pupil detection. Then, W is used together with the detected pupil for iris detection.

3.1 Pupil Detection

We point out that for the images in the CASIA-Iris-Interval Image database, pupil and eyelashes are always the darker areas. For the selection of these areas, we compute a binary version of the watershed partitioned image W. To this aim, we build a quantized version Q of the image I and will apply to Q image thresholding.

We build the gray level quantized version Q of the image I by assigning to all pixels in the same partition region R_i of W a unique representative gray level, computed as the arithmetic mean of the gray levels of all their homologous pixels in I. For the running example, the quantized image Q is shown in Fig. 3 right. By looking at Fig. 3 right and Fig. 1 left, we observe that in both Q and I, the pupil and some parts of the eyelashes are darker areas; on the contrary, light spots, clearly visible in the pupil of the input image I, and some parts of eyelashes result to be respectively darker and clearer in Q than they actually are in I. This difference between Q and I has a positive effect as far as the binarization of W is concerned. In fact, it reduces the number of parts into which the pupil is fragmented, and limits the number of foreground regions corresponding to eyelashes.

We apply the thresholding algorithm [10] to the quantized image Q, so as to identify three different thresholds, $\theta1$, $\theta2$ and $\theta3$. To this purpose, let l_{min} and l_{max} be respectively the lowest and the highest gray level in Q. The intermediate gray level l_{int} between l_{min} and l_{max} is computed as $l_{int}=(l_{max} - l_{min})/2+ l_{min}-1$. Since gray values larger than l_{int} are regarded as definitely too high to be in correspondence with the pupil, the three thresholds $\theta1$, $\theta2$ and $\theta3$ are orderly computed in the interval $[l_{min}, l_{int}]$.

Let Wp be the binarized version of W that will lead to pupil detection. All regions of W whose representative gray levels are smaller than $\theta2$ are assigned to the foreground of Wp. In this way, we ascribe to the foreground of Wp the regions of W that we regard as candidate to belong to the pupil or the eyelashes, while all other regions of W are assigned to the background of Wp. The result of this binarization for the running example can be seen in Fig. 4 left.

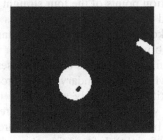

Fig. 4. Binarized version Wp of the watershed transform W, left, result of morphological operations and features extraction, right

We note that the foreground of Wp is likely to include part of the eyelashes. Moreover, the pupil may have been only partially assigned to the foreground of Wp, or may result to be affected by noisy holes. Thus, to remove holes, as well as components of the foreground corresponding to part of the eyelashes and possible links between pupil and eyelashes, morphological dilation and erosion are applied to Wp. For each connected component of the foreground remaining after the application of dilation and erosion, we compute the corresponding bounding box. This is used both to get rid of foreground components of small size and to evaluate the roundness of the remaining foreground components to detect the pupil.

We have experimentally observed that foreground regions whose bounding box has at least one side shorter than eight pixels can be considered as noise and can be safely considered background. For each remaining foreground component the ratio between the longest side and the shortest side of the relative bounding box is computed and is used to establish whether the bounding box can be interpreted as reasonably well approximating a square. This check is done since the pupil, due to its almost circular shape, is certainly enclosed by a bounding box shaped more or less exactly as a square. Only foreground regions for which the above ratio is smaller than 1.2 are regarded as delimiting a circular region. Of course, more than one foreground region may exist whose bounding box satisfies the above condition. If this is the case, we accept as (part of) the pupil the connected component with the bounding box better approximating a square, i.e., with the smallest ratio. If no bounding box exists that is shaped as a square, part of the pupil is detected as the foreground region with the largest area. Of course, once the foreground component detected as corresponding to (part of) the pupil has been selected, all other connected components are considered background. For the running example, the foreground component taken as pupil can be seen in Fig 4 right.

When the bounding box of the region selected as pupil is a square in the limits of the adopted tolerance, the selected region has almost circular shape. Thus, center and radius of the pupil can be computed as center and half the largest side of the bounding box, respectively. Otherwise, the selected region is only part of the pupil; this is likely to happen for the images in the database where the light spots appear very close to the boundary of the pupil. In this case, the points placed in the middle with respect to the first and to the last foreground pixel along each of the four sides of the bounding box are identified. The four straight lines passing through the homologous pairs of these points on opposite sides of the bounding box are considered. The distances between the center of the bounding box and the intersection points of the four straight lines are computed. The intersection point characterized by the smallest distance is taken as center of the pupil. The radius of the pupil is taken equal to the smallest distance from the detected center to the sides of the bounding box.

Once center and radius of the pupil have been computed, the circle representing the pupil can be easily generated. See Fig. 5 left, where the boundary of the circle is colored in blue. Then, the circle is used to identify as precisely as possible the pupil boundary. To this purpose, all regions of the watershed transform that are at least partially overlapping the circle are regarded as belonging to the pupil and are merged into a single region in W (shown in gray in Fig. 5 right). Information about the region representing the pupil will be used for iris detection.

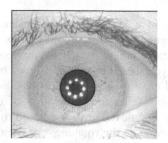 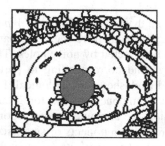

Fig. 5. Circle computed for the pupil, left. Detected pupil, right.

3.2   Iris Detection

A second binarization of W is performed, leading to iris detection. Let us call Wi the second binarized image. Regions of W that are not adjacent to the region selected as pupil in W and that are adjacent to the frame of the image are regarded as belonging to the sclera or to the eyelids. In both cases, these regions are certainly assigned to the background in Wi. The remaining regions of W, shown in white in Fig. 6 left, are tentatively assigned to the foreground of Wi. Actually, only the connected component with the largest area is considered as foreground in Wi. See Fig. 6 middle.

Fig. 6. Result after assignment to the background of the regions of *W* that are adjacent to the frame and are not adjacent to the pupil, left. Only the region with the largest area is taken as foreground in *Wi*, middle. Circular mask, right.

The bounding box of the detected foreground component of *Wi* is considered. The distances between the center of the pupil and the sides of the bounding box are computed and the largest one is taken as the radius of a circular mask to be centered in the center of the pupil (Fig. 6 right).

The circular mask is superimposed on *W* (Fig. 7 left), and is used to identify among the regions of *W* classified as belonging to the foreground in *Wi*, those that are completely overlapping the mask. The remaining regions of *W* are merged in *W* (Fig. 7 middle) and are assigned to the background in *Wi* .

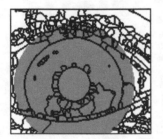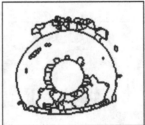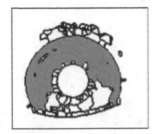

Fig. 7. Use of the circular mask for iris detection (see text)

The regions of *W* that correspond to foreground regions in *Wi* and are there adjacent to the background are interpreted as potentially belonging to the iris. Among them, the region having maximal area is selected (Fig. 7 right). The radius of the iris is computed as the arithmetic mean of the distances between the center of pupil and the pixels of the portion of the boundary separating the selected region from the background of *Wi*. The center of the pupil and the computed radius are finally used to obtain a circle fitting the iris. See Fig. 8, where the boundaries of the circles representing pupils and of the circles fitting irises are shown in blue for a few images. The running example is the top left image in Fig. 8.

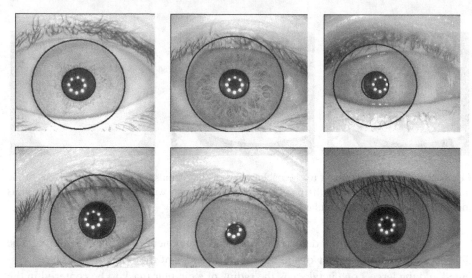

Fig. 8. The (blue) circles correspond to iris and pupil detected by our method

Once the circle fitting the iris has been detected, it is used together with the watershed transform to identify as precisely as possible the iris boundary. The regions of the watershed transform Wi that are at least partially overlapping the circle are regarded as belonging to the iris. For the running example, the obtained result is shown in Fig. 9.

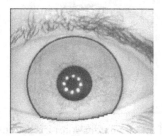

Fig. 9. The blue lines delimit the detected iris

The method has been tested on the images in the CASIA-Iris-Interval Image database Version 4.0. The obtained results have been evaluated by experts, who found them satisfactory. Only in a very few cases, the pupil or the iris were not correctly detected. In particular, in some cases the radius of the circle representing the pupil was slightly larger than expected. This happens when some eyelashes overlap the pupil causing the size of the connected component, included by the bounding box, to be larger than the pupil. In some other cases regions actually belonging to the eyelashes or the sclera were erroneously detected as belonging to the iris.

4   Conclusion

A new iris detection method has been suggested, based on the use of watershed segmentation. The Multi Otsu Threshold Algorithm and a quantized version of the input image, obtained by assigning to all pixels in the same watershed region a unique gray level, have been used to guide binarization of the watershed segmented image. The watershed transform is used for both pupil and iris detection. The method has been tested on the CASIA-Iris-Interval Image database, obtaining in general satisfactory results. Our future work will consist in evaluating the performance of the suggested method with respect to other methods in the literature.

References

1. Wildes, R.: Iris recognition: an emerging biometric technology. Proceedings of the IEEE **85**(9), 1348–1363 (1997)
2. Daugman, J.G.: How iris recognition works. IEEE Trans. Circuits and Systems for Video Technology **14**(1), 21–30 (2004)
3. Puhan, N.B., Sudha, N.: A novel iris database indexing method using the iris color. In: Proc. of the IEEE Conference on Industrial Electronics and Applications, pp. 1886–1891 (2008)
4. Special Issue on the Segmentation of visible wavelength iris images captured at-a-distance and on-the-move. Image and Vision Computing 28 (2010)
5. Special Issue on the Recognition of visible wavelength iris images captured at-a-distance and on-the-move. Pattern Recognition Letters 33 (2012)
6. http://www.idealtest.org/dbDetailForUser.do?id=4
7. Beucher, S., Lantuejoul, C.: Use of watersheds in contour detection. In: Proc. Int. Workshop on Image Processing, Real-Time Edge and Motion Detection/Estimation, France (1979)
8. Roerdink, J.B.T.M., Meijster, A.: The watershed transform: definitions, algorithms and parallelization strategies. Fundamenta Informaticae **41**, 187–228 (2001)
9. Liao, P.-S., Chung, P.-C.: A fast algorithm for multilevel thresholding. Journal of Information Science and Engineering **17**(5), 713–727 (2001)
10. Otsu, N.: A threshold selection method from gray-level histogram. IEEE Transactions on System Man Cybernetics **9**(1), 62–66 (1979)

Fast Iris Recognition on Smartphone by Means of Spatial Histograms

Andrea F. Abate, Michele Nappi, Fabio Narducci, and Stefano Ricciardi[✉]

BIPLab, DISTRA - Università degli Studi di Salerno, 84084, Fisciano (SA), Italy
{abate,mnappi,fnarducci,sricciardi}@unisa.it

Abstract. The iris has been proposed as a highly reliable and stable biometric identifier for person authentication/recognition about two decades ago. Since then, most work in the field has been focused on segmentation and matching algorithms able to work on pictures of whole face or eye region typically captured at close distance, while preserving recognition accuracy. In this paper we present an iris matching algorithm based on spatial histograms that, while showing good recognition performance on some of the most referenced public iris dataset, is also able to perform a one-to-one comparison in a small amount of time thanks to its low computing load, thus resulting particularly suited to iris recognition applications on mobile devices.

Keywords: Biometrics · Iris recognition · Smartphone · Spatial histograms

1 Introduction

Since the pioneering work of Daugman [1] in 1993, who assessed the statistical independence of two coded patterns originated from different eyes, the iris has been proposed as a biometric identifier. In his work, the author described a method for iris localization based on integro-differentials operators exploiting the 2D Gabor filters in order to extract iris texture features and a statistical-based approach to iris codes matching. A few years later, Wildes [2] focused his research effort on a non-invasive system for iris recognition and compared that to the one from Daugman. Both works mainly focused on achieving maximum accuracy in iris recognition under controlled conditions including specific enrollment protocols for the user to undergo.

In the following years, studies in the field of biometrics have progressively led to two main classes of issues. From one side the segmentation of the iris and from the other one its recognition. Nowadays, research efforts aim at facing those issues under less predictable acquisition conditions involving uncontrolled lighting and environmental factors which can result in noisy iris images (e.g., strong reflections over the cornea surface, blur, low contrast, etc.). Literature presents several solutions that have been proposed to this matter. Lim et al. [3] exploited the Haar wavelet transform to optimize the dimension of feature vectors to 87 bits, to the aim of reducing processing time without affecting accuracy of recognition. Combining the proposed descriptor with a method of initializing weight vectors and another one of determining winners for recognition in a competitive learning neural network, the authors were able to achieve a level of accuracy enough reliable even for "real world" applications. In [4]

© Springer International Publishing Switzerland 2014
V. Cantoni et al. (Eds.): BIOMET 2014, LNCS 8897, pp. 66–74, 2014.
DOI: 10.1007/978-3-319-13386-7_6

the authors suggested a representation of iris features by means of wavelet transform zero crossing. The most significant aspects of the descriptor are its invariance to translation, rotation, and scale as well as its robustness against variations in illumination and noise levels.

Particularly significant in the field of iris segmentation was the result of the NICE.I contest for the performance evaluation of recognition algorithms on noisy iris images by Proença and Alexandre in 2007 [5]. Focusing on performance in feature extraction and matching, Bowyer and Kevin recently resumed the results of the NICE.II Iris Biometric Competition [6] arguing that "since the top-ranked algorithms seem to have relatively distinct technical approaches, it is likely that a fusion of the top algorithms would result in further performance improvement". In this line of research, Jeong et al. [7] presented a new iris segmentation method that combines an AdaBoost detector for eyes detection and some color-based obstructions removal techniques. The results achieved and discussed by the authors let suppose that it could be successfully used to accurately extract iris regions from non-ideal quality iris images. Shin et al. [8] proposed an integrated iris recognition method that discriminates the left or right eye on the basis of the eyelash distribution and specular reflection and exploits iris region color and texture information to achieve a reliable classification.

The first attempt of demonstrating the possibility of developing it on mobile phones dates back to 2006 by a work of Jeong et.al. [9] who proposed to extract the iris code by means of Adaptive Gabor Filter (whose operating parameters depends on the amount of blurring and sunlight in captured image). To the aim of improving the robustness of iris recognition on mobile phones in various environments, Park et al. [10] presented a recognition method for mobile phones based on corneal specular reflections while Kang [11] proposed to pre-process iris through an automatic segmentation of pupil region, pupil and eyelids detection to remove the most noise from the iris image and improve recognition performance. On a similar line of research, Cho et al. [12] presented a pupil and iris localization method exploiting not only information of the pupil and iris, but also the characteristics of the eye images. In [13] pupil and iris localization is based instead on detecting dark pupil and corneal specular reflection by changing brightness and contrast value. Exploiting the ever-increasing computing power of mobile platforms, which makes them compared to that of low-end desktop computers, De Marsico et al. [14] have recently presented a combined face-iris mobile recognition system proving that multi-biometrics person authentication on mobiles can be a feasible option.

In this paper we describe a recognition algorithm based on spatial histograms with two main advantages. First of all it features a good recognition accuracy and, on the other hand, it achieves a fast iris matching requiring low computing power. Due to these reasons, it proves to suit mobile computing architectures, such as smartphones or tablet computers, very well, as our experimental results confirm.

The rest of this paper is organized as follows: in section 2 the proposed method is described with regard to iris segmentation, feature extraction and matching. Section 3 describes the experiments conducted and, finally, section 4 concludes the paper summarizing the lessons learned and the issues to be addressed in future work.

2   Description of the Proposed Method

As already introduced in the section 1., the purpose of this study aims at developing a complete system for iris-based person authentication suitable to mobile platforms. The processing pipeline is quite easy to describe as it consists of two main stages: detection/segmentation of the iris and features extraction/matching. Specifically concerning the segmentation of acquired iris, the approach proposed in IS_{IS} [15] was exploited. It is composed by four main stages: iris image pre-processing; pupil localization; image linearization and limbus localization. Following subsections provide details for each one of these steps.

2.1   Iris Segmentation

The pupil, which can be considered as a circular region with a homogeneous distribution of pixels, is a perfect candidate to the segmentation of an iris. The easiest assumption that could be done is that, typically, the darker region within the image is the pupil. However, the pupil changes its appearance in relation to the lighting making this assumption insufficient in uncontrolled or outdoor environments. On the contrary, the shape of the pupil allows to exploit concepts like homogeneity and separability that are successfully used for the selection of the best circle. For this reason, combining both approaches leads to a more robust method to pupil selection. The proposed function, based on the histogram H of gray tones in the region of the pupil, starts counting the number of occurrences of the same gray tone [0, 255]:

$$s_H = \max_i [H(i)] \bigg/ \sum_{i=1}^{255} H(i) \qquad (1)$$

The outline of the pupil, as well as for the limbo, has a zone in which it passes from a dark color to a lighter one. However this assumption becomes weaker when an iris dark in color is analyzed (in those cases the transition is more subtle). Therefore, we define an index of separability. Given a candidate circle C with center c=(c_x, c_y) and radius ρ in the image I, the Cartesian coordinates are given by:

- $x_C(\rho,\theta) = c_x + \rho \cos \theta$
- $y_C(\rho,\theta) = c_y + \rho \sin \theta$, where $\theta \in [0,2\pi]$

Considering the circle C_{IN}, internal to C, with radius $\rho_1 = 0.9\rho$ and the circle C_{OUT}, external to C, with radius $\rho_2 = 1.1\rho$; measuring the difference of gray tones, on the edge of the circle for each angle θ_i, using an operator similar to the Daugman's integro-differential operator, structured as follows:

$$D(i) = I\big(x_c(\rho_2,\theta_i), y_c(\rho_2,\theta_i)\big) - I\big(x_c(\rho_1,\theta_i), y_c(\rho_1,\theta_i)\big) \qquad (2)$$

where $i = 1, ..., 360$ represents the discrete value of the angle and then the index within the gradient vector h; while $\theta_i = i\pi/180$, is the same angle in radians. At the pupil, we expect a high and constant value for D. In other terms, a high average value and a low variance are expected. Based on these observations, the index of separability can be defined as:

$$s_D = \frac{\overline{D}}{\sigma(D) + 1} \tag{3}$$

By analyzing the polarized image of the eye in the horizontal direction, (see Figure 1), it is possible to accurately localize the limbo that appears in the region of separation between the iris and the sclera.

Considering that features like pores of the skin, eyelashes and eyelids can negatively impact on the detection of edges of the iris, the first stage of IS_{IS} implements an enhancement filter in order to eliminate interferences. A square window W of size $k \times k$, scans the entire image pixel by pixel. A histogram hW is computed and the value with the highest occurrence is replaced in the central position of the histogram.

A "canny" filter applied to the resulting image is exploited in order to locate the pupil. Ten different thresholds $th= 0.05, 0.010, 0.015, ..., 0.055$ are used and each frame at different threshold level is stored. For each of them, the connected components are identified. All components whose number of pixels exceeds a given threshold THC, are included in a list L. Then, the algorithm of Taubin [16] is applied to each element of the list to compute the corresponding circle. The circles that fall over the boundary of the image are promptly removed from the list L, which leads to the final list LC. Once obtained the list LC of potential connected components, homogeneity and separability criteria are applied on each of them to find the pupil. For each circle the value $S = S_H + S_D$ is calculated. In the end of this process, the circle shape that best approximates the pupil is the circle C_{max} with the highest value S_{max}.

At this stage, the algorithm looks for the pixels with highest ρ distance starting from the center of the localized pupil. The resulting sub image is transformed from Cartesian coordinates to polar coordinates, producing a new image $\hat{I}$ (Figure 1, right inset). The advantage of such transformation is that it makes easier to locate the boundary between the sclera and the iris. A median filter is also performed on the image $\hat{I}$ to further improve the sub image. Considering R as a row of the image and the neighborhood of each pixel P contained in R including $2q +1$ pixels (i.e., itself, q previous pixels and q following pixels). Then the neighborhood pixels are sorted and the pixel P takes the median value. It is possible to assert that for each column, which is located beyond ρ_J and the corresponding position on the horizontal axis of i and θ_i, the following weighted difference is calculated pixel wise:

$$\Delta(\rho_j, \theta_i) = \varphi(I, \rho_j, \theta_i) \cdot \left(I(p_j + \delta, \theta_i) - I(\rho_j - \delta, \theta_i) \right) \tag{4}$$

where:

$$\varphi(\hat{I}, \rho_j, \theta_i) = \begin{cases} 1 & \begin{array}{ll} if & \hat{I}(\rho_j + \delta, \theta_i) - \hat{I}(\rho_j - \delta, \theta_i) > 0 \\ and & \min\left(\hat{I}(\rho_j - \delta, \theta_i), \hat{I}(\rho_j + \delta, \theta_i)\right) > \varepsilon_G \end{array} \\ 0 & \quad\quad\quad\quad otherwise \end{cases} \tag{5}$$

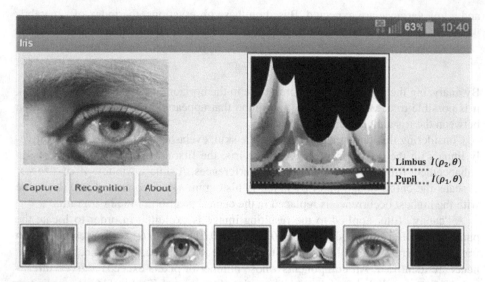

Fig. 1. Subject's eye-region captured (left inset), its iris correctly segmented and outlined in green (small inset below on the right), and mapped through polar coordinates (right inset above)

According to (5) the pupil occupies the lower part ρJ of the polarized image $\dot{I}$, followed by the iris and sclera. The sign of the difference is relevant as it is expected that the sclera is brighter than the iris. This indicates that the algorithm looks for changes with a positive sign, which represent the transition region between iris and sclera. In formula (5) the first inequality imposes a positive gradient; the second inequality excludes the pixels of the border between the pupil and iris, as it requires the darkest pixel in the pair to have a gray level greater than a threshold $\varepsilon \in [0,255]$. The area on the limb is composed of points that maximize the weighted difference (4) for each column θ_i in I.

2.2 Iris Matching by Means of Spatial Histograms

Before discussing the matching method, it is useful to clarify the difference berween histograms and spatiograms (or otherwise called spatial histograms) and how obtaining a spatiograms form a given image.

For a given discrete function $f: x \to v$, where $x \in X$ and $v \in V$, a histogram of f counts the number of occurrences for each element in the range of f. In particular, the histogram is $h_f: v \to Z^*$, where $v \in V$ and Z^* is the set of positive integers, and $h_f(v)$ is the number of elements $x \in X$ such that $f(x) = v$. The histogram h_f can also be seen as a binary function $g_f(x, v)$, where $g_f(x, v) = 1$ if $f(x) = v$ and $g_f(x, v) = 0$ otherwise. The moment of zero order of g on the dimension v is:

$$h_f(v) = \sum_{x \in X} g_f(x, v) \tag{6}$$

Histograms suit segmentation issue, and in this specific case the segmentation of the iris, because they ignore the information about the domain. This leads to an alternative representation that is invariant for one by one transformations of domain of the original function. A limited amount of information regarding the domain, can be extrapolated by means of higher order moments to the binary function g, where the i-th order moment is given by:

$$h_f^{(i)}(v) = \sum_{x \in X} x^i g_f(x, v) \tag{7}$$

This is defined as spatial histogram or simply spatiograms, because it captures the occurrences of information relating to the range of the function, as a common histogram does, but it also contains information related to the spatial domain. We define the k-th order spatiogram as a tuple containing all the moments up to k:

$$\langle h_f^{(o)}(v), \ldots, h_f^{(k)}(v) \rangle \tag{8}$$

In other terms, an histogram is only the zero-order moment of a spatiogram. As for histograms, the spatiograms efficiently calculate the differences between the correspondences of the images. Being more specific models, spatiograms retain information about the geometry of the region of image. In fact, they can be also seen as a geometric model that allows arbitrary transformations such as: translation, similarity, etc.

Differently from a simple co-occurrences comparison between arrays, spatiograms capture the global position of the pixels instead of the relation between their pairs. To understand how the comparison between two spatiograms works, let consider an image is a two-dimensional map $I: x \rightarrow v$ of pixel $x = [x, y]^T$ with v values. The pixel value may tipically represent an arbitrary value such as gray tones, colors, or the result of a preprocessing (quantization, the color transformation of the space, etc..). The second order spatiogram of the image can be represented as:

$$h_I^{(2)}(b) = \langle n_b, \mu_b, \Sigma_b \rangle \quad b = 1, \ldots, B \tag{9}$$

Where n_b is the number of pixels whose values are represented by the b-th bin, μb is the mean vector and Σ_b are the covariance matrices. $B = |V|$ is the number of bins in the spatiogram. Once defined the entities above, we are ready to define the similarity between two spatiograms h and h' as the weighted sum of the similarities between two histograms:

$$\rho(h, h') = \sum_{b=1}^{B} \psi_b \rho_n(n_b n_b') \tag{10}$$

For a zero-order spatiogram $\psi_b = 1$. For a second order spatiogram, ψ_b can be seen as the probability that x_b is calculated by a Gaussian distribution described by multiplying the probability in the reverse direction:

$$\psi_b = \eta \, exp\left\{-\frac{1}{2}(\mu_b - \mu_b')^T \hat{\Sigma}_b^{-1}(\mu_b - \mu_b')\right\} \tag{11}$$

Where η is the normalization constant Gaussian and $\hat{\Sigma}_b^{-1} = (\hat{\Sigma}_b^{-1} + (\hat{\Sigma}_b')^{-1})^{-1}$ is a covariance matrix. It should be noted that the values of the summation are the average of the two Mahalanobis distances, one between x and x' and the other between x' and x.

3   Experiments

We first wanted to assess the performance of the proposed iris recognition method described in section 3 on two reference datasets, UBIRIS [17] and UPOL [18]. Figure 2 and Figure 3 respectively show the ROC curve and the CMS resulting for both the aforementioned datasets as a combined view (actually a subset of UPOL composed by 173 elements as probe and 173 as gallery and a subset of UBIRIS including 114 elements as probe and 228 elements as gallery). In these first experiments the method performed well even if below state-of-the art algorithms. In particular, with regard to the ROC curve, spatiograms performed slightly better on UPOL than on UBIRIS until FAR 0.6 is reached, while after that point the two curves are very similar. For what concerns the CMS, the situation is almost reversed, as in this case the performance on UBIRIS is clearly better with a CMS value near 0.7 for rank 1 compared to rank 9 on UPOL.

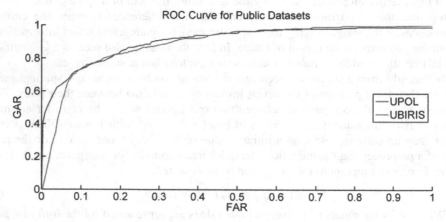

Fig. 2. Comparison of ROC curves for UPOL and UBIRIS datasets

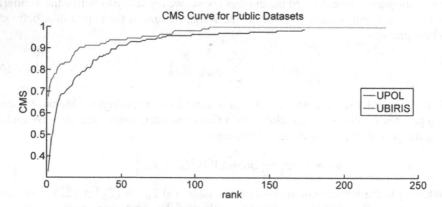

Fig. 3. Comparison of CMS curves for UPOL and UBIRIS datasets

Table 1. Average timing for iris detection and/or recognition on a Samsung S4 smartphone under Android rel 4.3. The timing is measured with regard to iris detection /segmentation and iris recognition, while total time is simply the sum of these two contributes.

GS4	Detection	1774,8	ms
Front Camera	Recognition	8,6	ms
1920x1080	Total time	1783,4	ms
GS4	Detection	4181,33	ms
Rear Camera	Recognition	9,67	ms
4128x2322	Total time	4191	ms

On a final note, we measured the average timing required for iris detection and recognition on a recent high-end smartphone, Samsung's S4 running Android rel. 4.3 (see Table 1). We measured these timing in case the acquisition is performed with either the front camera (featuring a Full-HD capture resolution of 1920x1080 pixels) or the rear camera (capable of 4128x2322 pixels), as the image size directly affects the computing time (and particularly the time required to segment the iris). Overall we can confirm that the smartphone version of the spatiograms based recognition algorithms is fast enough to make iris recognition a viable option in a mobile application scenario.

4   Conclusions and Future Works

In this paper, we presented an iris recognition algorithm that exploits spatiograms for feature matching. This approach applied to probes and gallery selected from public iris datasets UPOL and UBIRIS, provided a good performance in terms of both ROC and CMS curves, also featuring an average computing time for one-to-one comparison around 10ms on last generation multicore smartphones, such as Samsung's S4. These preliminary experiments suggest that the usage of iris biometric on smartphones and mobile devices is practically feasible in general. For this reason, we plan to perform an extensive experimentation involving subjects' enrollment and probes acquisition by means of built-in front and rear cameras of most advanced mobile devices. The main aim is to test the algorithm's robustness in uncontrolled environmental conditions and to evaluate its behavior in a real world scenario, though an extensive testing on a wider range of devices and acquisition condition is necessary to fully assert the feasibility of our approach.

References

1. Daugman, J.: High Confidence Visual Recognition of Persons by a Test of Statistical Independence. IEEE PAMI **15**(11), 1148–1161 (1993)
2. Wildes R.: Iris recognition: an emerging biometric technology. Proceedings of the IEEE 85(9) (1997)
3. Lim, S., Lee, K., Byeon, O., Kim, T.: Efficient Iris Recognition through Improvement of Feature O. Vector and Classifier. ETRI J. **23**(2), 61–70 (2001)

4. Boles, W.W., Boashash, B.: A Human Identification Technique Using Images of the Iris and Wavelet Transform. IEEE Transactions On Signal Processing **46**(4), 1185–1188 (1998)
5. Proenca, H., Alexandre, L.A.: The NICE.I: Noisy Iris Challenge Evaluation – Part I. In: Proceedings of the IEEE First International Conference on Biometrics: Theory, Applications and Systems (2007)
6. Bowyer, P., Kevin, W.: The results of the NICE.II Iris biometrics competition. Pattern Recognition Letters **33**(8), 965–969 (2011)
7. Jeong, D.S., Hwang, J.B., Kang, K., Won, C., Park, D., Kim, J.: A new iris segmentation method for non-ideal iris images. Image Vision Computing **28**(2), 254–260 (2010)
8. Shin, K., Nam, G., Jeong, D., Cho, D., Kang, B., Park, K., Kim J.: New iris recognition method for noisy iris images. Pattern Recognition Lett., Special Issue Recognition of Visible Wavelength Iris Images Acquired On-The-Move and At-A-Distance
9. Jeong, D.S., Park, H.-A., Park, K.R., Kim, J.H.: Iris Recognition in Mobile Phone Based on Adaptive Gabor Filter. In: Zhang, D., Jain, A.K. (eds.) ICB 2005. LNCS, vol. 3832, pp. 457–463. Springer, Heidelberg (2005)
10. Park, K.R., Park, H., Kang, B.Y., Lee, E.C., Jeong, D.S.: A study on iris localization and recognition on mobile phone. Eur. J. Adv. Signal Process, 1–12 (2007)
11. Kang, J.S.: Mobile iris recognition systems: An emerging biometric technology. In: International Conference on Computational Science (ICCS) (2010)
12. Cho, D.H., Park, K.R., Rhee, D.W.: Real-Time Iris Localization for Iris Recognition in Cellular Phone. In: Int',l Conf. Software Eng., Artificial Intelligence, Networking and Parallel/Distributed Computing, pp. 254–259 (2005)
13. Cho, D.H., Park, K.R., Rhee, D.W., Kim, Y.G., Yang, J.H.: Pupil and iris localization for iris recognition in mobile phones. In: Proc. SNPD, pp. 197–201 (2006)
14. De Marsico, M., Galdi, C., Nappi, M., Riccio, D.: FIRME: Face and Iris Recognition for Mobile Engagement. Image and Vision Computing (2014)
15. De Marsico, M., Nappi, M., Riccio, D.: ISIS: Iris Segmentation for Identification System. In: ICPR 2010, pp. 2857–2860 (2010)
16. Taubin, G.: Estimation Of Planar Curves Surfaces And Nonplanar Space Curves Defined By Implicit Equations, With Applications To Edge And Range Image Segmentation. IEEE Transactions on Pattern Analysis and Machine Intelligence **13**, 1115–1138 (1991)
17. Proença, H., Alexandre, L.A.: UBIRIS: A Noisy Iris Image Database. In: Roli, F., Vitulano, S. (eds.) ICIAP 2005. LNCS, vol. 3617, pp. 970–977. Springer, Heidelberg (2005)
18. Dobeš, M., Machala, L.: UPOL Iris Image Database (2008). http://phoenix.inf.upol.cz/iris/

A Contourlet Transform Based for Features Fusion in Retina and Iris Multimodal Biometric System

Morteza Modarresi[✉] and Iman Sheikh Oveisi

Biomedical Engineering Deptartment, Science and Research Campus,
Islamic Azad University, Tehran, Iran
{modaresi.bme,Iman.oveisi}@gmail.com

Abstract. Fusion biometric modal contributes in two aspects. It can not only improve the biometric recognition accuracy, but also gives a comparatively safe strategy, since it is difficult for intruders to achieve multi-biometric information simultaneously, especially the iris information. The contourlet transform is a new two-dimensional extension of the wavelet transform using multiscale and directional filter banks. The contourlet expansion is composed of basis images oriented at various directions in multiple scales, with flexible aspect ratios. In this paper, by using Contourlet transform, we extract the features of retina and iris, and fuse them at feature level and utilize Hamming distance for matching purpose to provide a higher accuracy than unimodal system. The experimental results show that our biometric system based on the integration of retina and iris traits achieve an EER= 0.0413%.

Keywords: Multimodal Biometric System · Feature Fusion Level · Contourlet Transform · Retina Recognition · Iris Recognition

1 Introduction

Biometric-based recognition systems represent a valid alternative to conventional approaches. Traditionally biometric systems, operating on a single biometric feature, have many limitations, which are as follows [1].

1) *Trouble with data sensors:* Captured sensor data are often affected by noise due to the environmental conditions (insufficient light, powder, etc.) or due to user physiological and physical conditions (cold, cut fingers, etc).

2) *Distinctiveness ability:* Not all biometric features have the same distinctiveness degree (for example, hand geometry- based biometric systems are less selective than the fingerprint-based ones).

3) *Lack of universality:* All biometric features are universal, but due to the wide variety and complexity of the human body, not everyone is endowed with the same physical features and might not contain all the biometric features, which a system might allow.

The multimodal biometric systems are a recent approach developed to overcome these problems. These systems demonstrate significant improvements over unimodal

© Springer International Publishing Switzerland 2014
V. Cantoni et al. (Eds.): BIOMET 2014, LNCS 8897, pp. 75–90, 2014.
DOI: 10.1007/978-3-319-13386-7_7

biometric systems, in terms of higher accuracy and high resistance to spoofing. Multimodal biometric systems address the shortcomings of unimodal systems.

The contourlet transform is a new two-dimensional extension of the wavelet transform using multiscale and directional filter banks. The contourlet expansion is composed of basis images oriented at various directions in multiple scales, with flexible aspect ratios. Given this rich set of basis images, the contourlet transform effectively captures smooth contours that are the dominant feature in natural images. There have been several other developments of directional wavelet systems in recent years with the same goal, namely a better analysis and an optimal representation of directional features of signals in higher dimensions.

At the feature level fusion, the information extracted from sensors of different modalities is stored in vectors on the basis of their modality. These feature vectors are then combined to create a joint feature vector, which is the basis for the matching and recognition process. Since the feature set contains richer information about the raw biometric data than the match score or the final decision, integration at this level is expected to provide better recognition results. In this paper, a feature level fusion algorithm resulting in a unified biometric descriptor and integrating retina and iris features for personal identification is presented. Successively, the Hamming Distance (HD) between two vectors is used to matching purpose to provide a higher accuracy than unimodal system.

The rest of this paper is structured as follows: Section 2 deals with Related Works. Section 3 deals with Proposed Multimodal Biometric System. Section 4 deals with Retina Preprocessing. Section 5 deals with Iris Preprocessing. Section 6 deals with Contourlet Transform. Section 7 deals with Feature Extraction. Section 8 deals with Fusion feature vector construction via combination of the retina and iris vector. Section 9 deals with Hamming Distance Based Matching. Section 10 deals with Experimental Results. Section 11 deals with Conclusion and Future Work.

2   Related Works

Multimodal biometric recognition system is the approach of using multiple biometric traits from a single user in an effort to improve the result of recognition process and to reduce error rates. Many researchers have demonstrated that the fusion process is effective, because fused scores provide much better discrimination than individual scores. Geetika *et al.* [2] develop Multimodal based fuzzy vault using iris retina and fingervein by fusion of extracted feature points (end points and bifurcations points from three biometric traits). Their method measures the security of the resultant vault by using min-entropy.

Some multimodal biometric fusion approaches include of iris: Wang *et al.* [3] adopt an efficient feature-level fusion scheme for iris and face in series, and normalizes the original features of iris and face using z-score model to eliminate the unbalance in the order of magnitude and the distribution between two different kinds of feature vectors, and then connect the normalized feature vectors in serial rule, which has proved to be effective. Besbes *et al.* [4] proposed a multimodal biometric system using fingerprint and iris features. They use a hybrid approach based on: 1) fingerprint minutiae extraction and 2) iris template encoding through a mathematical representation of the extracted iris region. This approach is based on two recognition modalities and every part provides its own decision. The final decision is taken by considering the unimodal decision through an "AND" operator. Meraoumia *et al.* [5] develop the multimodal biometric identification system based on palmprint and iris. They used (Unconstrained) minimum average correlation energy filter method for fusion at matching score level.

3   Proposed Multimodal Biometric System

Most of the problems and limitations of biometrics are imposed by unimodal biometric systems, which rely on the evidence of only a single biometric trait. Some of these problems may be overcome by multi-biometric systems and an efficient fusion scheme to combine the information presented in multiple biometric traits. In this paper, a multimodal biometric system on feature fusion level, based on retina and iris characteristics, is proposed. The following framework explains the workflow of the system in fig. 1.

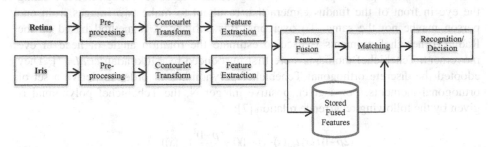

Fig. 1. Workflow of the proposed system

4   Retina Preprocessing

4.1   Retina Anatomy

The retina provides a higher level of security for recognition due to uniqueness and the stability of the blood vessel pattern during one's life. Fig.2 (a) shows a side view of the eye. A ray of light, after passing through the cornea, which partially focuses the image, passes through the anterior chamber, the pupil, and the lens, which focuses the image further, the vitreous and is then focused on the retina [6]. The retina is approximately *0.5mm* thick and covers the inner side at the back of the eye. In the center of the retina is the optical nerve or optical disk (OD), a circular to oval white area measuring about *2×1.5mm* across (about 1/30 of retina diameter). Blood vessels are continuous patterns with little curvature, branch from OD and have tree shape on the surface of retina (Fig. 2(b)). The mean diameter of the vessels is about *250μ*m (1/40 of retina diameter) [6].

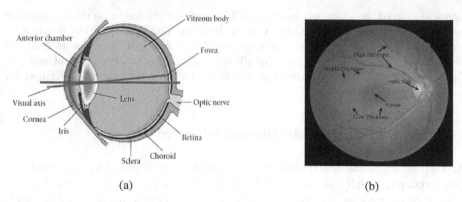

(a)   (b)

Fig. 2. (a) Side view of the eye (b) Sample retina image

4.2   Rotation Compensation Using Radial Tchebichef Moments

One of the most important problems in using retinal images for recognition is rotating the eye in front of the fundus camera that resultant to make two images from one person maybe not the same. To overcome this deficiency, a method based on the Radial Tchebichef moments is used to estimate the rotation angle of head or eye movement. Tchebichef moments were first introduced by Mukundan *et al.* [7]. They adopted the discrete orthogonal Tchebichef polynomials in order to derive a set of orthogonal moments. For a given positive integer N, the Tchebichef polynomial is given by the following recurrence relation [7]:

$$t_p(x) = \frac{(2p-1)\,t_1(x)\,t_{p-1}(x) - (p-1)(1 - \frac{(p-1)^2}{N^2}\,t_{p-2}(x))}{p} \tag{1}$$

with the initial conditions:

$$t_0(x) = 1 \tag{2}$$

$$t_1(x) = \frac{(2x+1-N)}{N} \tag{3}$$

The Tchebichef moment of order $(p+q)$ of an (N×M) image intensity function is defined as:

$$T_{pq} = \frac{1}{\rho(p,N)\,\rho(p,M)} \sum_{x=0}^{N-1} \sum_{y=0}^{M-1} t_p(x)\,t_q(x)\,f(x,y) \tag{4}$$

where p, $= 0, 1,..., N-1$ and $q=0, 1,...,M$. The Tchebichef polynomial satisfies the property of orthogonally with:

$$\rho(p,N) = \frac{N(1 - \frac{1}{N^2})(1 - \frac{2^2}{N^2})...(1 - \frac{p^2}{N^2})}{2p+1} \tag{5}$$

The moments defined in Equation (4) are not rotation invariant. Therefore, a rotation invariant method based on the Radial Tchebichef Moments is used to estimate the rotation angle of head or eye movement [8]. The basic functions of Radial-Tchebichef moments are products of one-dimensional Tchebichef polynomials in radial distance r and circular functions of the angle θ. For a given image of size, we require a discrete domain for these functions. The most appropriate mathematical structure for computing radial Tchebichef moments is a set of discrete concentric rings, where each ring represents a fixed integer value of radial distance r from the center of the image. In this method, the angle of rotation, α, is estimated using the relationship between the rotated and non-rotated radial Tchebichef moments [8]. If we denote the image intensity value at location (r, θ) by $f(r, \theta)$, then the radial Tchebichef moments of the non-rotated image, S_{pq}, of order p and repetition q are given by:

$$S_{pq} = \frac{1}{n.\rho(p,m)} \sum_{r=0}^{m-1} \sum_{\theta=0}^{n-1} t_p(r)\, e^{-jq\theta}\, f(r,\theta) \qquad (6)$$

where n denotes maximum number of pixels along the circumference of the circle, and m denotes the number of samples in the radial direction and the radial distance is defined in the range of $r = 0, 1, ...,$ $(N/2)-1$. The angle θ is a real quantity measured in radians and varies from 0 to 2π and calculated by:

$$\theta = \frac{2k\pi}{n}, \quad k = 0,1,2,...,(n-1), \qquad (7)$$

Radial Tchebichef moments of the rotated image with angle, $\theta_r = \theta + \alpha$, are given by:

$$S_{pq}^r = \frac{1}{n \cdot \rho(p,m)} \sum_{r=0}^{m-1} \sum_{\theta=0}^{n-1} t_p(r) e^{-jq(\theta+\alpha)} f(r,\theta) \qquad (8)$$

If an image is rotated about the origin $(r = 0)$ by an angle α, and if the intensity values are preserved during rotation, then the moments S_{pq} should ideally get transformed to S_{pq}^r, where α is computed by:

$$S_{pq}^r = S_{pq} \cdot e^{-jq\alpha} \qquad (9)$$

In the above equation, both r and θ take integer values. The mapping between (r, θ) and image coordinates x, y is given by:

$$\begin{cases} x = \dfrac{rN}{2(m-1)} \cos(\dfrac{2\pi\theta}{n}) + \dfrac{N}{2} \\[4mm] y = \dfrac{rN}{2(m-1)} \sin(\dfrac{2\pi\theta}{n}) + \dfrac{N}{2} \end{cases} \qquad (10)$$

Fig. 3(a) shows the typical rotated retinal image, Fig. 3(b) shows the Discrete Pixel Sampling of radial Tchebichef Moments in Polar Form and Fig.3(c) shows the rotation compensation retinal image.

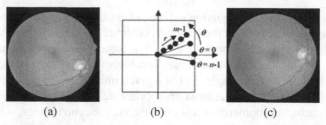

(a)   (b)   (c)

Fig. 3. (a) A typical rotated retinal image, (b) The discrete pixel sampling of Radial Tchebichef Moments in polar form, (c) Rotation compensation retinal image of (a)

5   Iris Preprocessing

The colored part of the eye is called the iris. It controls light levels inside the eye similar to the aperture on a camera. The round opening in the center of the iris is called the pupil. The iris is embedded with tiny muscles that dilate (widen) and constrict (narrow) the pupil size. The iris is flat and divides the front of the eye (anterior chamber) from the back of the eye (posterior chamber). Its color comes from microscopic pigment cells called melanin. The color, texture, and patterns of each person's iris are as unique as a fingerprint. A frontal view of the human eye is shown in Fig. 4 A very important characteristic of an iris is that it's a naturally protected organ and is stable without any variations including effects of an individual aging [9].

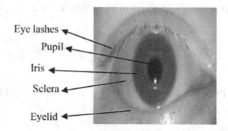

Fig. 4. A frontal view of the human eye

In this paper, the median filter is used to remove specular reflections from iris image, the canny Edge Detection and Hough Transform is adopted to estimate the iris boundary, then the Daugman's Rubber Sheet Model is used to normalize the iris image, and finally the Contourlet Transform is employed to extract the iris feature.

5.1   Reflection Removal from Iris Image

In order to remove specular reflections from iris image, we used the median filter. A median filter is a kernel based, convolution filter which blurs an image by setting a pixel value to the median of itself with its neighbors. For implement, we consult Perreault's paper [10], which describes an algorithm to create a median filter in linear time. The process (see algorithm 1) involves constructing individual column histograms and combining them to form histograms centered around a pixel, known as a kernel histogram.

The significant speed increase comes from the way in which the column histograms are updated and combined. For each pixel we remove an old column histogram from the kernel, shift a new column histogram down one pixel so it is centered on the required row and then add this new histogram to the kernel histogram. While this radically reduces the number of operations which need to be performed for each pixel, there is an initialization step for each row which has runtime linear in the size of the kernel histogram. This enabled the entire median filter to be applied in a matter of milliseconds.

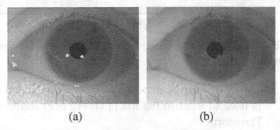

(a)   (b)

Fig. 5. Iris image preprocessing by median filter. (a) Before reflection removal (b) After reflection removal.

Algorithm 1. Median filtering algorithm as proposed

Input: Image X of size $m \times n$, kernel radius r.
Output: Image Y of size $m \times n$.
Initialize each column histogram $h_0, \ldots, h_{n-1}$ as if centered on row -1.
for $i = 1$ to m **do**
  Shift the first r column histograms $h_0, \ldots, h_{r-1}$ down 1 pixel.
  Combine these r column histograms to form the kernel histogram H.
  for $j = 1$ to n **do**
  Set pixel $Y_{i,j}$ equal to the median of H.
  Shift column histogram h_{j+r} down 1 pixel.
  Remove column histogram h_{j-r-1}.
  Add column histogram h_{j+r}.
  end for
end for

5.2 Circular Boundaries and Parameters Estimation

Due to the significant feature of handling spurious noisy images of canny operator, canny edge detection algorithm is used to generate the edge map of the iris image here. As pupil is a black circular region, it is easy to detect the pupil inside an eye image. Firstly, pupil is detected using thresholding operation. An appropriate threshold is selected to generate the binary image which contains pupil only. Morphological operator is applied to the binary image to remove the reflection inside the pupil region and other dark spots caused by eyelashes. Figure 6(b) shows the binary image after thresholding and morphological operator.

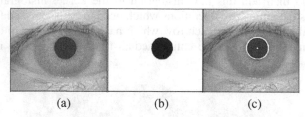

(a)   (b)   (c)

Fig. 6. (a) Original eye image (b) Binary image after thresholding and morphological operator (c) Pupil localization

Since the inner boundary of an iris can be approximately modeled as circles, circular Hough transform is used to localize the iris [11]. Fig 6(c) shows the iris localization by using Hough Transform.

5.3   Eyelid Detection

Two search regions were selected for the purpose of upper and lower eyelids detection. The search regions are confined within the pupil and area of the iris.

Width of search region = radius of iris - radius of pupil

The width of search region was 24 for CASIA database and upper and lower search region labeled as shown in Fig. 7. A horizontal edge map was used to find an eye image as eyelid part is present in upper or lower horizontal region. At each edge point within the search regions, a parabolic Hough transformation was applied for eyelids detection.

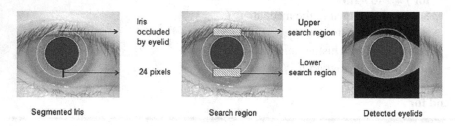

Fig. 7. Eyelids detection on CASIA database

5.4   Eyelash Segmentation

Two classes of eyelashes are defined in eyelash detection model, separable and multiple eyelashes [12]. Separable eyelashes are defined as the eyelashes that can be distinguished from other eyelashes and multiple eyelashes are the eyelashes that overlap in a small area.

5.4.1   Separable Eyelashes

By the definition of separable eyelashes, they can be distinguished from other eye-lashes; thus, the pixels around separable eyelash should not belong to other eyelashes. In fact, most of pixels around separable eyelashes are iris pixels. Because of the intensity difference between iris pixels and eyelashes pixels, a separable eyelash can be regarded as an edge in an image. Based on this property, a real part of Gabor filter is proposed to detect separable eyelashes, which, in the spatial domain has the following general form,

$$G(x, u, \sigma) = \exp\left\{\frac{x^2}{2\sigma^2}\right\} \cos(2\pi u x) \qquad (11)$$

where u is the frequency of the sinusoidal wave and σ is the standard derivation of the Gaussian envelope. The resultant values are small when a separable eyelash convolutes with the filter. In fact, the filter serves as an edge detector. If a resultant value of a point is smaller than a threshold, it is noted that this point belongs to an eyelash. Mathematically, it can be represented by:

$$f(x) * G(v, u, \sigma) < K_1 \qquad (12)$$

where K_1 is a pre-defined threshold that is -45 using in the following experiments and " *" represents an operator of convolution.

5.4.2   Multiple Eyelashes

For multiple eyelashes, many eyelashes overlap in a small area, which results in less intensity variation in this area. Thus, for detecting multiple eyelashes, if the variance of intensity in the area is less than a threshold, the center of the window is noted as a pixel of eyelash. It can be described by:

$$\frac{\sum_{i=-N}^{N} \sum_{j=-N}^{N} (f(x+i, y+j) - M)^2}{(2N+1)^2} < K_2 \qquad (13)$$

where M is the mean of intensity in the small window; $(2N + 1)^2$ is the window size and K_2 is a threshold. In the following experiments, K_2 is defined as 6 and $(2N + 1)^2$ as 5×5.

5.5   ROI Normalization and Enhancement

Normalization of the iris image involves unwrapping the iris and converting it into its polar equivalent. Here we use the Daugman's Rubber Sheet Model to achieve this goal [13]. Fig. 8(a) depicts the polar coordinate system for segmented iris image and the corresponding linearized visualization. For each Cartesian point of the segmented iris, image is assigned a polar coordinates pair (r, θ), with $r \in [R_1, R_2]$ and $\theta \in [0, 2\pi]$, where R_1 is the pupil radius and R_2 is the iris radius. In fig. 8(b) the normalized iris image is shown.

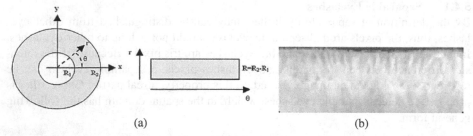

(a)   (b)

Fig. 8. (a) Polar coordinate system for an iris ROI and the corresponding linearized visualization. (b) Normalized Image.

In feature extraction process of the Retina and iris image, here we use the Contourlet Transform.

6   Contourlet Transform

Contourlet transform, developed by Do and Vetterli [14] provides a flexible image multi resolution presentation. Compared with wavelet and curvelet, contourlet represents richer directions and shapes while 2D wavelet transform can only capture information in horizontal, vertical and diagonal directions. Besides, contourlet transform performs better in depicting the geometrical structure of images. After contourlet transform, the low frequency sub-images gather most energy and consequently they suffer little impact caused by regular image processing. The resulting transform has the multiscale and time-frequency-localization properties of wavelets, but also offers a high degree of directionality and anisotropy.

Laplacian pyramid (LP) is used to perform a multi-resolution decomposition over the image to capture the singular points. Fig. 9 shows a multiscale and directional decomposition using a combination of a Laplacian pyramid (LP) and a directional filter bank (DFB).

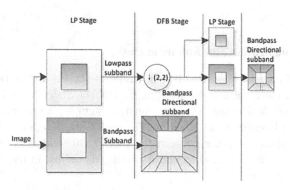

Fig. 9. The contourlet filter bank: first, a multiscale decomposition into octave bands by the Laplacian pyramid is computed, and then a directional filter bank is applied to each bandpass channel

It is simple with low computational complexity due to its single filtering channel and has higher dimension. LP is a multiscale decomposition of the $L^2(R^2)$ space in to a series of increasing resolution:

$$L^2(R^2) = V_{j_0} \oplus \sum_{j=j_0}^{w} (W_j)$$

(14)

where V_{j_0} is the approximation at scale 2^j and multi resolution W_j contains the added detail to the finer scale 2^{j-1}. By using L appropriate low pass filters, L low pass approximations of the image are created. The difference between each approximation and its subsequent down sampled lowpass version is a bandpass image. The result is a Laplacian pyramid with $L+1$ equal size levels; one coarse image approximation and L bandpass images. The original DFB is efficiently implemented via j-level binary tree leading to 2^j subbands with wedge-shaped frequency partitioning where j is the level of the directional filter. Fig. 10 depicts subsequent contourlet decomposition on a retina sub-image. For clear visualization, each image is only decomposed into three pyramidal levels, which are then decomposed into 4, 8 and 16 directional subbands. By performing the contourlet transform on the retina (and iris) we acquire diverse subbands, each one of these subbands interprets the characteristics of the image in particular direction.

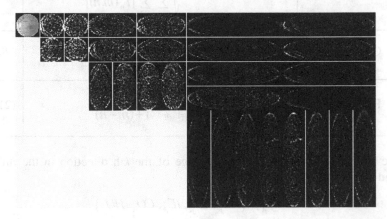

Fig. 10. Contourlet transform of the retinal image. The image is decomposed into three pyramidal levels.

7   Feature Extraction

Due to the iterated lowpass filtering the most relevant texture information has been separated, thus the retina and iris texture information is mainly contained in the directional subbands of each scale. As a result, the lowpass image is not taken into consideration when calculating the texture feature vector. A set of statistical texture features proposed in literature are evaluated in this study. This set is presented in Table 1. Mean energy, Standard deviation, Information entropy, Contrast and Homogeneity has been utilized for the contourlet domain in [15].

Table 1. List of the statistical measures used. I_{jk} is the subband image of the kth direction in the jth level. M_{jk} is the row size and N_{jk} the column size of the subband image I_{jk}.

Mean Energy	$ME_{jk} = \dfrac{1}{M_{jk} \cdot N_{jk}} \sum\limits_{n=1}^{N_{jk}} \sum\limits_{m=1}^{M_{jk}} [I_{jk}(m,n)]^2$	(15)
Standard Deviation	$SD_{jk} = \sqrt{\dfrac{1}{M_{jk} \cdot N_{jk}} \sum\limits_{n=1}^{N_{jk}} \sum\limits_{m=1}^{M_{jk}} (I_{jk}(m,n) - \mu_{i_k})^2}$	(16)
	$\mu_{jk} = \dfrac{1}{M_{jk} \cdot N_{jk}} \sum\limits_{n=1}^{N_{jk}} \sum\limits_{m=1}^{M_{jk}} I_{jk}(m,n)$	(17)
Information Entropy	$IE_{jk} = -\sum\limits_{n=1}^{N_{jk}} \sum\limits_{m=1}^{M_{jk}} p_{jk}(m,n) \cdot \log p_{j_k}(m,n)$	(18)
	$p_{jk}(m,n) = \dfrac{\left| I_{jk}(m,n) \right|^2}{\sqrt{\sum\limits_{n=1}^{N_{jk}} \sum\limits_{m=1}^{M_{jk}} [I_{jk}(m,n)]^2}}$	(19)
Contrast	$CO_{jk} = \sum\limits_{n=1}^{N_{jk}} \sum\limits_{m=1}^{M_{jk}} (m-n)^2 \cdot I_{jk}(m,n)$	(20)
Homogeneity	$ME_{jk} = \sum\limits_{n=1}^{N_{jk}} \sum\limits_{m=1}^{M_{jk}} \dfrac{I_{jk}(m,n)}{1+(m-n)^2}$	(21)

The feature vector of the subband image of the kth direction in the jth level is defined as:

$$f_{jk} = \{ME_{jk}, SD_{jk}, IE_{jk}, CO_{jk}, HO_{jk}\} \qquad (22)$$

A contourlet transform decomposition is referred as being J level when the retina and iris image is decomposed using a J level laplacian pyramid decomposition with a K_j subband DFB applied at the jth level, ($j = 1,2,...,J$). For a J level contourlet transform, the total number of directional subbands K_{total} is calculated as:

$$K_{total} = \sum_{j=1}^{J} K_j \qquad (23)$$

After calculating the feature vector of each subband image, these vectors are rearranged and combined to form the complete feature vector $F = \{ ME_i, SD_i, IE_i, CO_i, HO_i\}$, $i = 1, 2,..., K_{total}$, of the input image as shown on:

$$F = \{ME_1,...,ME_{K_{total}}, SD_1,...,SD_{K_{total}}, IE_1,...,IE_{K_{total}}, CO_1,...,CO_{K_{total}}, HO_1,...,HO_{K_{total}}\} \qquad (24)$$

Where ME_i, SD_i, IE_i, CO_i and HO_i refer to the respective statistical measure of the ith directional subband of the contourlet transform decomposition. At this feature vector, the number of elements increases exponentially with the level of DFB decomposition. Final feature vector, content of retina and iris features, is normalized between [0, 1].

8   Fusion Feature Vector Construction via Combination of the Retina and Iris Vector

In this paper, we used $3th$ level decomposition for retina and $2th$ level decomposition for iris images. After extracting the retina and iris features via Contourlet transform, we can get a m dimensional feature F_{retina} and n dimensional feature F_{iris} respectively, where $F_{retina} = \{F_{r_1}, F_{r_2}, ..., F_{r_m}\}$, $F_{iris} = \{F_{i_1}, F_{i_2}, ..., F_{i_n}\}$, then the min-max regularization principle is adopted to normalize the feature vector [16], thus the following equation can be acquired:

$$F'_{retina} = \frac{F_{retina} - \min(F_{retina})}{\max(F_{retina}) - \min(F_{retina})} \tag{25}$$

$$F'_{iris} = \frac{F_{iris} - \min(F_{iris})}{\max(F_{iris}) - \min(F_{iris})} \tag{26}$$

Finally, the new fusion vector can be acquired via the weighted concatenated way by the following equation:

$$F = \alpha\, F'_{retina} + \beta\, F'_{iris} \tag{27}$$

where α and β is the weight value of retina and iris feature while maintaining $\alpha + \beta = 1$. The fusion feature F in equation (27) will be the final multimodal feature adopted in the following recognition process.

9   Hamming Distance Based Matching

Comparing the feature vectors X_j and Y_j, the Hamming distance is defined as:

$$HD = \frac{1}{N} \sum_{j=1}^{N} XOR(X_j, Y_j) \tag{28}$$

where X_j is jth component of the sample feature vector, Y_j is jth component of template feature vector and N is the dimension of input feature vector. If the result of the XOR is zero, it means that the jth component of sample feature vector and template feature vector are the same.

10   Experimental Results

In this paper, we use DRIVE database for retina images and CASIA database for iris images in order to evaluate the performance of the proposed algorithm. 40 images from DRIVE (565 × 584 pixels) [17] was selected and then rotated randomly each image 10 times to obtain 400 images. Also 400 images from CASIA (320 × 280 pixels) [18] (100 unique eyes, each eye has 4 images) were selected randomly to perform our experiments. Fig. 11 shows some examples of retina and iris images in our experiments.

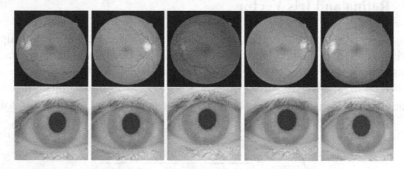

Fig. 11. Some example of DRIVE (top row) and CASIA images (down row) in our experiments

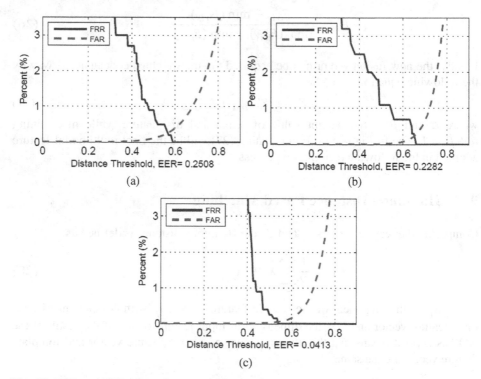

Fig. 12. FAR and FRR curves for proposed system with each EER. (a) In retina database (b) In iris database (c) In multimodal retina and iris database.

In order to better check the validity of proposed system, we used false acceptance rate (FAR), false rejection rate (FRR) and equal error rate (EER). Fig.12 (a) shows the FAR vs. FRR from bimodal retina database. In Fig.12 (b) show the FAR vs. FRR from bimodal iris database. Fig.12 (c) shows the FAR vs. FRR from multimodal retina and iris database. All EERs are taken in bottom of each figure, so that shown the EER in multimodal retina and iris database is better than in comparison of each bimodal database.

In order to better performance test of our proposed method, we test method based on contourlet transform in comparison of Haar wavelet transform. In our experiment, wavelet was decomposition in 5-th level and the contourlet was decomposition in 3-th level and the typical ROC curves of the experiment results are shown in Fig. 13. Therefore, it can be seen that the properties of the coarse coefficients of contourlet are very good in comparison of wavelet, and obtain higher recognition rate.

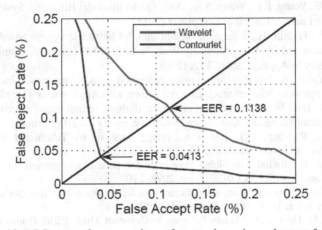

Fig. 13. ROC curves for comparison of contourlet and wavelet transform

Also for finding the better matching, we applied other matching algorithms based on Euclidean Distance and Manhattan distance. Table 2 shows the results of matching algorithms in our proposed method.

Table 2. Feature Matching Type

Feature Matching Type	EER
Hamming distance	0.0413
Euclidian Distance	0.0723
Manhattan distance	0.1162

11 Conclusion and Future Work

Biometric systems are widely used to overcome the traditional methods of authentication. But the unimodal biometric system fails in case of biometric data for particular trait. A feature level fusion scheme to improve multimodal matching performance has been proposed. The scheme has been tested on two relatively biometric systems, retina and iris images. Thus, we have attempt to present new insights by joint of retina and iris images at feature fusion level based on the Contourlet transform. Experiments results show that, the proposed multimodal biometric recognition method can achieve relatively high performance as compared to unimodal biometrics, thus it could be widely used in personal recognition applications in the future. Future work will include studying the effect of noisy data on the performance of our technique and the adoption of other biometric traits in this work.

References

1. Ross, A., Jain, A.: Information fusion in biometrics. Pattern Recogn. Lett. **24**, 2115–2125 (2003)
2. Manavjeet Kaur, G.: Multimodal Based Fuzzy Vault Using Iris Retina and Fingervein. In: IEEE – 31661. 4th ICCCNT (2013)
3. Wang, Z.F., Wang, E.F., Wang, S.S., Ding, Q.: Multimodal Biometric System Using Face-Iris Fusion Feature. Journal of Computers (2011)
4. Besbes, F., Trichili, H., Solaiman, B.: Multimodal biometric system based on fingerprint identification and Iris recognition. In: Proc. 3rd Int. IEEE Conf. Inf. Commun. Technol.: From Theory to Applications ICTTA (2008)
5. Rai, H., Yadav, A.: Iris recognition using combined support vector machine and Hamming distance approach. ScienceDirect, Expert Systems with Applications **41**, 588–593 (2014)
6. Goh, K.G., Hsu, W., Lee, M.L.: An automatic diabetic retinal image screening system. In: Medical Data Mining and Knowledge Discovery, pp. 181—210. Springer, Berlin (2000)
7. Mukundan, R., Ong, S.H., Lee, P.A.: Image Analysis by Tchebichef Moments. IEEE Transactions on Image Processing **10**, 1357–1364 (2001)
8. Mukundan, R.: Radial Tchebichef invariants for pattern recognition. In: Proc. of IEEE Tencon Conference TENCON2005, pp. 2098–2103 (2005)
9. Ma, L., Tan, T., Wang, Y.,et al.: Efficient Iris Recognition by Characterizing Key Local Variations. IEEE Trans. Image Processing (2004)
10. Perreault, S., Hebert, P.: Median Filtering in Constant Time. IEEE Transactions on Image Processing (2007)
11. Masek, L.: Recognition of human iris patterns for biometric identification (2003). http://www.csse.uwa.edu.au/opk/student projects/labor
12. Kong, W.-K., Zhangm, D.: Detecting Eyelash and Reflection for Accurate Iris Segmentation, Biometrics Research Centre Department of Computing, The Hong Kong Polytechnic University Kowloon, Hong Kong
13. Daugman, J.G.: High confidence visual recognition of persons by a test of statistical independence. IEEE Trans. Pattern Anal. Mach. Intell. **15**, 1148–1161 (1993)
14. Do, M.N., Vetterli, M.: The Contourlet transform: an efficient directional multi-resolution image representation. IEEE Transactions Image on Processing (2005)
15. Katsigiannis, S., Keramidas, E.G., Maroulis, D.: Contourlet Transform for Texture Representation of Ultrasound Thyroid Images. In: Papadopoulos, H., Andreou, A.S., Bramer, M. (eds.) AIAI 2010. IFIP AICT, vol. 339, pp. 138–145. Springer, Heidelberg (2010)
16. Viriri, S., Tapamo, J.R.: Integrating Iris and Signature Traits for Personal Authentication Using User-Specific Weighting. Sensors Journal **12**, 4324–4338 (2012). doi:10.3390/s120404324
17. Staal, J., Abr`amoff, M.D., Niemeijer, M., Viergever, M.A., van Ginneken, B.: Ridge-based vessel segmentation in color images of the retina. IEEE Transactions on Medical Imaging (2004)
18. Jonathon Phillips, P., Bowyer, K.W., Flynn, P.J.: Comments on the CASIA Version 1.0 Iris Data Set. IEEE Transactions on Pattern Analysis and Machine Intelligence (2007)

Speech Recognition

From Speaker Recognition to Forensic Speaker Recognition

Andrzej Drygajlo[✉]

Speech Processing and Biometrics Group,
Swiss Federal Institute of Technology Lausanne (EPFL),
CH-1015 Lausanne, Switzerland
andrzej.drygajlo@epfl.ch

Abstract. The goal of this paper is to review automatic systems for forensic speaker recognition (FSR) based on scientifically approved methods for calculation and interpretation of biometric evidence. The objective of this paper is not to promote one speaker recognition method against another, but is to make available to the biometric research community data-driven methodology combining automatic speaker recognition techniques and a rigorous forensic experimental background. Forensic speaker recognition is the process of determining if a specific individual (suspected speaker) is the source of a questioned speech recording (trace). This paper aims at reviewing forensic automatic speaker recognition (FASR) methods that provide a coherent way of quantifying and presenting recorded speech as biometric evidence, as well as the assessment of its strength (likelihood ratio) in the Bayesian interpretation framework compatible with interpretations in other forensic disciplines. Forensic speaker recognition has proven an effective tool in the fight against crime, yet there is a constant need for more research due to the difficulties involved because of the within-speaker (within-source) variability, between-speakers (between-sources) variability, and differences in recording sessions conditions.

1 Introduction

Fueled by the increasing identity fraud and theft, biometrics constitutes one of the most fast growing areas in the field of the security and forensic applications. Forensic speaker recognition (FSR) is a relatively recent combination of biometric and forensic methods for judicial purposes and particularly law enforcement.

1.1 Biometrics and Forensics

Biometrics is the science of establishing identity of individuals based on their biological and behavioral characteristics [14]. On the other side, forensics (forensic science) refers to the applications of scientific principles and technical methods to the investigation of criminal activities, in order to demonstrate the existence of a crime, and to determine the identity of its author(s) and their modus

© Springer International Publishing Switzerland 2014
V. Cantoni et al. (Eds.): BIOMET 2014, LNCS 8897, pp. 93–104, 2014.
DOI: 10.1007/978-3-319-13386-7_8

operandi [15]. Forensics means the use of science or technology in the investigation and establishment of facts or evidence in the court of law. The role of forensic practitioner is the provision of information (factual or opinion) to help answer questions of importance to investigators and to courts of law.

1.2   Forensic Speaker Recognition

Speaker recognition is the general term used to include all of the many different tasks of discriminating people based on the sound of their voices. In particular, forensic speaker recognition (FSR) is the process of determining if a specific individual (suspected speaker) is the source of a questioned voice recording (trace). This process involves the comparison of recordings of an unknown voice (questioned recording) with one or more recordings of a known voice (voice of the suspected speaker) [23].

There are several types of forensic speaker recognition [24]. When the recognition employs any trained skill or any technologically-supported procedure, the term technical forensic speaker recognition is often used. In contrast to this, so-called naïve forensic speaker recognition refers to the application of everyday abilities of people to recognize familiar voices.

The approaches commonly used for technical forensic speaker recognition include the aural-perceptual, auditory-instrumental, and automatic methods [24]. Aural-perceptual methods, based on human auditory perception, rely on the careful listening of recordings by trained phoneticians, where the perceived differences in the speech samples are used to estimate the extent of similarity between voices [19]. The use of aural-spectrographic speaker recognition can be considered as another method in this approach. The exclusively visual comparison of spectrograms in what has been called the voiceprint approach has come under considerable criticism in the recent years [4]. The auditory-instrumental methods involve the acoustic measurements of various parameters such as the average fundamental frequency, articulation rate, formant centre-frequencies, etc. [18,23,24]. The means and variances of these parameters are compared. In forensic automatic speaker recognition (FASR), the deterministic or statistical models of acoustic features of the suspected speakers voice and the acoustic features of questioned recordings are compared [10,16].

1.3   Forensic Automatic Speaker Recognition (FASR)

Forensic automatic speaker recognition (FASR) is an established term used when automatic speaker recognition methods are adapted to forensic applications [7]. Generally, automatic speaker recognition can be classified into two main methods: speaker verification and speaker identification. Recently, an investigation concerning the inference of identity in forensic speaker recognition has shown the inadequacy of the speaker verification and speaker identification (in closed set and in open set) techniques for forensic applications [5]. Speaker verification and identification are the two main automatic techniques of speech recognition used in security applications. When they are used for forensic speaker recognition they imply a final discrimination decision based on a threshold. Speaker verification is the task of deciding, given a sample of speech, whether a specified speaker is the source of it. Speaker identification is the task of deciding, given a sample of speech, who among many speakers is the source of it. Therefore, these techniques are clearly inadequate for forensic purposes, because they force the forensic expert to make decisions which are devolved upon the court.

The forensic experts role is to testify to the worth of the evidence by using, if possible a quantitative measure of this worth [1,7]. It is up to the judge and/or the jury use the testimony as an aid to the deliberations and decisions. Therefore, forensic automatic speaker recognition (FASR) methods should be developed on the basis of current state-of-the-art interpretation of forensic evidence, the concept of identity used in criminalistics, a clear understanding of the inferential process of identity and the respective duties of those involved in the judicial process. The forensic expert should base his opinion upon the four principles of balance, logic, robustness and transparency [3]:

- *Balance*: the expert should address at least two competing propositions (adversary system).
- *Logic*: the expert should address the probability of the evidence given the proposition and relevant background information and not the probability of the proposition given the evidence and background information.
- *Robustness*: the expert should provide opinion that is capable of scrutiny by other experts and cross-examination.
- *Transparency*: the expert should be able to demonstrate how he came to his conclusion in way that is suitable for a wide audience (i.e. participants in the justice system).

Results of FASR based case assessment and interpretation may be of pivotal importance at any stage of the course of justice, be it the very first police investigation or a court trial. In the forensic evaluative mode for a court trial, an opinion of evidential weight, based upon case specific propositions (hypotheses) and clear conditioning information (framework of circumstances) should be provided for use as evidence in court [13]. If there are two, mutually exclusive, competing propositions, exhaustive in the framework of circumstances of the case, then the odds form of Bayes' theorem can be used. The evaluative opinion of the forensic expert should be based around an assessment of a likelihood ratio (strength of evidence) of the observations given specific individual propositions (hypotheses) for the scientific findings. Consequently, three measures should be provided:

- *First Measure*: Biometric Evidence,
- *Second Measure*: Strength of Evidence,
- *Third Measure*: Evaluation of the Strength of Evidence.

Forensic automatic speaker recognition (FASR) offers data-driven biometric methodology for quantitative interpretation of recorded speech as evidence [9].

Commonly, in FASR the distribution of various features extracted from a suspect's speech is compared with the distribution of the same features in a reference population with respect to the questioned recording. The goal is to infer the identity of a source [1], since it cannot be known with certainty.

The paper is structured as follows. Section 2 highlights the meaning of biometric evidence in the forensic speech recognition. In Section 3 a general Bayesian framework for interpretation of the biometric evidence of speech is introduced. Section 4 presents evaluation of the strength of evidence using the Bayesian interpretation method. Section 5 concludes the paper.

2   Biometric Evidence in Forensic Automatic Speaker Recognition

The major scientific and technological aspect in the domain of forensic automatic speaker recognition (FASR) is that there is a critical need for developing forensic speaker recognition methods in the light of current state-of-the-art technology related to the interpretation of forensic evidence [1,6,18]. This approach needs biometric methods for recognition of individuals based on their biological and behavioural characteristics, as a common practice [14].

In one of such methods, univariate (scoring) method, the biometric evidence consists of the quantified degree of similarity between speaker-dependent features extracted from the trace and speaker-dependent features extracted from recorded speech of a suspect, represented by his or her model [2,10].

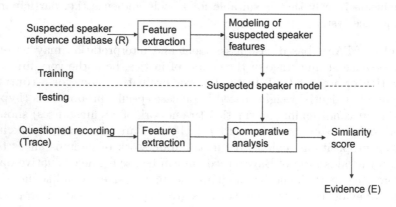

Fig. 1. Processing chain for calculating biometric speech evidence [10]

In another method, multivariate (direct) method, multivariate trace evidence is represented by the ensemble of features extracted from the questioned recording (trace) [2]. In both cases, the calculated evidence does not allow the forensic expert alone to make an inference on the identity of the speaker.

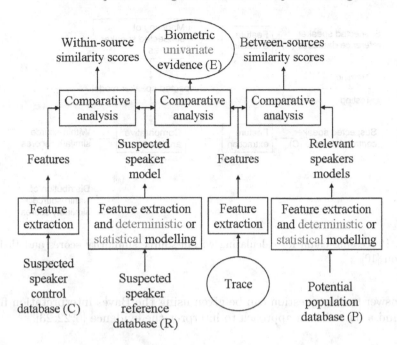

Fig. 2. General processing chain of feature extraction, comparative analysis and estimation of biometric evidence for univariate (scoring) method with deterministic or
statistical models of automatic speaker recognition

The interpretation of recorded speech as biometric evidence in the forensic
context presents particular challenges, including within-speaker (within-source)
variability, between-speakers (between-sources) variability, and differences in
recording session conditions.

Consequently, FASR methods must provide a probabilistic evaluation which
gives the court an indication of the strength of the evidence given the estimated
within-source, between-sources and between-session variabilities, and this evaluation should be compatible with other interpretations in other forensic disciplines [17,20,22]. The Bayesian interpretation framework, using a likelihood ratio
concept, offers such interoperability. At a high level of abstraction, Bayesian data
analysis is extremely simple, following the same, basic recipe: via Bayes Rule,
we use the data to update prior beliefs about unknowns [12]. Of course, there is
much to be said on the implementation of this procedure in any specific application, in particular FASR.

3 Bayesian Interpretation of Biometric Evidence

The court and investigative bodies are faced with decision-making under uncertainty. In a case involving FASR they want to know how likely it is that the
speech samples of questioned recording have come from the suspected speaker.

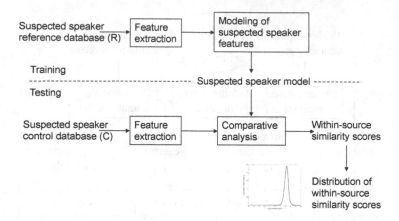

Fig. 3. Processing chain for calculating within-source similarity scores and their distribution [10]

The answer to this question can be given using the Bayes interpretation framework and a data-driven approach to interpret the evidence [6, 22, 23].

3.1   Bayesian Interpretation Framework

An interpretation framework, which relies on Bayes theorem becomes more and more accepted in many fields of forensic science [1, 3, 22], and has been adapted to speaker recognition. The preliminary research work done by the two research teams (EPFL School of Engineering and UNIL (University of Lausanne) School of Criminal Sciences) proves that a probabilistic model – the Bayes Theorem – is a useful tool for assisting forensic scientists in the assessment of the value of scientific evidence, jurists in the interpretation of scientific evidence and for clarifying the respective roles of forensic scientists and members of the court [10]. Bayes' theorem offers a practical, robust mechanism for inductive reasoning. The theorem provides a logical framework to appraise the value of new pieces of information and to update one's uncertainty about a questioned event. It is gaining wide acceptance as a robust approach to forensic science problems and it is the basis of the Case Assessment and Interpretation (CAI) model [13, 15].

The odds form of Bayes theorem shows how new data (questioned recording) can be combined with prior background knowledge (prior odds (province of the court)) to give posterior odds (province of the court) for judicial outcome (Eq. 1). It allows for revision based on new information of a measure of uncertainty (likelihood ratio of the evidence E (province of the forensic expert)) which is applied to the pair of competing hypotheses (propositions), e.g.: H_0 - the suspected speaker is the source of the questioned recording, H_1 - the speaker at the origin of the questioned recording is not the suspected speaker [5, 11, 18]:

$$\frac{p(H_0|E)}{p(H_1|E)} = \frac{p(E|H_0)}{p(E|H_1)} \cdot \frac{p(H_0)}{p(H_1)}. \tag{1}$$

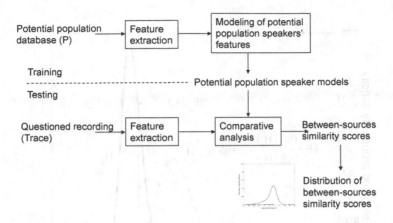

Fig. 4. Processing chain for calculating between-source similarity scores and their distribution [10]

3.2   Strength of Speech Evidence

The strength of speech evidence is the result of the interpretation of the biometric evidence, expressed in terms of the likelihood ratio of two alternative hypotheses $LR = p(E|H_0)/p(E|H_1)$. This interpretation consists of calculating the likelihood ratio using the probability density functions (pdfs) of the variabilities and the evidence. The likelihood ratio (LR) summarizes the statement of the forensic expert in the casework. It gives the degree of support for one hypothesis against the other. This way it allows the forensic expert to make an inference on the identity of the suspected speaker.

The value of a likelihood ratio depends critically on the choices one makes for describing the hypotheses and evidence, which depend on the feature extraction and speaker modelling processes.

3.3   Deterministic and Statistical Modelling of Speech

Automatic speaker recognition systems can be text-dependent or text-independent. In forensic applications, a text-independent automatic speaker recognition system is preferable to a text-dependent one, since the suspected speakers can be considered non-cooperative as they do not wish to be recognized. Classical speaker models can be deterministic or statistical [16]. In deterministic models, training and test feature vectors are directly, or after clustering, compared with each other with the assumption that either one is an imperfect replica of the other. Vector quantization (VQ) algorithms represent a rich family of deterministic models for text-independent recognition using a variety of clustering techniques. In statistical models, each speaker is modelled as a probabilistic source with fixed probability density function. The training phase is to estimate the parameters of the probability density function from a training sample. Comparison is usually done by evaluating the likelihood of the test

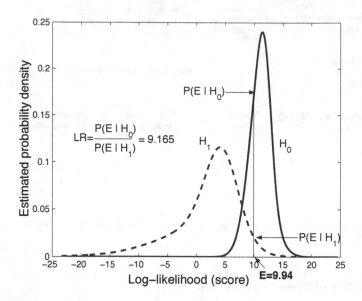

Fig. 5. The likelihood ratio (LR) estimation given the value of the evidence E and the probability density functions (pdfs) of the within-source and between-sources similarity scores [7, 10]

utterance with respect to the model. The Gaussian mixture model (GMM) is the most popular statistical models for text-independent recognition [21] but it needs much more data for training in comparison with deterministic VQ model.

Speaker recognition based on statistical modeling techniques such as Gaussian Mixture Modeling (GMM) has a useful property in that it directly returns a likelihood of whether an utterance can come from the statistical model created for a speaker [21]. As a consequence, in order to calculate the likelihood ratio we can follow two approaches, one directly using the likelihoods returned by the GMMs (multi-variate, direct method), and the other by modelling the distribution of these likelihood scores and then deriving the likelihood ratio on the basis of these score distributions (uni-variate, scoring method) [2].

Consequently, the state-of-the-art speaker recognition algorithms using vector quantization (VQ) and Gaussian mixture models (GMMs) for text-independent forensic tasks have to be adapted to the interpretation of the evidence using both direct and scoring methods. Generally, the latter approach is preferred, as it does not depend on the automatic speaker recognition technique (VQ or GMM) used [10].

4   Evaluation of the Strength of Evidence

The likelihood ratio (strength of evidence) summarizes the statement of the forensic expert in the casework. However, the greatest interest to the jurists is

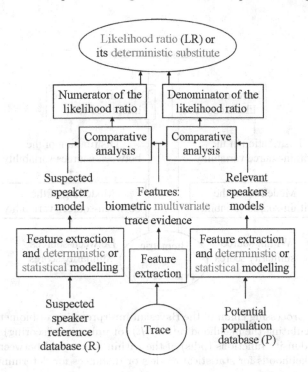

Fig. 6. General processing chain of the Bayesian interpretation of biometric multivariate trace evidence for calculating the likelihood ratio (LR) or its deterministic substitute for multivariate (direct) method using directly deterministic or statistical models of automatic speaker recognition

the extent to which the likelihood ratios correctly discriminate the same speaker and different-speaker pairs under operating conditions corresponding to those of the case in hand.

It should be criterial for the admissibility of scientific evidence to know to what extent the method can be, and has been, tested.

The principle for evaluation of the strength of evidence consists in the estimation and the comparison of the LRs that can be obtained from the evidence, on one hand when the first hypothesis is true (e.g., the suspected speaker truly is the source of the questioned recording) and, on the other hand, when the second hypothesis is true (the suspected speaker is truly not the source of the questioned recording).

The performance of an automatic speaker recognition method is evaluated by repeating the experiment described when calculating the strength of evidence, with several speakers being at the origin of the questioned recording, and by representing the results using experimental (histogram based) probability distribution plots and cumulative distribution functions in the form of Tippett plots [6,11].

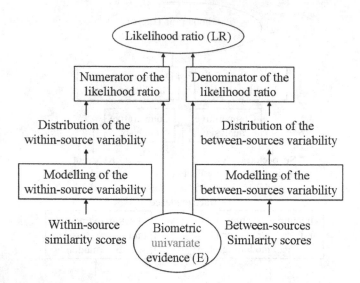

Fig. 7. General processing chain of the Bayesian interpretation of biometric univariate evidence for calculating the likelihood ratio (*LR*) for univariate (scoring) method using the probability density functions (pdfs) of the within-source and between-sources similarity scores (likelihoods for statistical models or distances for deterministic models)

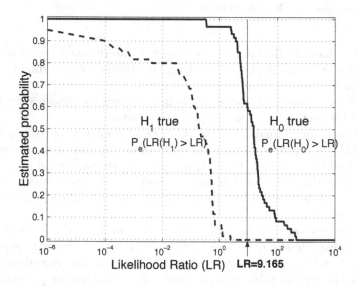

Fig. 8. Cumulative distribution functions in the form of Tippett plots corresponding to the probability density functions of likelihood ratios in Figure 5 [6,7,9]

5   Conclusions

Over the last decade telecommunication and biometric technology has become affordable and widely available to the population at large. With the increasing sophistication of communication devices and networks, there has also been an increase in the number and complexity of crimes in which the speech is used.Forensic speaker recognition experts have to adapt forensic casework techniques to this increasing sophistication. Therefore, there is a need to interpret speech as forensic evidence. With several different aspects of this specific biometric evidence, it is necessary to understand and deal with the dependencies that exist between them by using formal deterministic and statistical modelling in the Bayesian interpretation framework.

The main focus of this paper was to show what can be done in the domain of forensic automatic speaker recognition using deterministic and statistical evaluation of biometric speech evidence. It was shown that the data-driven based evaluation methodology using Bayesian framework provides a coherent way of assessing and presenting the biometric speech evidence of questioned recording.

This paper gives guidelines for the calculation of the biometric speech evidence and its strength under operating conditions of the casework. Bayesian framework methods such as calculation of likelihood ratios based on automatic (deterministic and statistical) pattern recognition methods, have been criticized, but they are the only demonstrably rational means of quantifying and evaluating the value of biometric speech evidence available at the moment. The future methods to be developed for interpretation of speech as forensic evidence should combine the advantages of automatic signal processing, pattern recognition and biometrics objectivity with the methodological transparency solicited in forensic investigations.

References

1. Aitken, C., Taroni, F.: Statistics and the Evaluation of Evidence for Forensic Scientists. John Wiley and Sons, Chichester (2004)
2. Alexander, A., Drygajlo, A.: Scoring and Direct Methods for the Interpretation of Evidence in Forensic Speaker Recognition. In: 8th International Conference on Spoken Language Processing (ICSLP 2004), Jeju, Korea, 2397–2400 (2004)
3. Association of Forensic Science Providers: Standards for the formulation of evaluative forensic science expert opinion. Science and Justice **49**, 161–164 (2009)
4. Bolt, R.H., et al.: On the theory and practice of voice identification. National Academy of Sciences, Washington (1979)
5. Champod, C., Meuwly, D.: The Inference of Identity in Forensic Speaker Identification. Speech Communication **31**(2–3), 193–203 (2000)
6. Drygajlo, A., Meuwly D., Alexander A.: Statistical Methods and Bayesian Interpretation of Evidence in Forensic Automatic Speaker Recognition. In: Proceedings of 8th European Conference on Speech Communication and Technology (Eurospeech 2003), Geneva, Switzerland, pp. 689–692 (2003)
7. Drygajlo, A.: Forensic Automatic Speaker Recognition. IEEE Signal Processing Magazine **24**(2), 132–135 (2007)

8. Drygajlo, A.: Statistical Evaluation of Biometric Evidence in Forensic Automatic Speaker Recognition. In: Geradts, Z.J.M.H., Franke, K.Y., Veenman, C.J. (eds.) IWCF 2009. LNCS, vol. 5718, pp. 1–12. Springer, Heidelberg (2009)
9. Drygajlo A.: Forensic Evidence of Voice. In: Li, S.Z. (ed.) Encyclopedia of Biometrics, pp. 1388–1395. Springer, New York (2009)
10. Drygajlo A.: Automatic Speaker Recognition for Forensic Case Assessment and Interpretation. In: Neustein, A., Patil, H. (eds): Forensic Speaker Recognition: Law Enforcement and Counter-Terrorism, ch. 2., pp. 21–39. Springer, New York (2011)
11. Gonzalez-Rodriguez, J., Drygajlo, A., Ramos-Castro, D., Garcia-Gomar, M., Ortega-Garcia, J.: Robust estimation, interpretation and assessment of likelihood ratios in forensic speaker recognition. Computer Speech and Language 20(2–3), 331–355 (2006)
12. Jackman, S.: Bayesian Analysis for the Social Sciences. John Wiley and Sons, Chichester (2009)
13. Jackson, G., Jones, S., Booth, G., Champod, C., Evett, I.: The nature of forensic science opinion-a possible framework to guide thinking and practice in investigations and in court proceedings. Science and Justice 46, 33–44 (2006)
14. Jain, A. et al. (eds).: Handbook of Biometrics. Springer, New York (2008)
15. Jamieson, A., Moenssens, A. (eds.): Wiley Encyclopedia of Forensic Science. John Wiley and Sons, Chichester (2011)
16. Kinnunen T., Li H.: An overview of text-independent speaker recognition: From features to supervectors. Speech Communication 52, 12–40 (2010)
17. Meuwly, D., Drygajlo, A.: Forensic Speaker Recognition Based on a Bayesian Framework and Gaussian Mixture Modelling (GMM). A Speaker Odyssey, The Speaker Recognition Workshop, Crete, Greece, pp. 145–150 (2001)
18. Morrison, G.: Forensic Voice Comparison and the Paradigm Shift. Science and Justice 49, 298–308 (2009)
19. Nolan, F.: The Phonetic Bases of Speaker Recognition. Cambridge University Press, Cambridge (1983) (reissued 2009)
20. Ramos Castro, D.: Forensic Evaluation of the Evidence using Automatic Speaker Recognition Systems. Ph.D. thesis, Universidad Autonoma de Madrid, Madrid, Spain (2007)
21. Reynolds, D., Quatieri, T., Dunn, R.: Speaker verification using adapted Gaussian mixture models. Digital Signal Processing 10(1), 19–41 (2000)
22. Robertson, B., Vignaux, G.: Interpreting Evidence. Evaluating Forensic Science in the Courtroom. John Wiley and Sons, Chichester (1995)
23. Rose, P.: Forensic Speaker Identification. Taylor and Francis, London (2002)
24. Rose, P.: Technical forensic speaker recognition: Evaluation, types and testing of evidence. Computer Speech and Language 20(2–3), 159–191 (2006)

Noisy Speech Endpoint Detection Using Robust Feature

Atanas Ouzounov[✉]

Institute of Information and Communication Technologies, Sofia, Bulgaria
atanas@iinf.bas.bg

Abstract. In this paper a new robust feature for speech endpoint detection is proposed. It combines the properties of the Modified Group Delay Spectrum (MGDS) and the Mean Delta (MD) approach in order to obtain the more robust endpoint detection. This feature is named as Group Delay Mean Delta (GDMD) feature. The effectiveness of proposed feature and other three features for trajectory-based endpoint detection is experimentally evaluated in the fixed-text Dynamic Time Warping (DTW) - based speaker verification task with short phrases of telephone speech. The analysed features are - Modified Teager Energy (MTE), Energy-Entropy (EE) feature and MD feature. The results of the experiments have shown that the GDMD feature demonstrates the best performance in endpoint detection tests in terms of verification rate.

Keywords: Teager energy · Speech activity detection · Group delay spectrum

1 Introduction

The errors in the automatic speech and speaker recognition systems designed to operate in noisy real-world environments are due to many reasons including the inaccurate detection of the endpoints of the analyzed speech utterance. The wrong Endpoint Detection (ED) increases the cases when the system processes data different from the actual speech utterance. These errors are crucial especially for recognition systems, which use short phrases with length of few seconds.

The ED algorithm consists of two main processing steps - feature extraction and decision step. In the first processing step, the features based on signal energy [3], [9], autocorrelation functions [27], spectral entropy [4], [6, 7], [23], group delay functions [8], [18], wavelets [21], bi-spectrum [10], etc., are extracted. In the second step, using the properties of the estimated features, the start and the end points of the utterance are estimated. This is accomplished by using a state automaton [9], [24] or some type of classification scheme, e.g., classification and regression tree [22], hidden Markov models [26], support vectors machines [20], etc.

In the study a new robust feature for endpoint detection is proposed. This is a Group Delay-Mean Delta (GDMD) feature. This feature utilized the Mean Delta approach proposed in [14] but the spectral autocorrelation function is defined, not with the power or magnitude spectrum, but with the Modified Group Delay Spectrum [5], [11]. The performance of the GDMD feature was compared with three additional features – the Mean Delta feature (MD) [14], [17], the Modified frame Teager Energy (MTE) [4], [6] and the Energy-Entropy feature (EE) [6]. These features are utilized in

© Springer International Publishing Switzerland 2014
V. Cantoni et al. (Eds.): BIOMET 2014, LNCS 8897, pp. 105–117, 2014.
DOI: 10.1007/978-3-319-13386-7_9

the trajectory-based real-world speech data endpoint detection paradigm. The state automaton and a set of thresholds are used and the endpoints are estimated based only on trajectory characteristics [17].

In order to estimate the performance of the considered endpoint detection algorithms two experiments are carried out. In the first experiment was measured the ED accuracy, i.e. the frames differences between manually labelled and detected endpoints [24]. The second one was conducted to estimate the effect of different ED algorithms on the recognition rate in the Dynamic Time Warping (DTW) fixed-text speaker verification task with short noisy telephone phrases in Bulgarian language [16].

The Z_{HTER} -test method proposed in [1] is applied to check whether the verification rate obtained by a given endpoint detection feature is statistically significantly different from the rate provided by another one.

2   Endpoint Detection Parameters

2.1   Mean-Delta Feature

The Mean-Delta (MD) feature was proposed by the author in [14] and it is defined as the mean absolute value of the Delta Spectral Autocorrelation Function (DSACF) of the power spectrum of speech signal. This function is obtained in a way similar to the delta cepstrum evaluation and its purpose was to remove the slope of the spectral autocorrelation function and enhance the peaks. For a particular frame, the DSACF $\Delta R_p(l)$ is computed utilizing only the frame's spectral autocorrelation lags as follows

$$\Delta R_P(l) = \frac{\sum_{q=-Q}^{Q} q R_P(l+q)}{\sum_{q=-Q}^{Q} q^2}, \tag{1}$$

where $l = 0,...,L$; L is the number of correlation lags and $R_P(l)$ is the biased spectral autocorrelation function defined with the power spectrum. The parameter Q determines the window width around the lag l and its effect on the accuracy of the approximation.

For the given frame the MD feature m_d is computed as follows

$$m_d = \left[\sum_{l=0}^{L} \left| \Delta R_p(l) \right| \right]^{0.5}, \tag{2}$$

where $\Delta R_p(l)$ is the DSACF in (1) for lag l , L is the number of lags. For more details about the MD feature, see [14].

The vector version of the MD feature is utilized in speech detection module as a part of speaker recognition tasks [15]. The results obtained in the trajectory-based endpoint detection task using the magnitude spectrum-based version of the MD feature are described in [17]. This version of the MD feature will be used in the current study.

2.2 Group Delay Mean Delta Feature

The Group Delay Spectrum (GDS) is defined as the negative derivative of the Fourier transform phase. If $x(n)$ is the given speech sequence then the GDS $\tau(\omega)$ can be computed from the signal according to [5], [11] as

$$\tau(\omega) = -\text{Im}\frac{d(\log(X(\omega)))}{d\omega} = \frac{X_R(\omega)Y_R(\omega) + Y_I(\omega)X_I(\omega)}{|X(\omega)|^2}, \tag{3}$$

where with subscripts R and I are noted the real and imaginary parts of the Fourier transform. $X(\omega)$ and $Y(\omega)$ are the Fourier transform of $x(n)$ and $nx(n)$, respectively. The GDS possesses two main properties – additive property and high-resolution property [5]. It is evident from the results presented in [5], [11] that the GDS is spikier than the magnitude spectrum, i.e. it possesses more clearly distinguished peaks. And due to the additive property there is a little influence between the peaks. As a consequence the closely spaced peaks (formants) in speech spectrum are resolved better in the GDS than in the magnitude spectrum. But if the denominator's term in (3) is a small value (spectrum's dip) then the GDS becomes very spiky and that complicate its usability in speech analysis. These small values (zeroes close to the unit circle in the vocal tract transfer function) can be due to the excitation source or to the short-term processing [5].

To overcome this drawback several approaches were proposed. One of them is the Modified Group Delay Spectrum (MGDS) and it is proposed in [5], [11]. The MGDS $\tau_m(\omega)$ is defined as

$$\tau_m(\omega) = \left(\frac{\tau(\omega)}{|\tau(\omega)|}\right)(|\tau(\omega)|)^\alpha, \tag{4}$$

where

$$\tau(\omega) = \left(\frac{X_R(\omega)Y_R(\omega) + Y_I(\omega)X_I(\omega)}{S(\omega)^{2\gamma}}\right), \tag{5}$$

and $S(\omega)$ is the cepstrally smoothed spectrum of $|X(\omega)|$. The parameters α and γ vary from 0 to 1 ($0 < \alpha \leq 1$) and ($0 < \gamma \leq 1$). These two parameters and the cepstrally-smoothed spectrum in denominator are introduced to decrease the spikes' amplitudes and to restrict the dynamic range of the MGDS. To control the level of cepstral smoothing of $S(\omega)$ the low-order cepstral window (lifter) l_w is used.

In the study a new robust feature named as Group Delay Mean Delta (GDMD) feature is proposed. This feature utilized the Mean Delta approach proposed in [14] but the spectral autocorrelation function is defined based on MGDS, not on the magnitude spectrum. The aim of this is to obtain peak-enhanced delta spectral autocorrelation function and thereafter more effective Mean Delta feature.

The biased spectral autocorrelation function $R_m(l)$ defined with the MGDS $\tau_m(k)$ is

$$R_m(l) = \sum_{k=0}^{K/2-l} \tau_m(k)\tau_m(k+l),$$ (6)

where K is the number of points in the discrete Fourier transform, $l = 0,...,L$; L is the number of correlation lags and $L = K/4$. The GDMD feature is calculated in an analogous manner as the MD feature according to the formulas (1) and (2) and using $R_m(l)$ instead of $R_P(l)$.

For each frame, the GDMD feature is computed into two steps as follows:

A. First step – calculation of the MGDS according to [5], [11]:

- let $x(n)$ is the given speech frame;
- compute the Fast Fourier Transform (FFT) with size K of the sequences $x(n)$ and $nx(n)$. Let these transforms are $X(k)$ and $Y(k)$, respectively.
- compute the $S(k)$ - cepstrally smoothed spectrum of $|X(k)|$ using low-order cepstral lifter l_w;
- compute the MGDS $\tau_m(k)$ as

$$\tau_m(k) = sign.\left|\frac{X_R(k)Y_R(k)+Y_I(k)X_I(k)}{S(k)^{2\gamma}}\right|^\alpha,$$ (7)

- where $sign$ is given by the sign of the term

$$\frac{X_R(k)Y_R(k)+Y_I(k)X_I(k)}{S(k)^{2\gamma}}.$$ (8)

- the parameters α, γ and l_w are adjusted according to the particular requirements.

B. Second step – calculation of the MD feature using the MGDS $\tau_m(k)$ (7) from previous step as:

- compute the average MGDS – averaged over all frames in the utterance;
- apply mean normalization - the frame MGDS is divided by the average MGDS;
- compute the non-normalized biased spectral autocorrelation function $R_m(l)$ by (6) with lags $L = K/4$ using the mean normalized MGDS;
- compute the delta spectral autocorrelation function $\Delta R_m(l)$ by equation (1) using $R_m(l)$ with $Q=3$ as

$$\Delta R_m(l) = \frac{\sum_{q=-Q}^{Q} q R_m(l+q)}{\sum_{q=-Q}^{Q} q^2} \tag{9}$$

- perform a trajectory smoothing for delta spectral autocorrelation function $\Delta R_m(l)$ (inter-frame processing) by J-order long-term spectral envelope algorithm with $J=3$ [19]. The obtained smoothed version of $\Delta R_m(l)$ is noted as $\Delta R_m^S(l)$;

- compute the GDMD m_{gd} by equation (2) using $\Delta R_m^S(l)$ as

$$m_{gd} = \left[\sum_{l=0}^{L} \left| \Delta R_m^S(l) \right| \right]^{0.5} \tag{10}$$

In Fig.1 are shown frame of the speech sound 'i' with length of 30 milliseconds (8 kHz sampling rate) and the corresponded FFT magnitude spectrum, the MGDS, the spectral and delta spectral autocorrelation functions. The MGDS parameters values are selected according to the recommendations in [5] and they are $\alpha=0.4$, $\gamma=0.9$ and $l_w = 8$.

2.3   Modified Frame Teager Energy Feature

The modified frame Teager energy is computed according to the algorithm described in [4], [6]. The MTE feature E_t for the given frame is

$$E_t = \left[\sum_{k=0}^{K/2} (k\Delta f)^2 \left| X(k) \right|^2 \right]^{0.5}, \tag{11}$$

where Δf is the frequency resolution, $\left| X(k) \right|^2$ is the FFT power spectrum and K is the FFT size;

2.4   Energy Entropy Feature

An endpoint detection feature, obtained by combination of the energy and the spectral entropy, is proposed in [4]. This combination of features is made in order to overcome the drawbacks of each other and to form a new feature more resistant to the some kind of noises. For the given frame the Energy-Entropy (EE) feature EE is computed as follows

$$EE = \sqrt{(1 + |E \times H|)}, \tag{12}$$

where E is the energy and H is the spectral entropy for the frame.

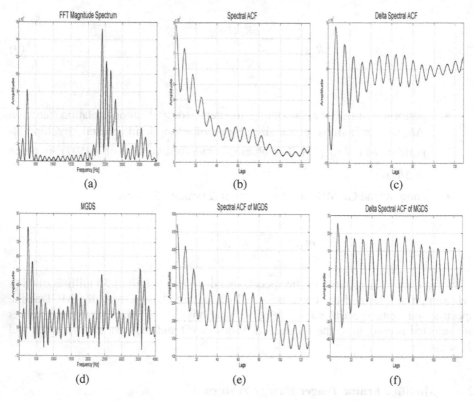

Fig. 1. Comparison of various spectra and corresponded parameters for part of speech sound 'i'. (a) FFT magnitude spectrum. (b) Spectral autocorrelation function of the FFT spectrum. (c) Delta spectral autocorrelation function of the FFT spectrum. (d) MGDS. (e) Spectral autocorrelation function of the MGDS. (f) Delta spectral autocorrelation function of the MGDS.

In order to make correct comparisons among different features, the limitation of the frequency range from 250 Hz to 3750 Hz (as was done in [4]), was not applied in our case.

For illustration in Fig.2 are shown the trajectories of the described above features for a record of the phrase obtained by a cell phone with a speaker standing on the noisy street. The clean version of the phrase is additionally obtained by a noise removal. The noise in Fig.2 (a) from 7.4 sec to 12 sec is due to the passing tram. In Fig.2 (c), (d), (e), (f) and (g) are shown the normalized features trajectories of the noisy phrase in Fig.2 (a). In Fig.2 are shown the trajectories of two versions of the GDMD feature – GDMD1 and GDMD2. The GDMD1 feature in Fig.2 (f) is obtained with parameters α, γ and l_w tuned according to recommendations in [5], i.e. $\alpha=0.4$, $\gamma=0.9$ and $l_w = 8$. While the GDMD2 feature in Fig.2 (g) is computed with parameters which provide best verification rate in the current study and they are $\alpha=0.6$, $\gamma=0.4$ and $l_w = 32$ (see 4.2).

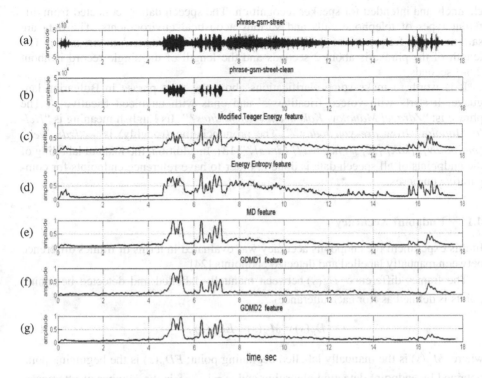

Fig. 2. An example of noisy speech: (a) original noisy speech data; (b) speech data after noise removal; (c) modified Teager energy contour; (d) energy entropy feature contour; (e) MD feature contour; (f) GDMD1 feature contour; (g) GDMD2 feature contour

3   Detection Algorithm

In the study the detection algorithm proposed in [17] is used. This algorithm is based on the single parameter trajectory variations and utilizes two fixed thresholds and six-state automaton. It is designed for endpoint detection of a word or single phrase with a short length (few seconds). For more details about detection algorithm, see [17].

4   Experiments and Discussion

In the study two experiments were carried out. In the first one the accuracy was evaluated in terms of frame difference between manually labelled and detected endpoints. The second experiment was conducted to evaluate the endpoint algorithms in terms of speaker verification performance.

The speech data used in the experiments are selected from the BG-SRDat corpus [13]. This corpus is in Bulgarian language and it is recorded over noisy telephone channels and intended for speaker recognition. The speech data is collected from different types of telephone calls and various acoustical environments. The data are sampled with frequency of 8 kHz at 16 bits, PCM format, and mono mode. The length of the phrase is about 2 seconds and the length of the single record is about 2.5-3 seconds.

It is worth to make some clarifications about the used phrase in Bulgarian language. It starts with voiced fricative 'z' and ends with unvoiced fricative 's'. The phrase is: "*Zdravei Manolov. Kak se chuvstvash dnes?*". Its English meaning is "*Hello Manolov! How are you today?*". The pronunciation (roughly) is – "*[zdra`vei:] [ma`nolov]! [kak] [se] [`tʃuvstvaʃ] [dnes]?*"[13]. In addition, the manual labelling of the endpoints of all speech data is done in order to have reference endpoints for comparative purposes.

4.1   Endpoint Accuracy

In this experiment the endpoints accuracy was evaluated in terms of frames difference between manually labelled and detected endpoints [24].

The frames difference $D_B(s)$ between manually labelled and detected beginning points is defined as (for each utterance)

$$D_B(s) = M_B(s) - ED_B(s),\tag{13}$$

where $M_B(s)$ is the manually labelled beginning point; $ED_B(s)$ is the beginning point obtained by endpoint detection algorithm and $s = 1,…,S$ is the number of utterances. The frames difference for ending points $D_E(s)$ is defined as

$$D_E(s) = M_E(s) - ED_E(s),\tag{14}$$

where $M_E(s)$ is the manually labelled beginning point; $ED_E(s)$ is the beginning point obtained by endpoint detection algorithm.

The histograms of D_B and D_E are presented in Figure 3. In Table 1 are shown for D_B and D_E the rates of distribution (in %) less than 5-frames and 10-frames differences, respectively. The used phrase begins with the following two phonemes 'z' and 'd' (it is the Bulgarian word '*zdravei*'). The stacked histogram in Fig.3 (a) has two modes. This is due to the fact that for some records all algorithms skip the voiced fricative 'z' and set the beginning point at the voiced stop consonant 'd' (after the voice bar). These errors correspond to the left mode with mean value of difference of about -10 frames, whereas the right mode corresponds to the correct beginning points. As seen in Table 1 for beginning points the rate is highest for the GDMD feature. The phrase ended with unvoiced fricative 's' which is difficult to detect in noise due to its noise-like characteristics. According to Table 1 the maximum rate of D_E belongs to the MTE feature.

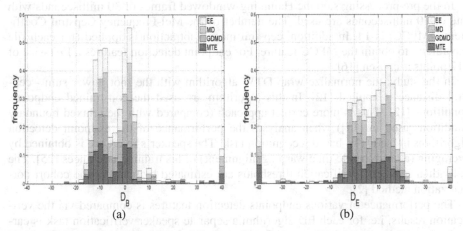

Fig. 3. The histograms of the frame differences between manually labeled and detected points: (a) D_B; (b) D_E

Table 1. The rate of distribution (%)

№	Features	ABS(D_B)		ABS(D_E)	
		≤ 5	≤ 10	≤ 5	≤ 10
1	MTE	39.69	68.70	37.02	61.83
2	EE	41.22	67.55	20.99	44.27
3	MD	40.45	74.80	29.00	51.52
4	GDMD	49.23	83.20	34.73	56.87

4.2 Speaker Verification Performance

The proposed endpoint detector is examined as a part of the fixed-text DTW-based speaker verification system. In the text below only a brief description of the speaker verification scheme is included.

The speech data used in the study include 262 records of a phrase collected from 12 male speakers. As the speech corpus is not large enough we cannot use two separate data set in training mode – one for reference template creation (training set) and another for thresholds settings (validation set). Therefore, in the study the training set is used directly as a validation set.

The different numbers of records per speaker (from 16 up to 34) and requirements to use equal number of records for speaker's reference creation [16] impose the following training procedure [16]. For reference creation are randomly selected 10 records per speaker. The rest of speaker's data are used for testing. This procedure is repeated 5 times. In the verification mode there are 142 client accesses or false rejection tests and 1562 impostor accesses or false acceptance tests. After 5 runs the total tests are: for false rejection - 710 and for false acceptance – 7810 [17].

In the pre-processing step the Hamming-windowed frames of 30 milliseconds with rate of 10 milliseconds are used. The number of the Mel-Frequency Cepstral Coefficients (MFCC) is 14. In addition, cepstral mean subtraction is applied (for each file separately) to obtain the MFCC feature. For endpoint detection features a FFT-size of 512 points is chosen [16].

In the study, the normalize-wrap DTW algorithm with the root power sum - cepstral distance is applied [12]. In this algorithm are used the constrained endpoints conditions [12]. This is more correct approach (compared with the relaxed boundary conditions used in [17]) when analyses the performance of the endpoint detection algorithms in the DTW-based recognition task. The speaker's reference is obtained by averaging (after dynamic time warping alignment) of his training utterances [25]. The individual speakers' verification thresholds are estimated by using of the cohort normalization method [2].

The performance of various endpoints detection features is compared via the verification results, i.e. for each ED algorithm a separate speaker verification task is carried out. Additional verification task is done with manually labelled endpoints.

The values of the parameters α, γ and l_w used in the MGDS estimation are crucial for the performance of the GDMD feature. In [5] as a result of exhaustive experimental work in speaker recognition, language identification and continuous speech recognition was found that the best across all tasks and all databases the MGDS parameters values are $\alpha=0.4$, $\gamma=0.9$ and $l_w = 8$. As the features in these experiments are utilized the cepstral coefficients obtained from the MGDS via the discrete cosine transform.

In the current study the MGDS is used slightly different in comparison to [5]. To estimate the actual values in the particular task it is necessary to perform line search for all parameters values. Based on the preliminary experiments with different values of the MGDS parameters and histogram analysis of the 5- and 10-frames differences was found the following set of values, performing best in terms of verification rate. This set of values for particular endpoint detection and verification framework is $\alpha=0.6$, $\gamma=0.4$ and $l_w = 32$. All experiments in the study were done with these values. Since the best values set was not obtained by the line search therefore another set of values, yielding better verification results might exist. This could be clarified in the future research.

For limited real-world data the single value error is not reliable estimation of the speaker verification performance [1]. Since this is our case it was decided to apply the methodology for performance estimation of the speaker verification proposed in [1].

The verification results are presented as rate ratios - False Rejection Rate (FRR), False Acceptance Rate (FAR) and the Half Total Error Rate (HTER) [1]. Also the 95% Confidence Interval (CI) for the HTER is shown computed according to [1]. The Z_{HTER} -test method proposed in [1] is applied to verify whether the given classifier is statistically significantly different than another. In Table 2 are shown the speaker verification results in rates and confidence interval for the HTERs. These rates are obtained for each feature and also for the manual end pointing. As seen in the table the GDMD feature performs the best among the features set.

Table 2. Speaker verification results

№	Features	FRR[%]	FAR[%]	HTER[%]	95% CI
1	Manual	6.90	4.98	5.94	±0.0096
2	MTE	11.83	10.47	11.15	±0.0123
3	EE	14.08	12.48	13.28	±0.0133
4	MD	10.56	8.06	9.31	±0.0116
5	GDMD	8.30	7.31	7.80	±0.0105

In Table 3 are shown the confidence values δ and standard deviations σ obtained from the Z_{HTER} -tests (independent case) [1]. With [A, B] are noted the two endpoints detection features A and B being tested.

Table 3. Confidence values

	[GDMD, MD]	[GDMD, MTE]
δ	93.88	99.99
σ	0.0080	0.0082

As seen in the Table 3, the GDMD feature is statistically significantly different from the MD and MTE features. For both tests the confidence values δ on their HTERs differences are greater than 90%.

It was found that there is not direct relationship between maximal rates in the frames differences histograms and verification rates. In other words, the maximal 5-frames differences rate obtained for a given feature does not lead to the maximal verification rate for that feature. The main reason for this is the phrases with serious endpoint detection errors. For them, the frames differences are greater than e.g. 20 frames (200 milliseconds). Since in the training mode are always used 10 utterances, no matter how accurate their endpoint detections are, these errors contribute to the poorly trained templates.

This observation is confirmed by the results shown in Table 1 where the GDMD feature possesses maximal rate for 5- and 10-frames differences for beginning points, but not for ending ones. Nevertheless, it provides the best verification rate as seen in Table 2. This is explained by the minimal number of the serious endpoint detection errors obtained for the GDMD feature, and is clearly seen in the histograms - in the last bar in Fig.3 (a), also in the first and in the last bars in Fig.3 (b).

5   Conclusions

In the study a new robust feature for endpoint detection, which combining the properties of the MGDS and the MD approach in order to obtain more robust endpoint detection is proposed. Its effectiveness was experimentally compared with three other features in the fixed-text DTW-based speaker verification task with short phrases of telephone speech. As seen in Table 2 the GDMD feature demonstrates the best performance in endpoint detection tests in terms of verification rate.

Future work in this area will be focused on three main objectives – the development of more efficient version for the GDMD feature with fewer adjustable parameters, the improvement of the endpoint detection accuracy especially for weak phonemes and the examination of the developed endpoint detector in the hidden Markov models framework for short phrases.

Acknowledgements. The author's participation into the workshop BIOMET'2014 was supported by the project AComIn "Advanced Computing for Innovation", grant 316087.

References

1. Bengio, S., Mariethoz, J.: A Statistical Significance Test for Person Authentication. In: ODYSSEY - The Speaker and Language Recognition Workshop, pp. 237–244 (2004)
2. Burileanu, C., Moraru, D., Bojan, L., Puchiu, M., Stan, A.: On Performance Improvement of a Speaker Verification System Using Vector Quantization, Cohorts and Hybrid Cohort-World Models. International Journal of Speech Technology (5), 247–257 (2002)
3. Gerven, S., Xie, F.: A comparative study of speech detection methods. In: Eurospeech, pp. 1095–1098 (1997)
4. Gu, L., Zahorian, S.: A new robust algorithm for isolated word endpoint detection. In: IEEE ICASSP, vol. IV, pp. 4161–4164 (2002)
5. Hegde, R., Murthy, H., Gadde, V.: Significance of the Modified Group Delay Feature in Speech Recognition. IEEE Transactions on Audio, Speech and Language Processing 15(1), 190–202 (2007)
6. Huang, L., Yang, C.: A Novel Approach to Robust Speech Endpoint Detection in Car Environment. In: IEEE ICASSP, pp. 1751–1754 (2000)
7. Jia, C., Xu, B.: An Improved Entropy based Endpoint Detection Algorithm. In: ISCSLP, pp. 96--100 (2002)
8. Krishnan, S., Padmanabhan, R., Murthy, H.: Robust Voice Activity Detection using Group Delay Functions. In: IEEE International Conference on Industrial Technology, pp. 2603–2607 (2006)
9. Li, Q., Zheng, J., Tsai, A., Zhou, Q.: Robust Endpoint Detection and Energy Normalization for Real-Time Speech and Speaker Recognition. IEEE Transaction on SAP 10(3), 146–157 (2002)
10. Mesa-Navarro, J., Moreno-Bilbao, A., Lleida-Solano, E.: An Improved Speech Endpoint Detection System in Noisy Environments by Means of Third-Order Spectra. IEEE Signal Processing Letters 6(9), 224–226 (1999)
11. Murthy, H., Gadde, V.: The modified group delay function and its application to phoneme recognition. In: IEEE ICASSP, vol. 1, pp. 68–71 (2003)
12. Myers, C., Rabiner, L., Rosenberg, A.: Performance Tradeoffs in Dynamic Time Warping Algorithms for Isolated Word Recognition. IEEE Transactions on ASSP 28(6), 623–635 (1980)
13. Ouzounov, A.: BG-SRDat: A Corpus in Bulgarian Language for Speaker Recognition over Telephone Channels. Cybernetics and Information Technologies 3(2), 101–108 (2003)
14. Ouzounov, A.: A Robust Feature for Speech Detection. Cybernetics and Information Technologies 4(2), 3–14 (2004)
15. Ouzounov, A.: Robust Features and Neural Network for Noisy Speech Detection. Cybernetics and Information Technologies 6(3), 75–84 (2006)

16. Ouzounov, A.: Cepstral Features and Text-Dependent Speaker Identification - A Comparative Study. Cybernetics and Information Technologies **10**(1), 1–12 (2010)
17. Ouzounov, A.: Telephone Speech Endpoint Detection Using Mean-Delta Feature. Cybernetics and Information Technologies **14**(2), 127–139 (2014)
18. Padmanabhan, R., Krishnan, P., Murthy, H.: A Pattern Recognition approach to VAD using Modified Group Delay. In: Proceedings of the National Conference on Communications, pp. 432–436 (2008)
19. Ramirez, J., Segura, J., Benítez, C., De la Torre, A., Rubio, A.: Efficient Voice Activity Detection Algorithms Using Long-Term Speech Information. Speech Communication **42**(3-4), 271–287 (2004)
20. Ramirez, J., Yelamos, P., Gorriz, J., Seguraet, J.: SVM-based speech endpoint detection using contextual speech features. Electronics Letters **42**(7), 426–428 (2006)
21. Seok, J., Bae, K.: A Novel Endpoint Detection using Discrete Wavelet Transform. IEICE Transaction on Inf. & Syst., E82-D(11) 1489–1491 (1999)
22. Shin, W., Lee, B., Lee, Y., Lee, J.: Speech/non-speech classification using multiple features for robust endpoint detection. In: IEEE ICASSP, pp. 1399–1402 (2000)
23. Wu, B.F., Wang, K.C.: Robust Endpoint Detection Algorithm based on the Adaptive Band-Partitioning Spectral Entropy in Adverse Environments. IEEE Transactions on SAP **13**(5), 762–775 (2005)
24. Yamamoto, K., Jabloun, F., Reinhard, K., Kawamura, A.: Robust Endpoint Detection for Speech Recognition Based on Discriminative Feature Extraction. In: IEEE ICASSP, vol. I, pp. 805–808 (2006)
25. Zelinski, R., Class, F.: A Learning Procedure for Speaker–Dependent Word Recognition System based on Sequential Processing of Input Tokens. In: IEEE ICASSP, pp. 1053–1056 (1983)
26. Zhang, Z., Furui, S.: Noisy Speech Recognition based on Robust End-point Detection and Model Adaptation. IEEE ICASSP **1**, 441–444 (2005)
27. Zhu, J., Chen, F.: The Analysis and Application of a New Endpoint Detection Method based on Distance of Autocorrelated Similarity. In: Eurospeech, pp. 105–108 (1999)

3D Ear Recognition

Appearance-Based 3D Object Approach
to Human Ears Recognition

Dimo T. Dimov[1(✉)] and Virginio Cantoni[2]

[1] Institute of Information and Communication Technologies, Bulgarian Academy of Sciences,
Sofia, Bulgaria
dtdim@iinf.bas.bg
[2] Department of Industrial and Information Engineering, Pavia University, Pavia, Italy
virginio.cantoni@unipv.it

Abstract. The paper presents an approach for recognition of 3D objects using a database (DB) of precedents. Each object of interest for recognition is presented in the DB through a sufficient number of 2D projections (images), each from a different view point. If it is available a CBIR method to access the DB that is to be fast enough and noise resistant, the number of necessary view positions for each 3D object can be substantially reduced, for example, to several tens or a few hundreds of images. The authors have already applied successfully this appearance-based approach two times: i) for recognition of palm signs from a sign language alphabet and ii) for human face recognition. The recent advance in 3D scanning technologies allow to fresh up the training phase of the proposed method, i.e. the DB gathering of the necessary appearance of precedents for 3D objects, now more accurately and simply. At the same time, the true recognition remains based on images from conventional 2D cameras. This study aims to experiment the mentioned approach for the case of human ears recognition, which, according to our research is of interest to the guild on Biometrics, in the country, in Europe and worldwide.

Keywords: Human ears recognition · 3D object recognition · Appearance-based 3D methods · Content Base Image Retrieval (CBIR) for 3D solids · Rapid and reliable CBIR

1   Introduction

The first activity in human identification by ears morphology has been in France more than a century ago [1]; new efforts were given with success in USA later by Iannarelli [2]. In fact, the human outer ear is usually segmented by six basic components: i) the outer helix, ii) the antihelix, iii) the lobe, iv) the tragus, v) the antitragus and finally vi) the concha. This shape evolves during the embryonic state from six growth nodules; its structure therefore is not completely random, in practice it is considered universal, unique and averagely permanent (even if it is still not demonstrated that ears of all people are unique, but it has been shown that it does not change consistently with aging [3]). A real explosion happened in the last decades so that we can here quote twelve surveys on ear biometrics starting from ten years [4-15]. Today, generally

© Springer International Publishing Switzerland 2014
V. Cantoni et al. (Eds.): BIOMET 2014, LNCS 8897, pp. 121–135, 2014.
DOI: 10.1007/978-3-319-13386-7_10

speaking, the most popular targets are identification (also known as recognition, "Who is he/she?"), authentication (also known as verification, "Am I who I claim I am?"), and surveillance. Identification implies matching a biometric sample against all records in a database of templates ("one to many matching"). The most commonly used biometrics for identification according to Ratha et al. [16] are fingerprints, face, voice, iris, signature, and hand geometry that are physiological characteristics that are based on data derived from direct measurements of a part of the human body. Biometric authentication requires comparing an enrolled biometric sample (biometric template) with a newly presented one. It is a "one-to-one matching" process. For authentication purposes the characteristics exploited frequently are voice and signature that even though they are person's physical characteristics they are behavioral biometric traits.

Following Jain et al. [17], human physiological or behavioral characteristic to be used in biometry must be universal, unique, permanent and collectable. That is each person should own a characteristic (universal feature) not shared with others (unique feature), that cannot change (permanent feature) and that is detectable to a sensor and reckonable (collectable feature). However in biometric systems there are more requirements, e.g. performance (system's accuracy and speed), acceptability in a daily routines and circumvention (how easy it is to fool the system).

Ear recognition for authentication has some advantages: it is more consistent compared to the variability due to expression, orientation and effect of aging. Furthermore, it has a more uniform distribution of color, and its appearance is fixed e.g. when converting the original image into gray scales. Data collection is convenient in comparison to the more invasive technologies like iris, retina, fingerprint etc. Other mammals like horses, dogs, and cats can articulate their ears to locate sound sources; humans instead can hardly articulate ears that are held rigidly in position on the side of the head, and this makes detection easier. Moreover, the acquisition of ear images does not necessarily require a person's cooperation, and is considered to be non-intrusive by most people; in fact the ear can easily be captured from a distance, even if the subject is not fully cooperative.

From visual complexity viewpoint face and ear are roughly similar. However note that since the face is symmetrical from a biometrics perspective the information on the left side usually reflects that on the right. Human ears have some degree of symmetry that can perhaps be systematically exploited, at the same time, thus the degree of asymmetry provides additional information about their identity and may be used in schemes that combine the face and ears information.

Nevertheless while face recognition is very popular, up to now ear recognition is not; but it is normally accepted that with the decreasing cost of the necessary 3D scanners and their increased performance the 3D ear biometrics is a promising "soft" biometric and is foreseen to be extremely useful in most real-world applications in the near future.

2   3D Ear Biometrics Approaches

Ear biometrics approaches are relying on morphological ear properties. Pattern recognition problem generally require the solution of two sub-problems: target representation and discriminant technique. Also ear recognition system follows this framework: description and feature extraction and the comparison strategy.

The ear color distribution is roughly monotone and the 3D appearance is due mainly to shading effects, thus it is morphology that characterizes look and trait. For this reason, pose and camera position variations are very critical features in 2D ear recognition. A 3D representation enriches the input data with depth information and can increase consistently the accuracy of ear recognition systems.

Chen and Bhanu [18] presented one of the first 3D ear recognition system that exploited the depth and structure of the ear's surface. The morphological components were characterized by a distribution of shape indices applied on profile images.

Chen et al. [19] proposed a 3D ear detection and recognition system using Iterative Closest Point (ICP) and a local surface descriptor for recognition, reporting a recognition rate of more than 90%.

Yan and Bowyer [20] developed an ear detection method which fuses 2D color images and images captured by a range scanner. The concha serves as the reference point, applies the active contour model and uses ICP registration.

Cadavid and Abdel-Mottaleb [21] developed a technique for ear recognition from videos. They reconstructed the 3D shape of an ear by using the Shape from Shading (SfS) technique. The ICP algorithm is then used to calculate the similarity between the 3D shapes of two ear videos.

Zhou et al. [22] train a 3D shape model based on the histogram of shape indexes. The ear descriptor is built from shape index histograms, which are extracted from sliding window of different sizes inside the image. A Support Vector Machine (SVM) classifier is trained to decide whether an image region is or not an ear segment.

A number of multimodal approaches that include ear recognition have also been mentioned, such as ear images and speech, face, various combinations of 2D Principal Component Analysis (PCA), 3D-PCA, and 3D-Edges. All these studies reported an increase in performance when using multimodal instead of individual biometrics. For further details of multi-modal ear and face biometrics see [23].

Prakash and Gupta [24] extend the quoted 2D approach to a 3D one. In this version the edges are computed as discontinuities in the depth image. Using the 3D representations of the same subset as in the 2D analysis they report an increase of the detection rate from 96.63% to 99.38%. In particular, this 3D graph-based approach looks robust to the influence by rotation and scale.

3   Our Approach Description

In this paper, an appearance based CBIR approach is considered for recognition of 3D objects using a DB of precedents. Every object of interest for recognition is presented in the DB through a sufficient number of 2D projections (images), each from a different view point. If it is available a CBIR method to access the DB that is to be fast enough and noise resistant, the number of necessary view positions for each represented 3D object can be substantially reduced, for example, to several tens or a few hundreds of images. Furthermore, for most applications for 3D solids, the appropriate viewpoints may be grouped together in a spatial sector of about from 90 up to 180 degrees. The approach is considered promising in recent surveys, like view based similarities [25] or image signatures [26], as it is relatively simple to implement and fits the consumer perceptions of effective marketability. There are two main problems to be solved here: (i) gathering of precedents for the DB and (ii) choosing a suitable CBIR method. We have already applied this appearance-based approach two times: for recognition of palm signs from a sign language alphabet, and for human faces recognition. The image DB (IDB) in these cases was collected through the so-called "circumvention film" by a conventional camera, with the help of a special mechanical construction for more accurate scanning of 3D objects. Now we use a modern 3D scanner to create an intermediate 3D computer model, to obtain from it the necessary number of 2D projections of the given object and to record them in the IDB, and so on for all 3D objects of interest. Of course, the input image for recognition is not required to act on such an expensive (now) 3D device; it can come from simple 2D camera as a video clip or even as a single still image. For the CBIR method to access the IDB, it is necessary to have enough processing speed, for example, proportional to $\log(|IDB|)$, where $|IDB|$ is the IDB volume in number of images. Our experience shows that it is desirable that the 2D projections of each 3D object, no matter how great their number is, are to be evenly distributed in the most likely stereo sector of inputs (positions of 2D camera). This allows an optimal noise immunity to be achieved by the chosen CBIR. The current study aims to experiment the mentioned approach in the case of human ears recognition. The paper text hereinafter is organized as follows: 3.1 The used IDB structure, 3.2 Our CBIR in brief, 3.3 General phases of the method, and finally – Experiments, Discussion, and Conclusion.

3.1   The Used IDB Structure

The Institute of Information and Communication Technologies (IICT) of the Bulgarian Academy of Sciences (BAS) has collected a 3D Ears' DB with the goal of providing data of higher definition than comparable collections. The DB contains 3D models of ears for ~20 subjects of various ages, gender, etc., gathered through a VIUscan 3D scanner[1] under optimal lighting conditions. Only 11 of the 3D models from this DB are used so far (the others are of relatively insufficient quality). An image example from the 3D Ears DB is shown in Fig. 1. The logical structure of this DB restriction respects the following rules:

- The necessary representative 2D projections (images) of a 3D object are considered positioned in a square grid over the experimental sector of visibility that for the current case of ears is considered the front stereo angle of about 90°;
- Two sets of images are implemented (a test set and a verification set) for each of the 10 used 3D models (one per a subject); one of the available 11 models is left in reserve for verification of false negative cases of searching the IDB.

---

[1] http://iict.bas.bg/acomin/smart_lab/Hand-held-3D-scanner.pdf

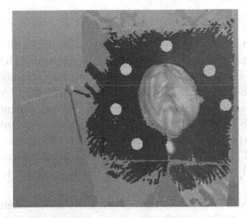 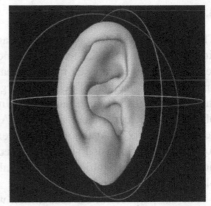

Fig. 1. A primary 3D ear model (directly after scanning, on the left), and after its post-processing (on the right)

- A square grid (10×10) is defined for the test images that divides evenly the experimental sector of vision, or a total of 100 nodes (view positions), each of them corresponding to a particular 2D projection (test image) for the given 3D ear object;
- One more square grid (9×9) is defined for the verification images that also divides evenly the experimental sector of vision totally on 81 view positions, each of them corresponding to a particular 2D projection (verification image) for the given 3D object;
- The verification grid is centrally located relatively to the test grid. Each verification image is positioned in the centre of a basic square of the test grid to represent "the worst case" of recognition by the proposed method;
- Thus, every 3D object should draw 100 test projections, one for each view position (node) of the test grid, as well as 81 verification projections, one for each verification view position.

The set of test projections for all 3D objects of recognition, i.e. the entire test set, was charged into the IDB. The set of all verification projections, i.e. the entire verification set is used to check the efficiency of the method here proposed.

Either the test set or the verification one consist of images (2D projections) obtained from a smoothed (by a spline approach) visualization of the corresponding 3D model. Thus, 2D projections received from the canonical triangular representation of the 3D model as well as other coarse visualizations of it can be considered as noisy versions of the basic 2D projections.

By default (according to the software used) the lighting of given 3D object originates from a centralized cohesive source, i.e. a point source located on the main focal axis, infinitely remote and of constant and sufficient power. Choosing different positions of lighting source(s), we can get other versions of the described test and/or verification sets and consider them as extra noisy versions.

3.2   Our CBIR Method in Brief

The time necessary for comparison of an input image with all the samples in the dictionary (i.e. our IDB) has to be short enough to ensure the operation in real-time. The realization of the proposed method idea is possible if we have enough noise tolerant and fast CBIR method of access to large IDB. Such CBIR methods are provided by the system EFIRS (Experimental Fast Image Retrieval System) that is a development of the SP&PR department of IICT-BAS, and can be associated with the so-called "early" CBIR [27]. At the same time, experiments show that EFIRS can be successfully extended for visual signature based [26] or view based [25], or multiple projections based 3D recognition [29], or finally as an appearance based CBIR approach to 3D recognition (this paper).

For our purposes of 3D recognition we will consider EFIRS primarily as a system for recognition by a more or less large vocabulary (IDB) of samples (precedent images). Besides of a sufficient number of images necessary, the images EFIRS operates with must comply with the basic restriction on its CBIR methods – the images have to be relatively "clean", i.e. to contain whole object of interest (ear) in color or gray scale on a white background, and if possible without any noise artifacts from the natural environment.

The currently used technologies for obtaining 3D models by our scanner (VIUscan of CreaForm) require additional manual and/or semi-automatic processing of the primary models (immediately after scanning); see also the brief description of respective software: VXElements (for the scanner), and MeshLab[2] (for 3D objects post-processing). By using "relatively clean" 3D models of the objects (human ears) we obtain the required "clean" images (2D projections) easily.

Their processing speed is of the order of $t.\log_2(N)$, in number of accesses into the computer HDD, where IDB resides, where N is the size of the IDB (in number of images), and t is the average access time of HDD. CBIR noise immunity of EFIRS covers any random linear transformations of the input (translation, rotation and scaling) as well as the so-called 'regular' noise in images. Thus, the current study can be seen also as an experimental evaluation of the available built-in noise tolerance of the CBIR methods of EFIRS. Moreover, EFIRS provides noise immunity against 'rough noise artifacts', but this is not interesting in our case because it is provided by the manual/semi-automatic processing of 3D models that is usually required immediately after scanning.

A Few Necessary Properties of CBIR Methods
- The input precedents (2D images), whose nearest similarity is sought in IDB, have to be normalized in advance (against random linear transformations and by intensity as well); the same normalization are also performed for all the images of IDB.
- All images, incoming for recognition or already recorded in IDB, are represented as fixed-length strings, each one composed of the values of the most informative features describing the corresponding image content. Each string is declared as a

---

[2] http://meshlab.sourceforge.net/

search key for IDB, through the corresponding index access method of the DBMS, implemented for the IDB performance and maintenance.

- Thus, seeing from the IDB side, all images are enriched by a linear (total) ordering according to their key values, i.e. the image feature space is reduced to 1D space. Additionally, for each image of IDB a similarity class can be defined as 1D area by both half distances to the corresponding two neighboring images. Noise tolerance for a given image, is determined by the size (width) of the corresponding 1D class, see Fig. 1 and 2.

Z-distance Between Two Images

We can define a distance by the number of positions to the end of the IDB keys, and we call it "Z-distance". Thus, the Z-distance between two images under comparison, in our case – the query image at the input, and the retrieved one from IDB, is measured as the maximal tail difference length between the respective image keys. The maximal tail difference length denotes the remainder from the key after position l, $l<L$, as to which the CBIR method considers both images similar enough, i.e.:

$$Z(K_1, K_2) = L - \max_{0 \le l < L}\left\{l : |k_{1,i} - k_{2,i}| \le \varepsilon, i = 0,1,..l\right\} , \tag{1}$$

where L is the length of the IDB keys, K_1 and K_2, $K=(k_0, k_1,...,k_{L-1})$ are the keys of compared images pair, and the positive constant ε reflects the EFIRS's built-in degree of noise tolerance.

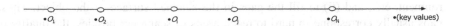

Fig. 2. Illustration of IDB objects ordered by their keys, that is a full ordering: $K(O)$ the key value associated to an object O

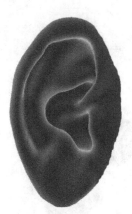 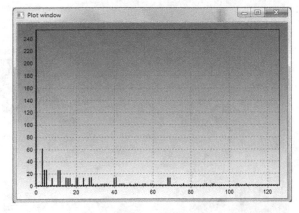

Fig. 3. An ear image and its key record into IDB

CBIR can be also considered a basic approach to pattern recognition that uses a large dictionary of image instances. This approach accents on preprocessing of images for adapting the applied recognition technique to the conventional retrieval methods of the DBMS used (to maintain the IDB of interest). We apply the EFIRS method based on our Polar-Fourier-Wavelets Transform (PFWT) definition of keys [30].

3.3   General Phases of the Method Proposed

Like the majority of recognition methods based on input precedents the proposed method consists also of two general phases:

1. Training phase: i.e. data collection for the IDB, through 3D scanning;
2. Operational phase: i.e. the actual recognition.

The Methodology for IDB Collection
The methodology consists of the following steps:

1. Obtain a 3D model of each 3D object of interest by 3D scanning of it: yet this operation requires certain practical skills of the operator of 3D scanner. To facilitate post-processing of the obtained 3D models we use a special helmet for the human head to paste the necessary markers that the 3D scanner needs for precise 3D orientation, see Fig. 4.
2. Post-process the scanner raw data: (i) to remove typical artifacts of 3D scanning, i.e. residues from the markers, artifacts corresponding to the scanned object environment, etc., and (ii) to fill the gaps in the scanned surface of the object. These gaps usually correspond to hard to reach areas of scanning; besides, the quality of soft filling is not acceptable for very large gaps. To post-process the raw data we use a combination of the basic software (VXElements) of the available scanner and the MeshLab software as well.

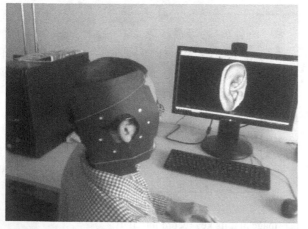

Fig. 4. 3D scanning of an ear using an optional helmet

3. Prepare the required number of 2D projections from the post-processed 3D model by combined use of MeshLab and a proprietary software written in Matlab and/or C++.
4. Load the necessary views (2D images) of the given 3D object into the IDB and re-index it. Images for all 3D objects of interest can be loaded also directly through EFIRS, in a batch mode. For this aim, some modules of EFIRS have been appropriately extended/modified.

At this phase of experiments we use 3D models of only the right ear (of each subject/person to be presented in the IDB). In previous applications of the proposed method [29], we organized the training phase through short video clips tracking the 3D object (face, or gesturing palm) by uniform scanning (in position and time) and for enough open spatial sector in front of the object. The necessary 2D projections had been extracted from the video clips of the so-called "surrounding filming" [29]. However, the use of a 3D scanner allows for greater precision of the experiments.

Operational Phase
The actual recognition scenario remains the same as in the above mentioned two applications, i.e. it is believed that the input data (2D image-precedents) used to

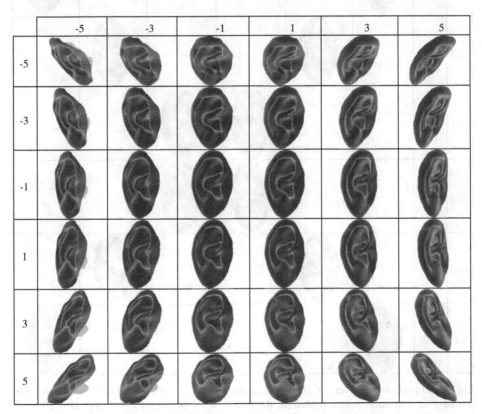

Fig. 5. 2D projections from an ear 3D model, evenly distributed in the expected stereo sector of visibility (for simplicity only odd rows/columns of the grid are shown)

extract/retrieve the most similar image from the IDB, is obtained by conventional 2D scanning devices, such as digital 2D cameras. The main idea is the true recognition scenario to be simple, fast and robust.

4   Experiments

An experimental study of the proposed approach is conducted through the system EFIRS, [28]. For the purposes of experiment, the EFIRS's test that operates on a single input image is extended for a series of input (verification) images. The EFIRS conventions are used to generate the necessary IDBs. The CBIR method chosen is PFWT, described in [30].

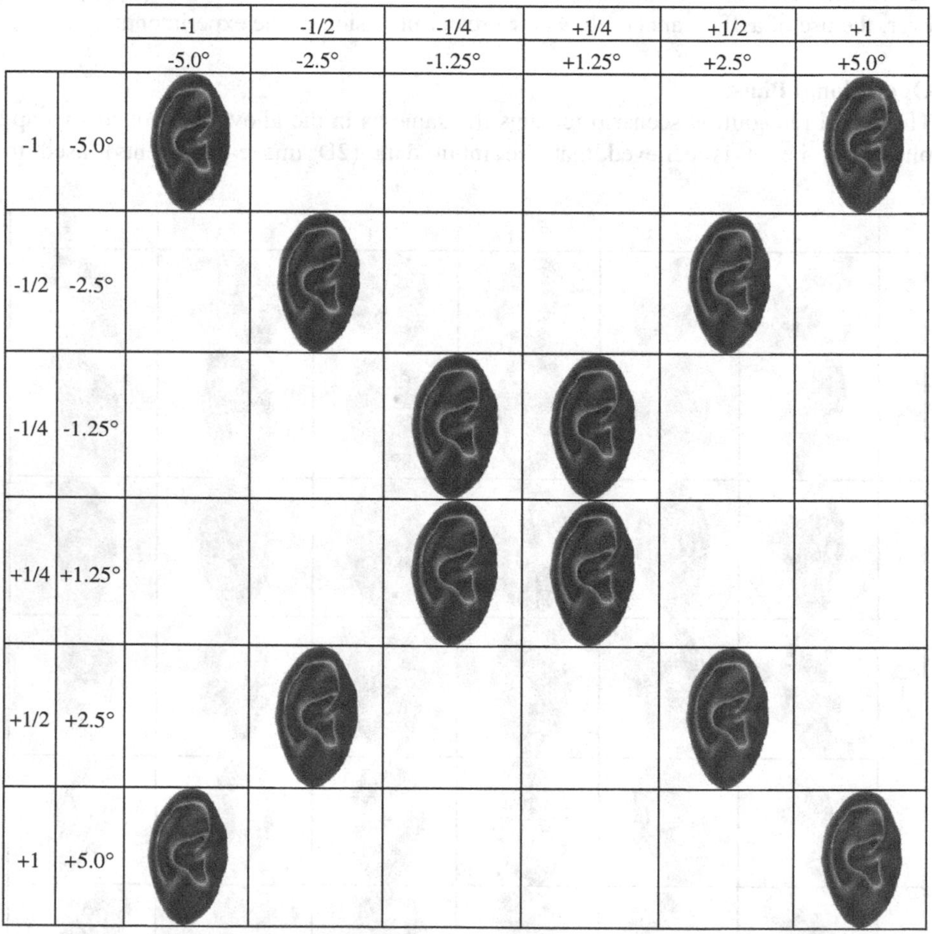

| | | -1 | -1/2 | -1/4 | +1/4 | +1/2 | +1 |
		-5.0°	-2.5°	-1.25°	+1.25°	+2.5°	+5.0°
-1	-5.0°						
-1/2	-2.5°						
-1/4	-1.25°						
+1/4	+1.25°						
+1/2	+2.5°						
+1	+5.0°						

Fig. 6. 2D projections of an ear 3D model, evenly distributed in the central zone of the IDB virtual grid. The outer square represents the nodes of the base grid 10×10 (i.e. $D = 10°$), the intermediate square – 20×20 extended grid (i.e. $D = 5°$), and the inner square – the densest grid 40×40 (i.e. $D = 2.5°$).

4.1 Nature of the Experiment

Ten 3D ear models are presented in our IDB. From each 3D model, a set of 100 (=10×10) 2D projections is generated to form the test set of projections (images) for the model. All images are in a "gray" scale, where the intensity of each true image object is inverted on a white background as required by EFIRS. Each image corresponds to a node of the visualization grid, see Fig. 5. The test sets for all 10 objects (human ear models) are loaded into the IDB, i.e. the basic version of IDB contains 1000 images.

Additionally, a set of 81(=9×9) 2D projections is also generated from the respective 3D model to form its verification set of projections (images). Thus, the total verification set (for the all 10 objects) consists of 324 images that are submitted sequentially to EFIRS recognition.

To realize the so-called "worst-case", each verification image is positioned in the center of a basic square of the chosen grid, see Fig. 6. This achieves the desired uniformity of distribution of the verification positions towards the IDB (test) images. The Error Recognition Rate (ERR) results for these basic verification sets are not very impressive, ERR ≈ 32.0%, see Table 1.

To improve the recognition ability, we reduced the basic distance D among test images of IDB; where D, i.e. the size of each basic square of the chosen grid, was initially chosen $D=D_0=10°$. To use the same verification set with the new experiment, we chose the new D as a half of previous D_0, i.e. $D=D_1=D_0/2=5°$. Thus, the new test set for a given 3D object should have 324 (=18×18) images that makes 3240 images for all 3D objects (10 human ear models), i.e. almost 3 times more. The ERR attained decreased to 10.4%, which was considered promising.

Table 1. Recognition results for the three IDB versions extracted from our 3D Ears DB

personal ID	verif.power	Test IDB$_0$ ⇔ 100 ear images per person		Test IDB$_1$ ⇔ 324 ear images per person		Test IDB$_2$ ⇔ 1156 ear images per person	
		errors	%	errors	%	errors	%
Φ_0	81	25	30.49	4	4.88	3	3.66
Φ_1	"	34	41.46	7	8.54	1	1.22
Φ_2	"	18	21.95	8	9.76	2	2.44
Φ_3	"	32	39.02	11	13.41	5	6.10
Φ_4	"	19	23.17	5	6.10	1	1.22
Φ_5	"	21	25.61	7	8.54	3	3.66
Φ_6	"	30	36.59	8	9.76	1	1.22
Φ_7	"	21	25.61	11	13.41	3	3.66
Φ_8	"	29	35.37	14	17.07	3	3.66
Φ_9	"	30	36.59	9	10.98	3	3.66
Totally:	810	259	31.98	84	10.37	25	3.09
Proc. speed [sec per input img]		0.54		0.57		0.63	

We conducted one more cut (by halves) of D_1, i.e. $D=D_2=D_0/4=2.5°$. This new test set of all 3D objects contains $11560 = 10×(34×34)$ images, and the achieved ERR became 3.1%.

Thus, we can consider that the expected trend of decreasing ERR, respectively increasing True RR (TRR), by reducing the basic (reference) distance D that means an increase in the number of necessary view positions for each 3D object, is experimentally confirmed.

4.2   Discussion of Results

The recognition results for the three experimented versions of IDB, based on our 3D Ears DB, are shown on the Table 1. The rows Φ_i, $i = 0$-9, represent the number of recognition errors and the appropriately ERR, in percentage of the number $(= 81)$ of the verification images per an ear. By columns the results for the 3 types of experiments conducted are grouped from left to right: for IDB_0, $|IDB_0|=1000$, i.e. with $D_0=10°$ (the basic version); for IDB_1, $|IDB_1|=3240$ with $D_1=5°$; and for IDB_2, $|IDB_2|=11560$ with $D_2=2.5°$ (the best version). In the penultimate row the corresponding average results are given and in the last line − the appropriate time to recognize a given input precedent (image); this is approximately constant because the time for accessing the IDB is proportional to the logarithm of the number of its records.

Below we systemize some directions for future research and improvement of the proposed method:

- At present, only the right ear is considered because of presumed symmetry, and for definiteness as usual.
- Ear region isolation, from scenes in still images and/or video, is considered outside of this paper scope. To this aim, it can be essentially used the obvious fact that the human ears are almost immovably fixed at the head, i.e. can be selected after global selection of a human face in the scene.
- The achieved TRR of ~ 97% is, of course, insufficient in practice. However, a more detailed treatment of the transitions from the true 2D object to its background in each of the images (as in the IDB and the input) is expected to lead to a substantial reduction of ERR, until about ERR <1%.
- A possible IDB alternative: the necessary experimental IDB could also be a less or more similar IDB, available by Internet. Thus, instead of a full grid of projections we will have only a few single images of an ear, which is insufficient for the proposed method, but better than nothing. Obviously, the images from these external databases should not be able to be find/recognized in our database (if the ears are really an unique characteristic of humans).
- By default (according to the software used), the lighting of a 3D object is produced from a centralized coherent source. Choosing different directions of the light, we can get other versions of the described testing and/or verification sets considering them as noisy versions. Thus, for the proposed method assessment, besides the basic (test and verification) sets we can also use extra sets as follows:

- A test set, in the basic grid nodes, but lightened from different positions. We ask for 8 surrounding positions of lighting angles ± 45°, horizontally and/or vertically that gives 8 extra sets of the "test" type (each one of the same power of 100).
- Similarly, for verification grid nodes we posed an extra total of 8 sets of the "verification" type (each one of the same power of 81).
- The verification 2D images produced for the selected 3D object are taken in the "worst case", in the square centre of the 4 (stereo-metrically) closest images from the test set. I.e., it is believed that the other cases of input image location, relatively to the test grid nodes are easier to recognize, i.e. TRR will be higher.
- 3D devices (like scanners) are expensive now, so we use them only for the collection of our IBD, while the input images for recognition are expected to be derived from conventional 2D cameras or other 2D scanning devices. The latter also needs specific ear selection techniques similar to the above mentioned for IDB gathering.
- If the input device is a simple camera (giving a video clip or a still image), a similar behavior of the method proposed is believed, with eventual differences in pre-processing and/or normalization of the input images (2D precedents).

5   Conclusion

An appearance-based 3D recognition method has been described and experimented for the case of human ears recognition. The experimentally achieved ERR ~3%, i.e. TRR ~97% is considered very promising to future extension/modification of the method proposed. The method is generally designed to application for human authentication and/or identification in several secure and pass control systems for large lists of subjects the system considers in its IDB. Even though its relatively not very high TRR, the method seems enough rapid, robust, reliable and probably firsthand one for the implementation in real-time systems, where all its recognition refusals (< 3%) are to be assigned to more sophisticated and probably slower extra developments. The method can be also fused (applied in combination) with other types of human identification modalities in a stand-alone multimodal system.

Acknowledgements. This research is partly supported by the project AComIn "Advanced Computing for Innovation", grant 316087, funded by the FP7 Capacity Programme (Research Potential of Convergence Regions).

References

1. Bertillon, A.: La Photographie Judiciaire: Avec Un Appendice Sur La Classification Et L'Identification Anthropometriques. Gauthier-Villars, Paris (1890)
2. Iannarelli, A.: Ear Identification. Forensic Identification Series. Paramont Publishing Company

3. Sforza, C., Grandi, G., Binelli, M., Tommasi, D.G., Rosati, R., Ferrario, V.F.: Age- and sex-related changes in the normal human ear. Forensic Sci. Int. **187**(1-3), 110e1–110e7 (2009)
4. Abaza, A., Ross, A., Herbert, C., Harrison, M.A.F., Nixon, M. S.: A survey on ear biometrics. ACM Computing Surveys 45(22), no.2 (2013)
5. Pflug, A., Busch, C.: Ear biometrics: a survey of detection, feature extraction and recognition methods. IET Biometrics. **1**(2), 114–129 (2012)
6. Ross, A., Abaza, A.: Human Ear Recognition. IEEE Computer Society. **44**(11), 79–81 (2011)
7. Ramesh, K.P., Rao, K.N.: Pattern extraction methods for ear biometrics – a survey. In: World Congress on Nature Biologically Inspired Computing, NaBIC 2009, pp. 1657--1660 (2009)
8. Bhanu, B., Chen, H.: Ear Biometrics, 3D. In: Li, S.Z., Jain, A.K. (eds.) Encyclopedia of Biometrics, pp. 241—248. Springer (2009)
9. Islam, S.M.S., Bennamoun, M., Owens, R., Davies, R.: Biometric approaches of 2D – 3D ear and face: a survey. In: Sobh, T. (edt.) Advances in Computer and Information Sciences and Engineering, pp. 509--514. Springer, Netherlands (2008)
10. Purkait, R.: Ear Biometric: An Aid to Personal Identification. In: Bhasin, V., Bhasin, M.K. (eds.) Anthropology Today: Trends, Scope and Applications, vol. 3, pp. 215—218. Kamla-Raj Enterprises (2007)
11. Hurley, D.J., Arbab-Zavar, B., Nixon, M.S.: The Ear as a Biometric. In: Jain, A.K., Flynn, P., Ross, A.A. (eds.) Handbook of Biometrics, pp. 131--150. Springer (2007)
12. Middendorff, C., Bowyer, K.W.: Multibiometrics Using Face and Ear. In:, Jain, A.K., Flynn, P., Ross, A.A. (eds.) Handbook of Biometrics, pp. 315–334, Springer (2007)
13. Choras, M.: Image feature extraction methods for ear biometrics – a survey. In: 6th Int. Conf. on Computer Information Systems and Industrial Management Applications, pp. 261--265 (2007)
14. Pun, K.H., Moon, Y.S.: Recent advances in ear biometrics. In: Proc. 6th IEEE Int. Conf. on Automatic Face and Gesture Recognition, pp. 164--169 (2004)
15. Lammi, H.K.: Ear biometics, Lappeenranta University of Technology, Department of Information Technology (2004)
16. Ratha, N.K., Senior, A.W., Bolle, R.M.: Automated Biometrics. In: Singh, S., Murshed, N., Kropatsch, W.G. (eds.) ICAPR 2001. LNCS, vol. 2013, pp. 447–455. Springer, Heidelberg (2001)
17. Jain, A.K., Ross, A., Prabhakar, S.: An Introduction to Biometric Recognition. IEEE Trans. on Circuits and Systems for Video Technology: Special Issue on Image and Video-Based Biometrics **14**(1), 4–20 (2004)
18. Chen, H., Bhanu, Bir.: Contour Matching for 3D Ear Recognition. In: Proc. of 7th IEEE Workshop Applications of Computer Vision, pp. 123--128 (2005)
19. Chen, H., Bhanu, B., Wang, R.: Performance Evaluation and Prediction for 3D Ear Recognition. In: Kanade, T., Jain, A., Ratha, N.K. (eds.) AVBPA 2005. LNCS, vol. 3546, pp. 748–757. Springer, Heidelberg (2005)
20. Yan, P., Bowyer, K.W.: Biometric Recognition Using 3D Ear Shape. IEEE Trans. on Pattern Analysis and Machine Intelligence **29**(8), 1297–1308 (2007)
21. Cadavid, S., Abdel-Mottaleb, M.: 3D Ear Modeling and Recognition from Video Sequences using Shape from Shading. IEEE Trans. on Information Forensics and Security 3(4), 709–718 (2008)

22. Zhou, J., Cadavid, S., Abdel-Mottaleb, M.: Histograms of categorized shapes for 3D ear detection. In: Fourth IEEE Int. Conf. on Biometrics: Theory Applications and Systems, pp.1--6 (2010)
23. Yan, P., Bowyer, K.W.: Multi-biometrics 2D and 3D Ear Recognition. In: Kanade, T., Jain, A., Ratha, N.K. (eds.) AVBPA 2005. LNCS, vol. 3546, pp. 503–512. Springer, Heidelberg (2005)
24. Prakash, S., Gupta, P.: An efficient technique for ear detection in 3D: invariant to rotation and scale. In: Fifth IAPR Int. Conf. on Biometrics, pp. 97--102 (2012)
25. Datta, R., Joshi, D., Li, J., Wang, J.Z.: Image Retrieval: Ideas Influences, and Trends of the New Age. ACM Computing Surveys 40(2), article 5, 5:1--5:60 (2008)
26. Tangelder, J.W.H., Veltkamp, R.C.: A Survey of Content Based 3D Shape Retrieval Methods. Journal of Multimedia Tools and Applications 39(3), 441–471 (2008)
27. Smeulders, A.W.M., Worring, M., Santini, S., Gupta, A., Jain, R.: Content-Based Image Retrieval at the End of the Early Years. IEEE Trans. on PAMI 22(12), 1349–1380 (2000)
28. Dimov, D.: Rapid and Reliable Content Based Image Retrieval. In: Lefebvre, E. (ed.) NATO ASI, Multisensor Data and Information Processing for Rapid and Robust Situation and Threat Assessment, pp. 384–395. IOS Press, Bulgaria (2007)
29. Dimov, D., Zlateva, N., Marinov, A.: CBIR over Multiple Projections of 3D Objects. In: Fierrez, J., Ortega-Garcia, J., Esposito, A., Drygajlo, A., Faundez-Zanuy, M. (eds.) BioID MultiComm2009. LNCS, vol. 5707, pp. 146–153. Springer, Heidelberg (2009)
30. Dimov, D.: A Polar-Fourier-Wavelet Transform for Effective CBIR. In: Morzy, T., Morzy. M., Nanopoulos, A. (eds.) ADMKD 2007, pp. 107--118.Bulgariapp (2007)

3D Ear Analysis by an EGI Representation

Virginio Cantoni[1], Dimo T. Dimov[2], and Atanas Nikolov[2(✉)]

[1] Department of Industrial and Information Engineering,
Pavia University, Pavia, Italy
virginio.cantoni@unipv.it
[2] Institute of Information and Communication Technologies,
Bulgarian Academy of Sciences, Sofia, Bulgaria
{dtdim,a.nikolov}@iinf.bas.bg

Abstract. In this paper, a new method to represent human ear for biometrics purposes is introduced. Even if ear has a uniform distribution of color, human external ear characteristics are considered unique to each individual and permanent during the lifetime of an adult. For these reasons ear biometrics approaches are relying on morphological ear properties. Even if ear biometrics is a young topic a variety of approaches have been proposed to characterize the ear geometry and topology. Moreover, note that the ear morphology is the biggest human head concavity, and that its convex hull complement is mainly convex. In this connection, the matching potential for ear discrimination can be effectively exploited through an Extended Gaussian Image (EGI) representation. The original EGI representation and its correspondent concrete data-structure are here applied to ear description and discussed for human authentication and identification purposes.

Keywords: Ear authentication · Ear biometrics · Ear identification · Ear recognition · Ear verification · Extended Gaussian Image

1 Introduction

In the computer society personal identification is emerging as a crucial problem: financial institutions, general computer networks, cellular phones, personal workstations, etc. have an ever-growing need to authenticate individuals. Traditionally the identity is established by means of passports, identity cards, badges, keys, or by userid, electronic passwords and personal identification numbers (PIN). These methods are based on possession or knowledge, but possessions can be lost, or stolen, and knowledge can easily be forgotten, or observed. For these reasons the biometrics science is rapidly evolving under the pressure of a large range of application in the civilian computer society. It can be applied in transactions conducted via telephone (exploiting voice recognition technology) and in e-business (exploiting cryptography and public/private password). Biometric methodologies offer today a much higher accuracy than the more traditional ones, and are now normally applied in a variety of applications ranging from personal laptop access to international border control.

© Springer International Publishing Switzerland 2014
V. Cantoni et al. (Eds.): BIOMET 2014, LNCS 8897, pp. 136–150, 2014.
DOI: 10.1007/978-3-319-13386-7_11

In this last decade, more than twenty databases of ears have been collected. These candidate benchmarks differ consistently by number of images, subjects and features. Some of them consider only right ear, or are characterized by variable lighting conditions, rotations, postures, occlusions, yaw and pitch poses, headdresses and earrings, side face, multi-scale, multi-race, ground truth ear's position, or exploitation of depth images (3D), successive sessions, indoor versus outdoor scene, multi-camera, cropped from video streams, etc. Each DB usually considers only a few of these features. For this reason the performances evaluated with the above variability are often not comparable, and the weighting with DB cardinality is certainly not sufficient. Only a few approaches and new proposals have been evaluated and compared on the same benchmark.

Following a very popular taxonomy most of the proposed solutions up-to now successfully proposed are classified as active modalities in which the tested candidate is conscious of the identification or authentication action. These require personal cooperation and will not work if one denies participation. The alternative modality does not require user's active participation, it is relating instead to a passive analysis which usually exploits approaches such as ear recognition or behavioral ones as gait analysis. These modalities can be successful also without that people even know that they are analyzed.

The human outer ear (or pinna) is usually segmented in six basic components: i) the outer helix; ii) the antihelix; iii) the lobe; iv) the tragus; v) the antitragus and finally vi) the concha. This shape in fact evolves during the embryonic state from six growth nodules; its structure therefore is not completely random. Moreover, the detailed structure of the human ear is considered universal and unique (however, it is still to be demonstrated that ears of all people are unique). Furthermore it is considered averagely permanent (the ear appearance does not change consistently when a person ages [1] and is normally collectable. Nevertheless, ear biometrics is not commonly used.

Face recognition has advantages; it can routinely be used in a covert manner, since a person's face is easily captured by video technology and individuals are identified by analyzing certain facial features, such as the medial and lateral corners of the eye or sides of the mouth, nose etc. But it has as well drawback: the face is the most changing part of the body due to facial expressions, during speech and when expressing emotions, and its appearance is often altered by make-up, spectacles, and beards and moustaches and hair styling, moreover there is the effect of age that brings changes in the facial morphology. The ear does not move and only has to support earrings, glasses frames, hearing aids, and it is often occluded by hair. As such, the ear is much less susceptible to interference than many other biometrics, with particular invariance to age.

From the visual complexity viewpoint, face and ear are roughly the same; it is accepted by the researchers that with the decreasing cost of the required 3D scanner and the increasing performance of the ear recognition techniques, ear biometric will be very useful in most practical applications in the near future.

2   Ear Biometrics Approaches

Even if ear biometrics is a young topic a variety of approaches have been proposed, from simple appearance-based methods such as principal component analysis to a whole new perspective based on scale-invariant feature transforms, local binary patterns, force fields, etc. Another proposed taxonomy is related to the general strategies pursued: based on shapes versus contours analysis; on the domain, spatial or transformed by Gabor, Fourier, Hough, Ray, Haar, or by wavelet transformations; considering the pursued ear alignment technique e.g. rigid motion evaluated with the concha area [2, 3] versus the external triangle [4, 5, 6].

Following another taxonomy proposed by Pflug and Busch [7] the proposed solutions are classified on the bases of the input ear image dimensionality (2D or 3D) and then on a quad hierarchy: holistic, local, statistical or hybrid approaches.

The holistic approach is characterized by description of the components as they are mutually interconnected and integrated to compose the ear. A method developed by Burge and Burger [8] is based on the ear representation through a graph model built by the Voronoi diagram on the edge and curve segments extracted from the intensity image, and applies graph matching as discriminant technique. A different model to describe the ear, [9] is built by treating every pixel as an attractor following the Newton's law of gravitation (pixels have a mutual attraction proportional to their intensities and inversely to the square of the distance between them), and the ear is represented by a force field. The discrimination is founded on force field comparison. In [10] the ear image is subdivided into a number of equally large tiles and the self-similarity is evaluated by affine transform of image sub regions. If one tile is occluded, the other tiles may contain a sufficiently distinctive set of features and this make the approach robust to occlusion. In [11] the authors compose six different feature vectors by using seven moment invariants. The moment invariants are robust against changes in scale and rotation. The feature vectors are applied to a back propagation neural network which is trained to classify the feature sets.

Among the holistic methods a large number of proposals exploit classical computer vision transforms. In [12] the generalized Hough transform is used to detect the edges distribution. The cumulative approach make the ear detection Hough transform-based robust to extraction edge misplacement and to pose variation. Extra edges can be due to earing and glasses or hair (mainly strait lines). In [13] a method exploiting the ray transform, which is robust to detect ear in different poses and extra straight edges, is developed. The ray transform is based on the light ray analogy; the simulated ray is reflected by the curved structures like the outer helix in bright regions, hence highlighting these regions in the transformed image. In [14] a Fourier descriptor into frequency space for rotation and scale invariant feature representation is adopted. The ear images have to be aligned and (as in other approaches) the concha region is used to fix a reference point for the alignment step. In [15] a multi-resolution Trace transform and the Fourier transform are exploited to build a feature vector invariant to rotations and scale. In [16] the feature vector consists of some selected wavelet coefficients from Haar-wavelet compression. Applying iteratively a four-level wavelet transform on the ear image, at each iteration new derived coefficients are produced and stored. In [17] the distinctiveness of different feature extraction methods is compared. In particular, the performance of Fourier descriptors, Gabor transform, moment invariants and statistical features are compared, and the conclusion is that the highest recognition rate is achieved by using moment invariants and Gabor transform.

It is worth to point out the original proposal [18] which develops an ear biometric system based on the acoustic properties of the ear. The method is founded on the estimation of the acoustic transfer function of the ear by stimulating the ear though a sound wave and evaluating the reflected signal.

Basic primitives of the local approach are landmark assessment and local binary pattern. Scale invariant feature transform (SIFT) is known to be a robust way for landmark extraction and can also be used for estimating the rotation and translation between two normalized ear images. A proposal exploiting this approach is [12] in which a reference landmark model, containing a small number of non-redundant landmarks, constitutes the training set. This landmark model is used for filtering the SIFT landmarks, which were initially detected in the reference ear; it is then possible to assign the landmarks with its counterpart. This assignment becomes critical with pose variations and in highly structured regions.

In [19] is proposed 2D ear detection based on edge segmentation through concavity and convexity and then represented in a connectivity graph. A convex hull is applied to the edge in order to detect the ear region. This approach has been extended (with some updating) to the 3D ear analysis.

The keywords of the Statistical approach are principal component analysis (PCA), independent component analysis (ICA), and locally linear embedding (LLE). PCA is by far the most widely adopted method used in ear biometrics; the goal is to reduce the feature vectors dimension. In [20] the performances of PCA when applied on face and ear recognition are compared. In their experiments, the performance of face based recognition overcomes the one of ear based recognition. However, in [21] it is reached (in similar experiments) a different conclusion: no appreciable difference was found between face and ear in terms of recognition performance.

In [22] the performance in ear identification by neural network classifiers is investigated. The ear image is represented by outer ear points, information collected from ear shape and folds, and macro features assessed by compression network. The conclusion was that compression network support the best performance.

In [4] the outer contour of the ear is located by searching for the top, bottom and left points of the detected ear boundary; these points form a triangle and its barycenter is selected as reference point for image alignment and consequently for the matching process.

An example of the hybrid approach is given in [23, 24] that use the active shape model for extracting the outline of the ear. In [23] manually cropped ear images are used. A feature extractor stores selected points on the outline of the ear together with their distance to the tragus which is selected as reference. Before applying a linear classifier, the dimensionality of the feature vectors is reduced by PCA.

3   Extended Gaussian Image

A 3D mesh model, approximating a 3D object, is represented by a set of triangles (see Fig. 1a):

$$T = \{T_1, \ldots, T_N\}, \; T_i \subset R^3, \tag{1}$$

where N is the number of triangles of the object mesh.

Each triangle T_i consists of a set of three vertices:

$$T_i = \{P_{A_i}, P_{B_i}, P_{C_i}\} \tag{2}$$

Being w_i and $\bar{n}_i$ respectively the center and the normal of a triangle T_i (see Fig. 1b), the surface area A_i of triangle T_i, and the area A of the mesh are given by:

$$w_i = (P_{A_i} + P_{B_i} + P_{C_i})/3 \tag{3}$$

$$\bar{n}_i = (P_{C_i} - P_{A_i}) \times (P_{B_i} - P_{C_i}) \tag{4}$$

$$A_i = \tfrac{1}{2}\left|(P_{C_i} - P_{A_i}) \times (P_{B_i} - P_{C_i})\right| \tag{5}$$

$$A = \sum_{i=1}^{N} A_i \tag{6}$$

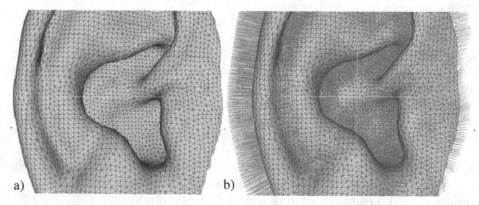

a)   b)

Fig. 1. a) A 3D triangular mesh model; b) normal vectors to mesh triangles; Both images are scaled and respectively cropped for better visualization of the triangular mesh

The Extended Gaussian images (EGI) of a 3D object or shape is the histogram of orientations that represents the distribution of surface area with respect to surface orientation (see Fig. 2) [25].

Each surface patch is mapped to a point on the unit Gaussian sphere according to its surface normal. The weight for each surface normal (represented by a point on the Gaussian sphere) is the total sum of area of all the surface patches having that surface normal.

The EGI can be easily built from needle or depth maps generated by range or stereo devices. In fact, for an effective digital representation the Gaussian sphere is discretized by a triangular tessellation (sometimes called geodesic dome). Starting with a regular polyhedron (e.g. the icosahedron herewith adopted), recursively in a more detailed description level each triangle is split into four smaller triangles (see Fig. 3). Being k the number of iterative subdivision steps, the number of triangles is $m = 2^{2k}K_0$, where K_0 is the number of faces of the starting polyhedron (20 for the icosahedron) and the area (solid angle) of the single cell is $A_\Delta = \pi/(2^{2(k-1)}K_0)$ respectively [26].

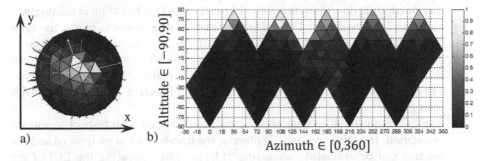

Fig. 2. a) & b) 3D/2D EGI histograms: in each EGI bin (oriented triangle from discretized polyhedron) the triangle areas with the same orientation were accumulated.

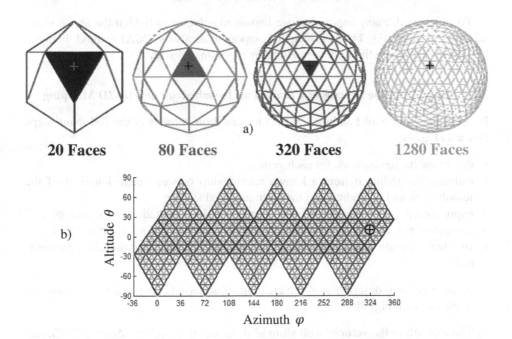

Fig. 3. a) From left to right: hierarchical refinement of successive searching for maximum dot product between the normal vector of an input patch and the icosahedron ones or of the three polyhedrons with 80, 320, and 1280 faces; b) 2D representation of the face positions of the four polyhedrons (expressed by azimuth and altitude of triangle vertices). The representation of a given input orientation ⊕ is also shown.

Main properties of the EGI for convex polyhedrons and for general convex objects are:

- Rotation of the polyhedron corresponds to an equal rotation of the EGI, and vice versa, since the surface normal vectors rotate with the object.
- Being the total mass of the EGI obviously just equal to the total surface area of the polyhedron, and being the same the projected area when viewed from any pair of opposite directions, the center of mass of an EGI has to lie at the origin.
- Herman Minkowski in 1897 demonstrated that a convex object is fully described by the area and orientation of its faces, that is, two different convex polyhedrons have different EGIs. Vice versa two different EGIs represent two different polyhedrons. Moreover, this property is maintained for a general convex object: in case of convex objects, there is an injective correspondence with their EGI.
- The EGI is invariant to translation being a distribution with respect to surface orientation. In registering two 3D objects, the translation can be ignored and the rotation can be evaluated minimizing $e(R)$ i.e. just comparing the EGI of the model $M_{\hat{n}}$ and the EGI $S_{\hat{n},R}$ of the shape rotated by R:

$$e(R) = \sum_{\hat{n} \in m} \left(M_{\hat{n}} - S_{\hat{n},R} \right)^2 \qquad (7)$$

To this regard, many approaches are known to solve or to lighten the above minimization problem, e.g. by the Principal Component Analysis (PCA) method, both the 3D objects can be preliminary normalized by position and size.

3.1   Describing the Process of Creation an Icosahedron and Its 2D Mapping

In brief, the process of building a 3D/2D icosahedron consists of the following steps (see also Fig. 4):

- determine the azimuth φ_i for each vertex;
- estimate the radius ρ from a known relationship between edge length a of the icosahedron and the radius r of the circumscribed sphere;
- express each (x, y) coordinate of the vertices of the icosahedron by ρ and φ_i ;
- compute the z coordinate of the vertices by the radiuses ρ and r, $(r = 1)$;
- find both altitude levels $+\theta_1$ and $-\theta_1$, which are necessary for the 2D representation.

A more detailed description of the creation of an icosahedron and its 2D mapping is given here (see Fig. 4):

1. The azimuth to the vertices with altitude θ_1 is equal to: $\varphi_i^+ = i \, \Delta\varphi = i \, 2\pi/5$, and respectively for the vertices with altitude $-\theta_1$, the azimuth is: $\varphi_i^- = i \, \Delta\varphi - \Delta\varphi/2 = \pi/5(2i - 1)$, where $i = 0 \div 4$. The azimuth of the top and bottom vertex is zero.

2. It is known that if the edge length of an icosahedron is a, the radius r of the circumscribed sphere around the icosahedron is: $r = a \sin\left(\frac{2\pi}{5}\right)$.

In our case $(r = 1) \Rightarrow a = \frac{1}{\sin\left(\frac{2\pi}{5}\right)} \approx 1.0515$ and the radius ρ:

$$\rho = a \left(2 \sin\left(\frac{\Delta\varphi}{2}\right)\right)^{-1} = \left(2 \sin\left(\frac{\pi}{5}\right) \sin\left(\frac{2\pi}{5}\right)\right)^{-1} \approx 0.8944.$$

3. The (x, y) coordinates of vertices on θ_1 altitude level are: $x_i^+ = \rho \cos(\varphi_i^+)$, $y_i^+ = \rho \sin(\varphi_i^+)$. Respectively for vertices on $-\theta_1$ altitude level: $x_i^- = \rho \cos(\varphi_i^-)$, $y_i^- = \rho \sin(\varphi_i^-)$, $i = 0 \div 4$. The (x, y) coordinates of the top (N) and bottom (S) vertex are $(0, 0)$.

4. The distance $\overline{OO_+} = \sqrt{r^2 - \rho^2} = \sqrt{1 - \rho^2} \approx 0.4472$, which actually is $\rho/2$. So the z coordinates of vertices lying on θ_1 and $-\theta_1$ levels are $\pm\rho/2$. The top and bottom vertex has $z = \pm 1$.

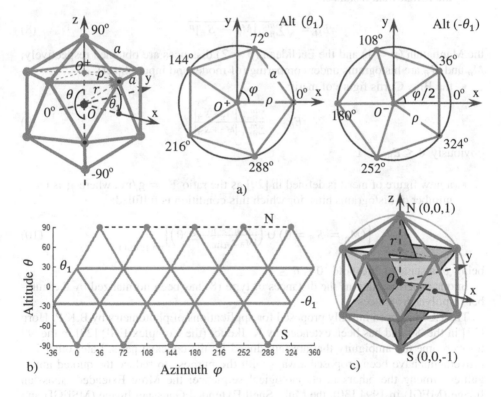

Fig. 4. a) Parameters description of an icosahedron: radius $(r = 1)$ of the circumscribed unit sphere; icosahedron edge length a; azimuth $\varphi \in [0, 360]$; altitude $\theta \in [-90, 90]$; radius ρ of the O_{xy}^+ and O_{xy}^- 2D sections; altitude levels θ_1 and $-\theta_1$ of the vertices belonging to the both 2D sections of the icosahedron; b) the same icosahedron mapped into 2D plane, represented by azimuth φ and altitude θ of its triangular faces; c) the icosahedron, inscribed in a unit sphere, and formed by three mutually orthogonal 'golden rectangles', whose sides ratio is equal to the golden ratio $(1 + \sqrt{5})/2 \approx 1.6180$

5. The altitude levels $\pm\theta_1$, can be estimated as: $\pm\theta_1 = \arccos\left(\frac{\sqrt{x^2+y^2}}{r}\right) \approx 26.57^\circ$, for any (x, y) point on these levels, where $r = 1$.

The above data is enough for building a 3D icosahedrons and its 2D mapping. It is worth mentioning that higher discretization levels from an icosahedron can be achieved by computing the vertices coordinates, dispatching each triangle into four new ones.

3.2   Evaluation of Similarity Between EGI Histograms

Among the matching indexes adopted to determine a geometrical score of similarity with EGI applications, we have considered the following [27]:

- the Minkowski distance:

$$E_M = \sqrt[p]{\sum_{\hat{n}=1}^{m}|M_{\hat{n}} - S_{\hat{n}}|^p} \tag{8}$$

the Manhattan ($p = 1$) and the Euclidean ($p = 2$) distances are obtained respectively; $M_{\hat{n}}$ and $S_{\hat{n}}$ are histograms under comparing (of model and input object).

- the Bray Curtis figure of merit:

$$E_{BC} = \frac{\sum_{\hat{n}=1}^{m}|M_{\hat{n}} - S_{\hat{n}}|}{\sum_{\hat{n}=1}^{m}|M_{\hat{n}} + S_{\hat{n}}|} \tag{9}$$

obviously $0 \leq E_{BC} \leq 1$;

- a new figure of merit is defined in [29] as the ratio $E_Z = g/m$, where g is the number of histograms bins, for which this condition is fulfilled:

$$\left\{(M_{\hat{n}} = S_{\hat{n}} = 0) \cup \left(\frac{|M_{\hat{n}} - S_{\hat{n}}|}{[M_{\hat{n}}, S_{\hat{n}}]_{max}} \leq \theta\right)\right\}_{\forall\hat{n}, 1 \leq \hat{n} \leq m} \tag{10}$$

being θ a suitable threshold, $0 \leq \theta \leq 1$.

In our experimentations the distances of type (8) has been normalized by the number of polyhedron faces.

The EGI has been initially proposed for applications of photometry by B.K.P. Horn [25] in the '80 and has been extended by K. Ikeuci (the Complex-EGI) [29] in the '90 to overcome the ambiguity that are introduced by the concave parts. Later other improvements have been proposed always with the purpose to reduce the quoted ambiguities, among the others in chronological sequence: the More Extended Gaussian Image (MEGI) in 1994 [30], the Multi-Shell Extended Gaussian Image (MSEGI) and the Adaptive Volumetric Extended Gaussian Image (AVEGI) in 2007 [31], and the Enriched Complex Extended Gaussian Image (EC-EGI) in 2010 [32].

In this preliminary work our experiments are limited to the EGI, because it constitutes a compact and effective representation of a 3D object. Besides, the feeling is that being an ear basically a cavity (certainly with convexities) the EGI can be both effective and efficient [33]. After suitable experiments, other more precise solutions, but not only limiting to derivations of the EGI, can be adopted too.

4   Experimental Analysis

The Institute of Information and Communication Technologies (IICT) of the Bulgarian Academy of Sciences (BAS) has collected an ear dataset with the goal of providing more high definition data than comparable collections. The dataset now represents 11 subjects of various ages and consist of 66 3D ear models in total. For each subject, the dataset contains 6 3D ears (where 5 are intentionally noised). All 3D ear models are taken under optimal lighting conditions through a VIUscan 3D scanner. This type of scanners is composed of a laser cross beam and of two HD cameras surrounded by a set of LEDs, thus allowing the laser triangulation and 3D data acquisition. The scanner can reach a geometry resolution of 0.1mm, an accuracy of 50μm, and 24 bits of texture colors. In Fig. 5, some examples of 2D frontal projections from the 3D dataset are shown.

The preprocessing of the ears consists of cropping the ear from the background and holes filling by the VIUscan 3D scanner's software (VXelements). Then in a postprocessing phase by an open source system for the processing and editing of 3D triangular meshes - MeshLab, the final result of Fig. 5 is obtained. Note that this phase is applied just for the model construction that is an off-line procedure.

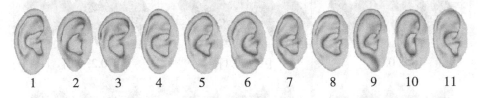

Fig. 5. The current test dataset of 11 original 3D ear models

One of the aims of our experiments is to determine the most appropriate distances for similarity evaluation between EGI histograms (see section 3), as well as their robustness to noise for object recognition. This noise is introduced to represents different accuracy of 3D scanning systems. For this purpose, a uniform noise in a given range was generated, and added to each 3D vertex coordinate of the scanned objects (Fig. 6a). It could be easily seen that: the higher noise, the more uniform the orientation histogram (see Fig. 6b, c), and the more challenging the recognition process.

For each ear in the dataset the corresponding EGI represented by 3D/2D histograms are built. There, in each EGI bin (see Fig. 2) all the areas of object's triangle having the same orientation are accumulated. In order to do this, the histogram bin is selected by the maximum dot product between the input patch orientation and the coarse-to-fine set of triangles' normals of the polyhedron (see Fig. 3). Thus, the total area of the EGI histogram is equal to the object's area.

Before forming the 3D/2D EGI histograms, the PCA method was used to equalize position and scale of the 3D objects in a global coordinate system. Thus, all ears models become invariant to scaling and only their morphology is taking into account. Obviously the eigenvectors and eigenvalues can be applied (and are more and more applied) for recognition purposes, but in our experimentation we use them just for alignment and scaling using as discriminant characteristics only the EGI.

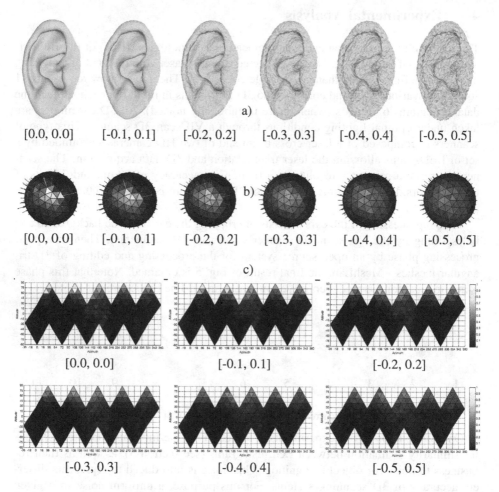

Fig. 6. a) An ear model corrupted with uniform noise in a given range, added to each of its (x, y, z) coordinates, thus simulating the varying accuracy of a 3D scanning device; b) & c) the corresponding 3D/2D EGI histograms of the noisy ears

So far, our primary recognition strategy is based on the classical approach of the nearest neighbor, i.e. the shortest distance is pursued between an EGI histogram of given noisy input ear, compared to all ear model histograms, using (8), (9) and (10). As an example, in Table 1, on rows, the distances between input noisy ears with uniformly distributed noise in range [-0.1, 0.1] and all original ears (models) are given, using matching index E_{BC}. To have true recognition of given noisy ear, the minimal distance in every row must lie on the main diagonal (green cells). If this is not the case, a false detection is attained – as in the case in Table 2 (the red cells). Furthermore, in addition to have true recognition, it is important to evaluate its reliability. Therefore, an evaluation of the recognition reliability is given in the last column of each table. It represents the ratio between the true matches and the first false one. The smaller its value, the better the reliability. If the reliability value $\eta \geq 1$, it is a false recognition detection.

A set of analogous 20 tables for each of the 4 mentioned distances ($E_{M(p=1|2)}$, E_{BC} and E_Z) and for 5 ranges of the noise have been computed in order to view the impact of noise on these distances reliability. All the results of true and false detections are summarized in Table 3, where the True Recognition Rate (TRR) and average reliability $\bar{\eta}$ for each of 20 tables (cases) is presented.

Table 1. The matching index E_{BC} is used between input noisy [± 0.1] ears and model ears. The last column represents the ratio η between the true matches and the first false one (in gray)

Model / Noisy	1	2	3	4	5	6	7	8	9	10	11	η
1	0.099	0.321	0.276	0.211	0.224	0.259	0.255	0.235	0.255	0.264	0.218	0.468
2	0.318	0.099	0.327	0.307	0.308	0.251	0.294	0.280	0.306	0.285	0.330	0.394
3	0.285	0.321	0.089	0.297	0.273	0.305	0.286	0.298	0.309	0.307	0.290	0.325
4	0.222	0.305	0.288	0.079	0.242	0.262	0.234	0.218	0.232	0.275	0.213	0.370
5	0.230	0.316	0.275	0.234	0.087	0.223	0.262	0.237	0.255	0.240	0.243	0.390
6	0.250	0.246	0.299	0.257	0.231	0.093	0.252	0.251	0.265	0.251	0.243	0.404
7	0.263	0.290	0.298	0.234	0.254	0.266	0.089	0.257	0.222	0.274	0.255	0.401
8	0.230	0.285	0.295	0.210	0.227	0.253	0.253	0.096	0.243	0.261	0.249	0.458
9	0.235	0.293	0.292	0.206	0.235	0.246	0.214	0.234	0.104	0.236	0.218	0.507
10	0.267	0.280	0.308	0.264	0.224	0.239	0.268	0.269	0.249	0.101	0.246	0.452
11	0.237	0.321	0.284	0.212	0.238	0.243	0.241	0.250	0.242	0.244	0.090	0.426
											AVG	**0.418**

Table 2. The matching index E_{BC} is used between input noisy [± 0.4] ears and model ears. The last column represents the ratio η between the true matches and the first false one (gray | red)

Model / Noisy	1	2	3	4	5	6	7	8	9	10	11	η
1	0.215	0.298	0.235	0.226	0.228	0.249	0.228	0.237	0.258	0.283	0.232	0.954
2	0.282	0.208	0.296	0.279	0.283	0.233	0.265	0.261	0.291	0.283	0.293	0.892
3	0.263	0.308	0.213	0.272	0.268	0.286	0.260	0.276	0.289	0.307	0.293	0.821
4	0.249	0.310	0.262	0.203	0.237	0.259	0.224	0.247	0.245	0.284	0.237	0.905
5	0.230	0.311	0.247	0.230	0.208	0.236	0.220	0.240	0.258	0.279	0.247	0.946
6	0.256	0.265	0.264	0.252	0.245	0.206	0.232	0.252	0.271	0.286	0.262	0.887
7	0.283	0.315	0.281	0.267	0.265	0.271	0.204	0.276	0.263	0.311	0.268	0.775
8	0.230	0.302	0.259	0.218	0.227	0.232	0.223	0.216	0.245	0.281	0.241	0.988
9	0.235	0.309	0.265	0.222	0.240	0.249	0.211	0.255	0.223	0.271	0.228	1.055
10	0.233	0.285	0.269	0.212	0.225	0.236	0.244	0.238	0.246	0.211	0.233	0.994
11	0.248	0.315	0.265	0.229	0.246	0.259	0.221	0.256	0.259	0.282	0.219	0.992
											AVG	**0.928**

Table 3. True Recognition Rate (TRR) and corresponding average reliabilities $\tilde{\eta}$ (the smaller, the better), based on different combinations of the investigated distances and ranges of noise

Distance \ Noise	± 0.1		± 0.2		± 0.3		± 0.4		± 0.5	
$E_M(p = 1)$	100%	0.415	100%	0.655	100%	0.828	72.7%	0.939	36.4%	1.002
$E_M(p = 2)$	100%	0.427	100%	0.705	63.6%	0.917	45.5%	1.031	36.4%	1.101
E_{BC}	100%	0.418	100%	0.657	100%	0.830	90.9%	0.928	54.5%	0.987
E_Z	100%	0.776	100%	0.847	90.9%	0.927	72.7%	0.966	36.4%	1.019

According to these experiments, it seems that the figure of merit E_{BC} is the most robust to this kind of uniform noise with the highest TRR and the best average reliability $\tilde{\eta}$ of recognition. A little bit worse for high noise data are the results for the $E_M(p = 1)$ metric.

The E_Z index shows good performance, but it ranks on third place by goodness of TRR. This result is subject to the experimentally chosen threshold which is here set to 0.5.

The last $E_M(p = 2)$ distance gives the lowest TRR.

The experiments show that the results are very promising, i.e. even the simplest EGI representation of ear models could distinguish them very well each other, no matter that their surface is not entirely convex. Also it would be interesting to use 2D mapping of EGI representation not only for overall better observing the resulting histograms, but also for applying the well-known or new adopted 2D recognition approaches on it.

5   Conclusion

In this paper a new approach suitable for ear authentication and identification has been proposed. The first results look promising for considering these new strategies among the candidates for a practical exploitation. Certainly it is necessary to extend the investigation to more general conditions for the acquisition and experiment also in the large variety of cases and people. Moreover, the computer demanding preprocessing phase is easily supported because it is offline, certainly it must be investigated the amount of preprocessing necessary for the online authentication and identification to be applied to the ear under test. Nevertheless, these preliminary results show robustness to image degradation that looks very encouraging.

The near future activity is related to a few tuning aspects of the current implementation. In particular we will consider: i) relationship between input 3D ear image quality and EGI resolution; ii) speed-up analysis considering simpler data representations, e.g. 2D EGI descriptions as in Fig. 2 b); iii) analysis if there are cases for which more complex EGI representations are required (e.g. Complex EGI, Enriched C-EGI, etc.).

Acknowledgements. This research is partly supported by the project AComIn "Advanced Computing for Innovation", grant 316087, funded by the FP7 Capacity Programme (Research Potential of Convergence Regions).

References

1. Sforza, C., Grandi, G., Binelli, M., Tommasi, D.G., Rosati, R., Ferrario, V.F.: Age- and sex-related changes in the normal human ear. Forensic Sci. Int. **187** (1–3), 110e1–110e7 (2009)
2. Yan, P., Bowyer, K.W.: Biometric recognition using 3D ear shape. Pattern Anal. Mach. Intell. **29**, 1297–1308 (2007)
3. Choras, M.: Perspective methods of human identification: ear biometrics. Opto-Electron. Rev. **16**, 85–96 (2008)
4. Attarchi, S., Faez, K., Rafiei, A.: A New Segmentation Approach for Ear Recognition. In: Blanc-Talon, J., Bourennane, S., Philips, W., Popescu, D., Scheunders, P. (eds.) ACIVS 2008. LNCS, vol. 5259, pp. 1030–1037. Springer, Heidelberg (2008)
5. Mu, Z., Yuan, L., Xu, Z., Xi, D., Qi, S.: Shape and Structural Feature Based Ear Recognition. In: Li, S.Z., Lai, J.-H., Tan, T., Feng, G.-C., Wang, Y. (eds.) SINOBIOMETRICS 2004. LNCS, vol. 3338, pp. 663–670. Springer, Heidelberg (2004)
6. Rahman, M., Islam, R., Bhuiyan, N.I., Ahmed, B., Islam, A.: Person identification using ear biometrics. Int. J. Comput. Internet Manage. **15**, 1–8 (2007)
7. Pflug, A., Busch, C.: Ear biometrics: a survey of detection, feature extraction and recognition methods. IET Biometrics. **1**(2), 114–129 (2012)
8. Burge, M., Burger, W.: Ear biometrics in computer vision. Proc. Int. Conf. on Pattern Recognition **2**, 822–826 (2000)
9. Hurley, D.J., Nixon, M.S., Carter, J.N.: Force field energy functionals for image feature extraction. Image Vision Comp. J. **20**, 311–317 (2002)
10. De Marsico, M., Michele, N., Riccio, D.: HERO: human ear recognition against occlusions. IEEE Computer Society Conf. on Computer Vision and Pattern Recognition Workshops, p. 178 (2010)
11. Wang, X.q., Xia, H.y., Wang, Z.l.: The research of ear identification based on improved algorithm of moment invariants. Third Int. Conf. on Inf. and Computing, p. 58 (2010)
12. Arbab-Zavar, B., Nixon, M.S.: On Shape-Mediated Enrolment in Ear Biometrics. In: Bebis, G., Boyle, R., Parvin, B., Koracin, D., Paragios, N., Tanveer, S.-M., Ju, T., Liu, Z., Coquillart, S., Cruz-Neira, C., Müller, T., Malzbender, T. (eds.) ISVC 2007, Part II. LNCS, vol. 4842, pp. 549–558. Springer, Heidelberg (2007)
13. Alistair, H., Cummings, A.H., Nixon, M.S., Carter, J.N.: A novel ray analogy for enrolment of ear biometrics. Theory Applications and Systems, Fourth IEEE Int. Conf. on Biometrics (2010)
14. Abate, A.F., Nappi, M., Riccio, D., Ricciardi, S.: Ear recognition by means of a rotation invariant descriptor. 18th Int. Conf. on Pattern Recognition **4**, 437–440 (2006)
15. Fooprateepsiri, R., Kurutach, W.: Ear based personal identification approach forensic science tasks. Chiang Mai J. Sci. **38**(2), 166–175 (2011)
16. Sana, P.P.R., Gupta, A.: Ear biometrics: a new approach. Advances in Pattern Recognition, pp. 1–5 (2007)
17. Wang, X., Yuan, W.: Human ear recognition based on block segmentation. Int. Conf. on Cyber-Enabled Distributed Computing and Knowledge Discovery, pp. 262–266 (2009)
18. Akkermans, A.H.M., Kevenaar, T.A.M., Schobben, D.W.E.: Acoustic Ear Recognition for Person Identification. Fourth IEEE Workshop on Automatic Identification Advanced Technologies, pp. 219–223 (2005)
19. Gupta, P., Prakash, S.: An efficient technique for ear detection in 3D: invariant to rotation and scale. Fifth IAPR Int. Conf. on Biometrics, p. 97–102 (2012)

20. Victor, B., Bowyer, K.W., Sarkar, S.: An evaluation of face and ear biometrics. Proceedings of International Conference on Pattern Recognition, pp. 429–432 (2002)
21. Chang, K., Bowyer, K.W., Sarkar, S., Victor, B.: Comparison and combination of ear and face images in appearance-based biometrics. IEEE Transaction on Pattern Analysis of Machine Intelligence. **25**, 1160–1165 (2003)
22. Moreno, B., Sanchez, A., Velez, J.F.: On the use of outer ear images for personal identification in security applications. In: Proceedings of IEEE Conference on Security Technology, pp. 469–476 (1999)
23. Lu, L., Xiaoxun, Z., Youdong, Z., Yunde, J.: Ear recognition based on statistical shape model. First Int. Conf. on Innovative Computing, Inf. and Control, pp. 353–356 (2006)
24. Yuan, L., Mu, Z.: Ear recognition based on 2D images. First IEEE Int. Conf. on Biometrics: Theory, Applications, and Systems, pp. 1–5 (2007)
25. Horn, B.K.P.: Extended Gaussian images. Proc. of the IEEE. **72**, 1671–1686 (1984)
26. Cantoni, V., Gaggia, A., Lombardi, L.: Essay: Extended Gaussian Image for pocket-ligand matching. Definitions: EGI; CEGI e ECEGI. In: W. Dubitzky, O. Wolkenhauer, K. Cho & H. Yokota (eds.) Encyclopedia of Systems Biology. LLC. Springer (2012)
27. Gaggia, A.: System for protein-ligand interaction analysis, PhD Thesis, Pavia University (2013)
28. Zhang, J.: Content-based 3D Model Retrieval Based on Volumetric Extended Gaussian Image Shape Representation. PhD Thesis of the City University of Hong Kong (2007)
29. Kang, S.B., Ikeuchi, K.: Determining 3-D object pose using the complex extended Gaussian image. In: IEEE Computer Society Conference on Computer Vision and Pattern Recognition, pp. 580–585 (1991)
30. Matsuo, H., Iwata, A.: 3-D Object Recognition Using MEGI Model from Range Data. In: Proc. 12th Int. Conf. Pattern Recognition, pp. 843–846 (1994)
31. Wang, D., Zhang, J., Wong, H.-s., Li, Y.: 3D Model Retrieval Based on Multi-Shell Extended Gaussian Image. In: Qiu, G., Leung, C., Xue, X.-Y., Laurini, R. (eds.) VISUAL 2007. LNCS, vol. 4781, pp. 426–437. Springer, Heidelberg (2007)
32. Hu, Z., Chung, R., Fung, K.S.M.: EC-EGI: enriched complex EGI for 3D shape registration. Machine Vision and Applications. **21**, 177–188 (2010)
33. Cantoni, V., Gaggia, A., Lombardi, L.: A data structure for protein-ligand morphological matching. In: New Tools and Methods for Pattern Recognition in Complex Biological Systems, Nuovo Cimento C, vol. 35, no. 5, suppl. 1, pp. 89–97 (2012)
34. Iannarelli, A.: Ear Identification. Paramont Publishing Company, Forensic Identification Series (1989)

Face and Facial Attributes Analysis

Biometrics in Forensic Science: Challenges, Lessons and New Technologies

Massimo Tistarelli[1]([✉]), Enrico Grosso[1], and Didier Meuwly[2]

[1] Computer Vision Laboratory Porto Conte Ricerche, University of Sassari,
Tramariglio, Alghero, Italy
{tista,grosso}@uniss.it
http://visionlab.uniss.it
[2] Netherland Forensic Institute, The Hague, The Netherlands
d.meuwly@nfi.minvenj.nl
http://www.forensischinstituut.nl

Abstract. Biometrics has historically found its natural mate in Forensics. The first applications found in the literature and over cited so many times, are related to biometric measurements for the identification of multiple offenders from some of their biometric and anthropometric characteristics (tenprint cards) and individualization of offender from traces found on crime-scenes (e.g. fingermarks, earmarks, bitemarks, DNA). From sir Francis Galton, to the introduction of AFIS systems in the scientific laboratories of police departments, Biometrics and Forensics have been "dating" with alternate results and outcomes. As a matter of facts there are many technologies developed under the "Biometrics umbrella" which may be optimised to better impact several Forensic scenarios and criminal investigations. At the same time, there is an almost endless list of open problems and processes in Forensics which may benefit from the introduction of tailored Biometric technologies. Joining the two disciplines, on a proper scientific ground, may only result in the success for both fields, as well as a tangible benefit for the society. A number of Forensic processes may involve Biometric-related technologies, among them: Evidence evaluation, Forensic investigation, Forensic Intelligence, Surveillance, Forensic ID management and Verification.

The COST Action IC1106 funded by the European Commission, is trying to better understand how Biometric and Forensics synergies can be exploited within a pan-European scientific alliance which extends its scope to partners from USA, China and Australia.

Several results have been already accomplished pursuing research in this direction. Notably the studies in 2D and 3D face recognition have been gradually applied to the forensic investigation process. In this paper a few solutions will be presented to match 3D face shapes along with some experimental results.

1 Introduction

Forensic science is defined as the body of scientific knowledge and technical methods used to solve questions related to criminal, civil and administrative law.

© Springer International Publishing Switzerland 2014
V. Cantoni et al. (Eds.): BIOMET 2014, LNCS 8897, pp. 153–164, 2014.
DOI: 10.1007/978-3-319-13386-7_12

Biometric technologies are the set of automated methods used for the recognition of individuals using their physiological and behavioral traits. Forensic biometrics can be defined as the scientific discipline that makes use of the biometric technologies for the demonstration of the existence and the investigation of infringements, the individualization of perpetrators and the description of modus operandi. These tasks are embedded in several forensic processes: forensic investigation, forensic evaluation, forensic intelligence, automated surveillance and forensic identity management.

Methods like, the forensic anthropometry (Bertillon), the forensic dactyloscopy (Galton) and "le portrait parlé" (Reiss), exploiting physiological and behavioral traits, since the end of the 19th century have been used for the identification of criminals as well as for the transmission of the information relevant for remote identification. From the 1960s the development and implementation of automatic fingerprint identification systems (AFIS) represent the first forensic deployment of biometrics, with the automation of the identity verification process [1]. This is also used for the automation of the first step of the individualization process (selection/rejection of candidates). In the 1980s the discovery of forensic DNA profiling led to identity verification process from DNA reference material and the individualization process from biological traces.

In the 1990s the development of computer science and signal processing allowed a performance breakthrough of biometric technologies, offering practical solutions for access control based on several modalities. Speaker, face and gait recognition became of interest for forensic biometrics, as a consequence of the development of mobile telecommunication and surveillance technologies (CCTV). During the same decade the first solutions integrating biometric technologies and the Bayesian inference framework were proposed for forensic individualization, with the aim of ensuring a logical and transparent approach for the evaluation of the biometric forensic evidence.

In the last decade interest has arisen in so-called soft biometric modalities, based on biometric features such as height, weight, gender, hair, skin and clothing color. This interest is mainly due to their availability of data, allowing capture without constraint that is a prerequisite in surveillance environments. However, their limited typicality enhanced the necessity to consider the fusion of several modalities. Some aspects of this technological progress are potentially interesting for forensic biometrics, for example the estimation of the body height and body weight from individuals present on still and live images. Attempts to combine several biometric modalities are not only of interest for forensic biometrics but for forensic science in general, as it is related to the combination of forensic evidence [2,3]. The critical gap is the analysis of all the forensic processes that can integrate biometric technologies, to understand their specificities and translate them in clear needs, for the biometric community to be able to propose specific solutions.

A number of Forensic processes may involve some sort of Biometric-related technology, among them:

- Evidence evaluation. Likelihood ratio-based method to quantify the evidential value of biometric traces
- Forensic investigation. List of putative sources of biometric traces from one or several combined modalities
- Forensic Intelligence. Grouping of putative sources of biometric traces on basis of one or several combined modalities
- Surveillance. Capture of biometric traces and detection of putative sources on the basis of one or several combined modalities
- Forensic ID management and ID Verification. ID infrastructure and management, ID processes (create, challenge (access control / ID verification) and end an identity)

Several results have been already accomplished pursuing research in this direction. Notably the studies in 2D and 3D face recognition are being gradually applied to the forensic investigation process. [4]

2   Biometric Challenges in Forensics

Obtaining and using biometric evidence from the multimedia content available on social networking sites is a promising forensic activity for which the forensic community lacks biometric solutions. On the other hand the biometric community has developed technologies that are still not fully implemented in all the possible forensic processes:

- Even though uniqueness is not an issue in some forensic processes [5], several law enforcement applications still require the extent to which fingerprints coded in AFIS systems are unique to individuals.
- The role of the human operator in comparing the results of automated processing of fingerprints, facial images, etc.
- Systems engineering approaches to the application of biometric recognition in a forensic context
- Coding of scars, marks and tattoos; and a quantitative assessment of their contribution to identification or verification of identity
- The role of international standards and codes of practice to support research as well as in the interchange of forensic information
- Establishing robust test procedures (on the lines of work undertaken in the testing of biometric devices, software and systems in the ISO 19795 series of standards)
- Development of privacy-enhancing techniques to reduce privacy invasion in the collection and processing of material relating to people who are only incidentally involved in a capture event (e.g. processing a video stream in a crowded public place, where many hundreds of individuals are involved).

The EU COST Action IC1106 "Integrating Biometrics and Forensics for the Digital Age" represents an ideal opportunity for the Biometric and Forensic communities to join and understand each others needs, challenges and opportunities in a realistic manner. These synergies will lead to the development of a coherent joint vision and its dissemination across disciplinary and geographical borders [6].

2.1   Biometric Evidence for Forensic Evaluation and Investigation

Biometric data analysis may be of pivotal importance at any stage of the course of justice, be it the very first police investigation or a court trial. In the police investigative mode, reasoning follows a process of generating likely explanations, testing these with new observations and eliminating or re-ranking the explanations. In the forensic evaluative mode for a court trial, an opinion of evidential weight, based upon case specific propositions (hypotheses) and clear conditioning information (framework of circumstances) should be provided for use as evidence in court. The main objective of this task is to establish a robust methodology for forensic automatic biometric recognition based on statistical and probabilistic methods. Such a methodology should provide guidelines for the calculation of biometric evidence value and its strength and the evaluation of this strength under operating conditions of casework. This theoretical approach and corresponding design methodology are intended to bridge the gap between forensics and biometrics. This task involves several aspects of the forensic casework process: from the collection of evidence to the evaluation of the strength of evidence, to provide a unified framework which models the assumptions, conditions, and uncertainty implicit in the casework. A complete set of interpretation methods, based on the likelihood ratio approach, needs to be defined independently of the baseline biometric recognition system [7]. It should also define the integration procedure of these interpretation methods with the state-of-the-art automatic biometric recognition algorithms.

2.2   Audiovisual Biometrics for Forensics Examination

Nowadays digital evidence rather than physical evidence is increasingly getting easier to acquire from the scene of crime or cyber-crime.[1]

In fact, the Internet, computers, video surveillance cameras, mobile phones, telephone networks, social networks are all examples of methods for generating, collecting and sharing information on a massive scale. Therefore, by exploiting biometric technologies it will be possible to capture identity information from strong biometric data left on the scene of a crime, like:

- facial imaging (face, ear, iris) which can be acquired from both single images and surveillance video recordings, etc.;
- voice recording acquired from video sequences, ambient microphones, phone call recordings;
- Audio-visual recording containing lip-motion and faces;
- gait information acquired from video sequences.

In many cases, face and iris samples are not ideal since they depend on the camera position, occlusions, and the degree of cooperation of the suspected person. This

---

[1] Some of the forensic concepts developed for physical evidence may be transposed to digital evidence, some other not, due to the property of digital information. It is desirable to define the extent and limits of such a transposition. For example the question of chain of evidence is different for the physical and digital evidence.

information must be complemented with other sources of evidence like voice recording, lip-motion, gait information, etc.

Audio-visual speech can be also useful to determine the authenticity of a recorded media. This is a challenging task because of the enormous amount of recorder data and the non-cooperative acquisition scenario, which may reduce the recognition accuracy. Interactive multimodal biometric authentication techniques, using quality and reliability measures, offer a potential solution. In the near future, audiovisual biometrics could be regarded as the best starting point of forensic investigations, also to orient the collection of physical traces.

2.3   Soft Biometrics for Forensics Examination

Soft biometrics like age, gender, ethnicity, height, weight, eye color, hair style, can not be used to authenticate individuals since they lack of sufficient permanence and distinctiveness. Nevertheless, they can be used as ancillary information to support the forensic evaluation process to either narrow down the field of search or if only partial strong biometrics data are available. Moles, freckles, birthmarks, scars, marks, and tattoos possess higher discriminative capabilities. Being permanent imprints on the body, they can be used to assist the process of people identification in forensic applications or disaster recovery. Automating the accrual of evidential value, based on soft biometrics, would provide experts a valuable tool for: supplementing the decision made from other biometrics (like face, iris, etc); improving the identification accuracy: increasing the search speed in a database with hierarchical searches; improving the strength of evidence, also when partial information is available.

2.4   Forensic Behavioral Biometrics

From a forensic perspective, it is becoming increasingly important being able to infer various aspects about criminal activities. As such, biometric data are not only usable in forensic science for inference of identity of source, but also for inference at activity level. Either single user or crowd behavioral analysis is one of these aspects. Given an audio visual or visual scene is there any unusual or abnormal event taking place in the scene? Are there any specific contexts or events that will change the behavior of the scene dynamics by triggering other events without necessarily leading to unusual events? For instance, it is expected that when a train is near its departure time, that many individuals start running to catch it. One of the major difficulties in extracting useful information from a long dynamic visual flow, is the identification of that small portion of data that contains important information. Algorithms that could automatically detect unusual events within streaming or archival audio/video would significantly improve the analysis efficiency and save valuable human attention for only the most salient content. For example, algorithms for real time scene analysis, fight scene detection, weapon detection, etc. The outcome of this research task is to associate Actions/events with a group, identifying the role of the various individuals leading up to the potentially criminal activities. In this framework special focus will be on real time analysis of the actions to detect a suspect behavior in order to prevent crime.

2.5   Biometric Analysis of Crime Scene Traces and Their Forensic Interpretation

The collection of forensic traces from a crime scene involves a number of different processes which may be used for evidential purpose. Biometric technologies can be deployed to process data from:

- latent fingerprints and palmprints;
- written documents (signatures and handwriting analysis, etc.).

At the crime scene, fingerprints and palmprints can be found on many different surfaces [8]. Although fingerprints have been studied for decades, both in the forensic and in the biometric community, the progress made followed parallel and almost never convergent tracks. The potential convergence can be investigated by adopting high resolution optical capturing devices, to obtain non destructive quality measurements. For example, recovering the age of a latent fingerprint can be very important to determine if the suspect was present before or after a crime took place.[2] Moreover, the use of the *whole* electromagnetic spectrum (from infrared to X-rays) may track potential biometrics, even in a covert mode, such as latent finger and palm marks, for a subsequent forensic analysis (e.g. contaminations, DNA, etc.).

Novel means of fingerprints and palmprints visualization can be addressed. Especially when a conventional treatment is unlikely to work, such as on metal surfaces subject to extreme conditions [9]. Techniques that extend the range of treatments available for latent fingerprint visualization, all of which would extend the usefulness of an AFIS database in searching for offenders, would be very useful.

Written documents represent another source of physical evidence that is used by forensic experts and whose analysis can benefit from the studies conducted in the biometric field on both signature and handwriting analysis. The focus of this research should be on the development of pattern recognition algorithms, to complement and expedite the experts judgment. Algorithmic solutions for a semantic analysis, i.e. for extracting and representing the contextual usage meaning of words, by means of statistical processes applied to a large corpus of text, can be also exploited to infer the users identify.

2.6   Combination of Multimodal Biometrics with Other Forensic Evidence

Data fusion may involve the same biometric trait, acquired from different devices, or different traits from different sources. For example, the same walking individual can be acquired by different surveillance cameras placed in different locations. On the other hand, several data like gait, face, ear, voice, can be acquired

---

[2] Research on datation in forensic science exists (in the fingerprint field and others) and has proven extremely difficult as the environmental parameters are unknown.

from the same video. This data needs to be properly represented, with feature extraction techniques, and fused. In the forensic community, little or no effort has been devoted to the multimodal integration and fusion of data from multiple sensory channels. On the contrary, multimodal data fusion has been extensively studied by the biometrics community. This may resort in a multidisciplinary approach where techniques for effective evidential evaluation, based on fragmentary evidence, object and behavior recognition, are concurring to provide a robust support for the case, in agreement with the appropriate privacy/legal requirements and recommendations. Soft biometrics may be also exploited, together with other sources of evidence, to provide support to the hypothesis of criminal behaviour.

2.7 Ethical and Societal Implications of Emerging Forensic Biometrics

It is of crucial importance for law enforcement practices to accomplish with key democratic principles and fundamental human rights. Three main areas of intervention should be considered:

- Impact on Fundamental Rights: according to the Strategy for the effective implementation of the Charter of Fundamental Rights by the European Union (COM(2010) 573 final, the Charter Strategy) adopted by the Commission on 19 October 2010, all EU policies should be assessed against their impact on fundamental rights. This holds true in particular for RTD policies and technologies concerning justice and law enforcement.
- Impact on Privacy and Data Protection: the likely impact of new and emerging biometrics on privacy and data protection should be assessed and specific guidance issued. In particular, the possibility to adopt a privacy by design approach to forensic biometrics, should be explored. Policy issues concerning international biometric data sharing for forensic purposes and the establishment of crossborder biometric forensic databanks, are also relevant.
- Impact on vulnerable and disadvantaged groups: the risk that the implementation of new forensic biometrics may produce discrimination against ethnical and religious minorities, low income or geographically dispersed populations, children and minors, persons with disabilities and aging population, should be carefully assessed and minimized.

This process may result in increasing the understanding of non-technical challenges of emerging forensics biometrics among the international scientific community and in strengthening the Biometric-Forensic EU COST IC1106 network.

3   3D to 2D Face Recognition

The analysis of 3D face data is very promising in improving the identification performances of individuals. 3D acquisition systems are also becoming affordable, user friendly and easy to install in different environments. For these reasons it is envisaged that, in the near future, 3D face acquisition and matching can be successfully employed in forensic applications as well.

There are different scenarios where three-dimensional data can be acquired and used to to provide forensic evidential value to face images in criminal investigations:

- (3D to 3D) The conventional face mug shots taken from arrested criminals are substituted with a full 3D representation of the face. A 3D face can be obtained from a video acquired by a surveillance camera in the crime scene. The degree of similarity of two 3D faces is computed to accrue evidence for a potential suspect.
- (3D to 2D) As in the previous case, a 3D face representation is available from a list of suspects, but only a 2D face image is available from the crime scene. The 3D face representation is used to generate a synthetic 2D view of the face and perform the matching with the face image taken from the crime scene.

In order to perform the 3D to 2D matching a number of salient features are extracted from the two face images. The similarity is determined by comparing the two feature-based representations.

4   Pattern Matching Algorithm

3D face data is acquired for enrolment while 2D face images are used for identification. This is the case of convicted criminals whose 3D faces were acquired and stored, while 2D snapshots or a video clip is available from the crime scene. In this case the police officer should be able to identify the criminal whose face is depicted in the captured image or video. In most cases identification from images taken from a surveillance camera is quite difficult because the face is often rotated with respect to the camera. Having 3D face data allows to re-project face images with any orientation and use these images to perform the matching.

To perform the matching a series of 2D views were first produced, corresponding to 9 different head orientations, spaced 30 degrees along the horizontal and vertical axes. The 2D projections and the test images are aligned and scaled according to the positions of the eyes and the mouth. To ensure the proper scale and position on the 2D image plane a simple planar affine transformation is adopted. The image brightness is also normalized with a multi-window histogram equalization technique. Finally all 2D projections of all subjects are matched against the probe 2D face image.

The face matching algorithm is based on the comparison of the Scale Invariant Feature Transform (SIFT) feature sets extracted from the probe and gallery (3D projected) images [20]. One of the interesting features of the SIFT approach is the capability to capture the main gray-level features of an object's view by means of local patterns extracted from a scale-space decomposition of the image.

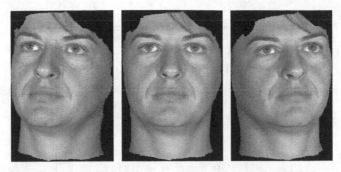

Fig. 1. Sample 2D images obtained by projecting the 3D texture mapped model

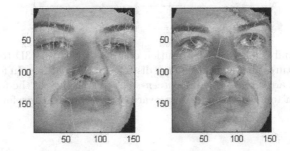

Fig. 2. (left) SIFT computed from a 2D test face image. (right) SIFT extracted from the corresponding pose-projected 3D face from training.

In order to perform the matching the SIFT features are first extracted from the gray scale images [21]. The matching score is computed, as proposed in [20], by counting the number of most similar SIFT features in the probe and gallery images. As several views are projected for each subject it is expected that the 2D projection corresponding to the closest head orientation of the probe image produces the smallest matching score.

Several tests were performed to determine the expected performances of the proposed biometric technology as a potential forensic application. Six out of the total nine 2D projected images of one subject are shown in figure 1. In figure 2 the test and probe image, with the same head orientation and registered with the extracted SIFT features are shown. The genuine and impostor score distributions, obtained by performing a complete matching test on the acquired dataset, are shown in figure 3. The equal error rate computed from the two distributions is equal to 4%.[3]

---

[3] It is worth noting that even though the EER provides a good performance indication for the technology evaluation, in the forensic evaluation scenario, some more appropriate metrics have been developed, such as [22]:

- Tippet plot, rates of misleading evidence (RMEP, RMED);
- Empirical Cross Entropy (ECE) and Cost Log Likelihood Ratio (Cllr);

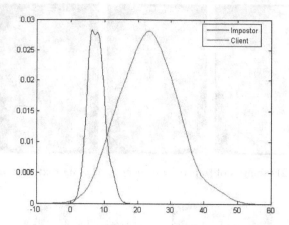

Fig. 3. Impostor and client score distribution computed with the 3D to 2D matching using the SIFT features and using the global distance of the features. In forensic science these distributions are often termed *"between-source* variability of the features for the relevant population" and the *"within-source* variability of the features for the suspected person".

5   Conclusion

Biometrics and Forensics have an undiscussed strong potential for mutual cross-fertilization. Several forensic processes may be automated and rationalized by the introduction of biometric classification algorithms. Several forensic traces and sources of evidence in criminal cases may be better analyzed and represented by means of feature extraction techniques. Different traces and evidence sources could be more efficiently combined by means of multibiometric techniques. Some examples of how biometrics may complement forensic science have been discussed. Practical implementations and further studies are the subject of a newly started pan-European network (EU COST Action IC1106) aiming to the development of a task force to properly address and solve these as well as other emerging issues in forensic biometrics.

Face-based identification has been extensively used in forensic applications. Generally 2D face images are captured both from convicted criminals and in the crime scene. We argue that 2D face images do not convey enough information to perform automatically a reliable matching of a probe and gallery pair. Extremely different acquisition conditions between the enrollment set-up and the crime scene make it difficult to compare images from the same subject. While mug shots are taken from criminals with a camera directly looking at the subject's face, the pictures taken from the crime scene generally originate from surveillance cameras looking at faces from above. A viable solution is to exploit the information content of a full 3D face, at least for the enrollment phase.

In this paper a forensic scenario has been considered where a 3D face representation is available from a list of suspects, but only a 2D face image is available from the crime scene. The 3D face representation of the suspect is used to generate a synthetic 2D view of the face and perform the matching with the face image taken from the crime scene. 3D to 2D experiments are presented producing promising results. Improvements are expected by increasing the number of synthetic head pose variations in the training set.

References

1. Maltoni, D., Maio, D., Jain, A.K., Prabhakar, S.: Handbook of Fingerprint Recognition, 2nd edn. Springer (2009)
2. Ross, A., Nandakumar, K., Jain, A.K.: Handbook of Multibiometrics. Springer (2006)
3. Tistarelli, M., Chellappa, R., Li, S.Z.: Handbook of Remote Biometrics. Springer (2009)
4. Meuwly, D., Veldhuis, R.: Forensic biometrics: From two communities to one discipline. In: Proc. of the International Conference of the Biometrics Special Interest Group (BIOSIG). IEEE (2012)
5. Cole, S.A.: Forensics without uniqueness, conclusions without individualization: the new epistemology of forensic identification. Law, Probability and Risk 8(3), 233–255 (2009)
6. The Proposers of the COST Action IC1106. Integrating Biometrics and Forensics for the Digital Age. Memorandum of Understanding of the European Commission (2012)
7. Neumann, C., Evett, I.W., Skerett, J.: Quantifying the weight of Evidence from a forensic fingerprint comparison, a new paradigm. J. R. Statist. Soc. A 175(2), 1–26 (2012)
8. Champod, C., Lennard, C., Margot, P., Stoilovic, M.: Fingerprints and other ridge skin impressions. CRC Press (2004)
9. Tahtouh, M., Kalman, J., Roux, C., Lennard, C., Reedy, B.: The Detection and Enhancement of Latent Fingermarks Using Infrared Chemical Imaging. J. Forensic Sci. 1(1), 1–9 (2005)
10. Abate, A.F., Nappi, M., Riccio, D., Sabatino, G.: 2D and 3D face recognition: A survey. Pattern Recognition Letters 28, 1885–1906 (2007)
11. Besl, P., McKay, N.: A method for registration of 3-D shapes. IEEE Transactions on Pattern Analysis and Machine Intelligence 14(2), 239–256 (1992)
12. Bronstein, A.M., Bronstein, M.M., Kimmel, R.: Three-dimensional face recognition. Int. Journal of Computer Vision 64(1), 5–30 (2005)
13. Cadoni, M., Bicego, M., Grosso, E.: 3D Face Recognition Using Joint Differential Invariants. In: Tistarelli, M., Nixon, M.S. (eds.) ICB 2009. LNCS, vol. 5558, pp. 279–288. Springer, Heidelberg (2009)
14. Mpiperis, I., Malassiotis, S., Strintzis, M.G.: 3-D face recognition with the geodesic polar representation. IEEE Transactions on Information Forensics and Security, 2(3) (pt. 2), 537–547 (2007)
15. Al-Osaimi, F.R., Bennamoun, M., Mian, A.: Integration of local and global geometrical cues for 3D face recognition. Pattern Recognition 41(2), 1030–1040 (2008)
16. Colombo, A., Cusano, C., Schettini, R.: 3D face detection using curvature analysis. Pattern Recognition 39(3), 444–455 (2006)

17. BenAbdelkader, C., Griffin, P.A.: Comparing and combining depth and texture cues for face recognition. Image and Vision Computing **23**(3), 339–352 (2005)
18. Beumier, C., Acheroy, M.: Face verification from 3D and grey level cues. Pattern Recognition Letters **22**, 1321–1329 (2001)
19. Bowyer, K., Chang, K., Flynn, P.: A survey of approaches and challenges in 3D and multi-modal 3D + 2D face recognition. Computer Vision and Image Understanding **101**, 1–15 (2006)
20. Lowe, D.: Distinctive image features from scale-invariant keypoints. Int. Journal of Computer Vision **60**(2), 91–110 (2004)
21. Bicego, M., Lagorio, A., Grosso, E., Tistarelli, M.: On the use of SIFT features for face authentication. In: Proc. of Int Workshop on Biometrics, in Association with CVPR 2006 (2006)
22. Ramos, D.: Forensic Evaluation of the Evidence Using Automatic Speaker Recognition Systems. EURASIP Library of Phd Theses, Universidad Autonoma de Madrid (November 2007)

Facial Expression Classification Using Supervised Descent Method Combined with PCA and SVM

Agata Manolova, Nikolay Neshov[⊠], Stanislav Panev, and Krasimir Tonchev

Faculty of Telecommunications, Technical University of Sofia, Sofia, Bulgaria
{amanolova,nneshov,s_panev}@tu-sofia.bg, k_tonchev@tu-sofia.bg

Abstract. It has been well known that there is a correlation between facial expression and person's internal emotional state. In this paper we use an approach to distinguish between neutral and some other expression: based on the displacement of important facial points (coordinates of edges of the mouth, eyes, eyebrows, etc.). Further the feature vectors are formed by concatenating the landmarks data from Supervised Descent Method, applying PCA and use these data as an input to Support Vector Machine (SVM) classifier. The experimental results show improvement of the recognition rate in comparison to some state-of-the-art facial expression recognition techniques.

Keywords: Supervised Descent Method · SVM · PCA · Facial expression · Emotion recognition

1 Introduction

Face plays significant role in social communication. This is a 'window' to human personality, emotions and thoughts. The face we look at is a mix of both physical characteristics and emotive expressions. According to the psychological research, nonverbal part is the most informative channel in social communication. Verbal part contributes about 7% of the message, vocal – 34% and facial expression -55% [8]. Due to that, the face is a subject of study in many areas of science such as psychology, behavioral science, medicine and finally computer science.

One of the grand challenges for computational intelligence is to understand how people process and recognize each other's face and expression and to develop automated and reliable face recognition systems. In the field of computer science much effort is put to explore the ways of automation the process of face detection and segmentation. Several approaches addressing the problem of facial feature extraction have been proposed [8, 25]. The main issue is to provide appropriate face representation, which remains robust with respect to diversity of facial appearances.

The objective of this paper is to outline the problem of facial expression recognition that is a great challenge in the area of computer vision. Advantages of creating a fully automatic system for facial action analysis are constant motivation for exploring this field of science. The emotion recognition system is a considerably challenging task to generate such an intelligent system that is able to identify and understand

© Springer International Publishing Switzerland 2014
V. Cantoni et al. (Eds.): BIOMET 2014, LNCS 8897, pp. 165–175, 2014.
DOI: 10.1007/978-3-319-13386-7_13

human emotions for various vital purposes, e.g. security, society, entertainment, health care, human-computer interaction, industrial and personal robotics, surveillance and transportation.

Some already developed emotion recognition applications have demonstrated their capabilities in different areas of everyday life; for instance, they can predict the criminal's behavior by analyzing the images of their faces that are captured by the surveillance camera. Furthermore, such system is very useful and powerful in signed language recognition that deals with deaf people. Additionally, it is used to build the intelligent automobile systems that will allow the car to recognize the physical condition of its driver (in case of heart attack for example). The emotion recognition system has had a considerable impact on the game and entertainment fields besides its use to increase the efficiency of robots for specific tasks such as caring services, military tasks, medical robots, and manufacturing servicing. In general, the intelligent computer with the emotion recognition system can be used to improve our daily lives.

The scientists have analyzed the human emotions and realized that human emotion recognition can be achieved by analyzing speech or the facial expressions. There are many algorithms which study the speech [26-28] or the 2D or 3D facial expressions [29] in order to discern the emotion. According to many studies, both kinds of algorithms succeed in classifying the emotions but the facial expression algorithms have been revealed to be more accurate than the speech algorithms [30].

The goal of the facial expression recognition system is to imitate the human visual system in the most similar way. This is very challenging task in the area of computer vision because not only it requires efficient image/video analysis techniques but also well-suited feature vector used in machine learning process.

The first principle of this system is that it should be effortless and efficient. That is connected with full automation, so that no additional manual effort is required. The system should be able to avoid limitations on body and head movements which could also be an important source of information about displayed emotion. The constraints about facial hair, glasses or additional make-up should be reduced to minimum. Other important features that are desired in this kind of a system are user and environment independence. The former means that, the algorithm must be invariant to skin color, age, gender or nation.

Despite 40 years of research, however, today's recognition systems are still largely unable to handle the extraordinary wide range of appearances and facial expression assumed by people in typical images or video sequences.

The rest of the paper is organized as follows: In the next section we present a brief survey on popular automatic facial feature extraction algorithms a necessary step for the emotion recognition. In Section 3 we present the approach Supervised Descent Method (SDM) for facial feature extraction that will be used later for the facial expression analysis. In Section 4 we will present the proposed method in several steps: Viola-Jones for face detection followed by SDM, PCA for feature vector dimensionality reduction and SVM for data classification. Section 5 will illustrate the experimental results for the classification of the processed data with various classification techniques and we will present a comparison between similar methods. Finally section 6 conclude the paper.

2   Brief Survey on Existing Automatic Facial Feature Extraction Algorithms

On fig. 1 is illustrated the basic structure of a facial expression analysis system.

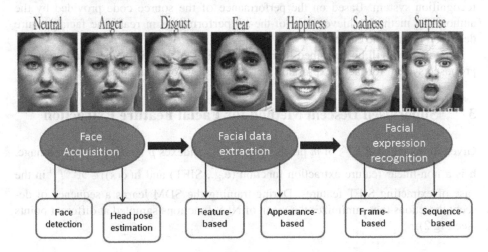

Fig. 1. Basic structure of facial expression analysis systems

One of the most important steps of the facial expression analysis is the face feature extraction and representation. Deformation of facial features are characterized by shape and texture changes and lead to high spatial gradients that are good indicators for facial actions and may be analyzed either in the image or the spatial frequency domain. The latter can be computed by high-pass gradient or Gabor wavelet-based filters [31], which closely model the receptive field properties of cells in the primary visual cortex. They allow to detect line endings and edge borders over multiple scales and with different orientations. These features reveal much about facial expressions, as both transient and intransient facial features often give raise to a contrast change with regard to the ambient facial tissue. They have shown to perform well for the task of facial expression analysis and were used in image-based or frame-based approaches [13, 14, 20].

Model-based approaches constitute an alternative to image-based deformation extraction. Appearance-based model approaches allow to separate fairly well different information sources such as facial illumination and deformation changes. Lanitis et al. [21] interpreted face images by employing active appearance models (AAM) [22, 23]. Faces were analyzed by a dual approach, using both shape and texture models. Active shape models (ASM) allow to simultaneously determine the shape, scale and pose by fitting an appropriate point distribution model (PDM) to the object of interest. A drawback of appearance-based models is the manual labor necessary for the construction of the shape models. The latter are based on landmark points that need to be precisely placed around intransient facial features during the training of the models.

Huang and Huang [24] used a point distribution model to rep-resent the shape of a face, where shape parameters were estimated by employing a gradient-based method.

Recently in [4] a new method is proposed based on a Supervised Descent Method (SDM) for minimizing a Non-linear Least Squares (NLS) function. This method is fast and reliable and can be used to detect facial features necessary for the expression recognition system. Based on the performance of the source code provided by the authors the method achieves state-of-the-art performance in real time facial feature detection from static camera.

This method will be described in the next section and it will be used further in the proposed system for facial expression recognition developed in our research.

3   Supervised Descent Method for Facial Feature Extraction

Given an image $d \in \Re^{m \times 1}$ of m pixels, $d(x) \in \Re^{p \times 1}$ indexes p landmarks in the image. $\mathbf{h}$ is a non-linear feature extraction function (e.g., SIFT) and $\mathbf{h}(d(x)) \in \Re^{128 p \times 1}$ in the case of extracting SIFT features. During training the SDM learns a sequence of descent directions that minimizes the mean of NLS functions sampled at different points (see Fig 2).

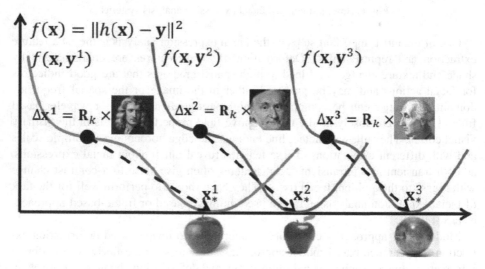

Fig. 2. a) Using the training set SDM learns a generic set of descent directions $\{R_k\}$. Each parameter update (Δx^i) is the product of R_k and an image specific component (y^i) [4].

So we will assume that the correct p landmarks (in our case 66) are known, and we will refer to them as x∗ (see Fig. 3 a).

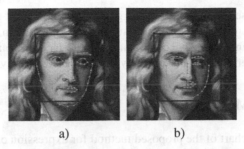

a)   b)

Fig. 3. a) Manually labeled image with 66 landmarks. Blue outline indicates face detector. b) Mean landmarks, x_0, initialized using the face detector [4].

Also, to reproduce the testing scenario, we ran the face detector on the training images to provide an initial configuration of the landmarks (x_0), which corresponds to an average shape (see Fig. 3b). In this setting, face alignment can be framed as minimizing the following function over Δx, so for a particular face the Δx can be learned:

$$f(x_0 + \Delta x) = \left\| h(d(x_0 + \Delta x)) - \varphi_* \right\|_2^2 \tag{1}$$

where $\varphi_* = h(d(x_*))$ represents the SIFT values in the manually labeled landmarks (SIFT features from ground truth shape x_*). In the training images, φ_* and Δx are known and $\varphi_0 = h(d(x_0))$ are the SIFT features from initial shape x_0.

In Eq. 1 we do not learn any model of shape or appearance beforehand from training data. We align the image w.r.t. a template φ_*. For the shape, the model will be a non-parametric one, and we will optimize the landmark locations $x \in \Re^{2p \times 1}$ directly. The proposed non-parametric shape model is able to generalize better to untrained situations (e.g., asymmetric facial gestures). Then, the SIFT features extracted from patches around the landmarks are used to achieve a robust representation against illumination. Observe that the SIFT operator is not differentiable and minimizing Eq. 1 using first or second order methods requires numerical approximations (e.g., finite differences) of the Jacobian and the Hessian. However, numerical approximations are very computationally expensive. The goal of SDM is to learn a series of descent directions and re-scaling factors (done by the Hessian in the case of Newton's method) such that it produces a sequence of updates $x_{k+1} = x_k + \Delta x_k$ starting from x_0 that converges to x_* in the training data.

During the learning stage for a large number of faces in the dataset a general or common sequence of descent directions R_k and bias terms b_k can be learned. Assume that we are given a set of face images   and their corresponding hand-labeled landmarks   . For each image R_k and b_k are obtained by minimizing the expected loss between the predicted and the optimal landmark displacement under many possible initializations:

$$\arg\min_{R_k b_k} \sum_{d^i} \sum_{x_k^i} \left\| \Delta x_*^{ki} - R_k \varphi_k^i - b_k \right\|^2 \tag{2}$$

SDM is a supervised technique learning generic set of descent directions. It is able to overcome many drawbacks of second order optimization schemes, such as nondifferentiability and expensive computation of the Jacobians and and Hessians and at the same time it performs in an extremely fast and accurate way.

4   Proposed Method

The processing flowchart of the proposed method for expression classification is illustrated on fig. 4. In the subsections below we describe each stage.

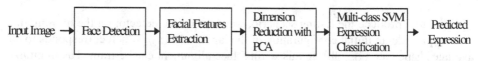

Fig. 4. Overview of the proposed system

4.1   Face Detection

As first stage, the input image is analyzed for face presence and determination of its location. There are many face detection methods available in the literature [1]. In our system we used an open source code library (OpenCV) that implements algorithm based on Viola-Jones [2] which is known to be a very fast and efficient. Fig. shows an example image from CK+ database [3] (©Jeffrey Cohn) and located face (bounded is square) using the OpenCV face detector.

Fig. 5. An illustration of example image from CK+ database and detected face using OpenCV

4.2   Facial Features Extraction

For features extraction we obtain the coordinates of important facial points using the Supervised Descent Method (SDM) presented in [4]. The source code and models we used are provided by the authors[1]. Afterwards the feature vector is computed by subtracting the coordinates of each pair of two neighbor landmarks. To explain this, let's denote the set of coordinates of keypoints for given face as: $\{(x_1,y_1), (x_2,y_2), (x_3,y_3),\dots, (x_N,y_N)\}$, where $N = 49$. Then the future vector is 96 dimensional and is formed as follows:

$$f = \{(x_2 - x_1), (x_3 - x_2), (x_4 - x_3), \dots, (x_N - x_{N-1}),$$
$$(y_2 - y_1), (y_3 - y_2), (y_4 - y_3), \dots, (y_N - y_{N-1})\} \tag{3}$$

In this way the feature vector is invariant with respect to the location of detected face. Fig. 6 depicts the keypoints obtained after applying the SDM method.

Fig. 6. An example image and detected keypoints

4.3 Dimension Reduction with Principal Component Analysis

One of the main advantages of PCA is its ability to reduce the dimensionality without much loss of information. In our experiments PCA is used to reduce the size of feature for each image to 24 dimensional vector. This vector is input into the Support Vector Machine (SVM) classifier.

4.4 Multi-class Support Vector Machine Expression Classification

SVM is very popular and powerful method for binary and multi-class classification as well as for regression problems. For two class separation, SVM applies a maximum margin manner that estimates the optimal separating hyper-plane. In our investigation we used the LibSVM library[2] [5]. In general SVMs can only solve binary classification problems. For multi-class classification, LibSVM computes decision surfaces for all class pairs (one-against-one technique) and then find the correct class by a voting mechanism.

---

[1] http://www.humansensing.cs.cmu.edu/intraface/
[2] http://www.csie.ntu.edu.tw/~cjlin/libsvm/

Let us given sample and label pairs $(x^{(i)}, y^{(i)})$, where $x^{(i)} \in R^m$, $y^{(i)} \in \{-1;1\}$ and $i = 1,..., K$. Here, for class "1" and for class "2", $y^{(i)} = 1$ and $y^{(i)} = -1$, respectively. We also define a feature map - $\phi: R^m \to H$, where H denotes Hilbert-space. The kernel implicitly performs the dot product calculations between mapped points: $k(x, y) = \langle \phi(x), \phi(y) \rangle_H$. Now, the SVM can be formulated as following optimization problem:

$$\min_{w,b,\xi} \frac{1}{2} w^T w + C \sum_{i=1}^{K} \xi_i, \tag{4}$$

$$\text{s.t. } y^{(i)} (w^T \phi(x^{(i)}) + b) \geq 1 = \xi_i, \ \xi_i \geq 0, \tag{5}$$

where $\xi_i (i = 1,..., K)$ are slack variables which measure the degree of misclassification of their associated training data points with respect to the current decision boundary and margin.

In our experiments, we used non-linear classifier with Gaussian kernel.

5   Experimental Results

In our experiments we used the Cohn-Kanade Extended Facial Expression Database (CK+) [3]. This database is developed for evaluation and comparison of methods and algorithms for facial expression analysis. It contains 123 different subjects and 593 image sequences. From these, 118 subjects are annotated with 7 universal emotions: anger, contempt, disgust, fear, happy, sad and surprise (Table 1). The corresponding labels are used as the "ground truth" data.

Table 1. Distribution of emotion labels for 118 subjects from CK+ database

Emotion	anger	contempt	disgust	fear	happy	sad	surprise
Number of images per emotion	45	18	59	25	69	28	83

We trained a multi-class SVM using leave-one-subject-out cross validation method in which all images of the test subject were excluded from the training data.

The conducted results of the classification accuracy are shown in Table 2. It can be seen that emotions with large displacement of keypoints (such as surprise and happy) gave more than 97% correct classification. For the worst case (fear), the accuracy is 76%. The average recognition rate is 86,27%.

Table 2. Emotion classification confusion matrix for CK+ database using the proposed method

%	anger	contempt	disgust	fear	happy	sad	surprise
anger	**82,22**	6,67	6,67	0,00	2,22	2,22	0,00
contempt	16,67	**77,78**	0,00	5,56	0,00	0,00	0,00
disgust	8,47	0,00	**89,83**	0,00	0,00	1,69	0,00
fear	4,00	0,00	0,00	**76,00**	4,00	4,00	12,00
happy	2,90	0,00	0,00	0,00	**97,10**	0,00	0,00
sad	14,29	0,00	0,00	0,00	0,00	**82,14**	3,57
surprise	0,00	1,20	0,00	0,00	0,00	0,00	**98,80**
Recognition Rate (Avg.)	86,27						

Looking at the results produced by the most accurate implementations of the Active Appearance Model (AAM) that utilizes shape and texture information [3] and the Constrained Local Model (CLM) that uses only texture information [6], it can be seen that with our proposed method, the average recognition accuracy is higher (from 83,3% and 74,4% to 86,27% respectively). We can also see some reasonable improvement of classification rate by comparing our work with different learning methods, including SVMs and the Grassmann manifold [7] (from 85,8% to 86,27%). However we should note that direct comparison analysis is misleading because the results in [7] are reported on the first version of the CK dataset with different emotion labels. These works are summarized in Table 3.

Table 3. Comparison of the results for CK+ database with other methods

%	An.	Co.	Di.	Fe.	Ha,	Sa.	Su.	Avg.
AAM-SVM (Shape) [3]	35	25	68,4	21,7	98,4	4	100	50,3
AAM-SVM (Texture) [3]	70	21,9	94,7	21,7	100	60	98,7	66,7
AAM-SVM (Texture and Shape) [3]	75	84,4	94,7	65,2	100	68	96	83,3
CLM-SVM (Texture) [6]	70,1	52,4	92,5	72,1	94,2	45,9	93,6	74,4
G-KLDA [7]	65,7	-	86,8	83	95,1	85,7	98,6	85,8
E-SVM [7]	62,8	-	78,9	74,4	91,3	80,3	97,2	80,8
G-SVM [7]	65,7	-	78,9	74,5	95	85,7	97,2	82,8
Proposed method	82,2	77,8	89,8	76	97,1	82,1	98,8	86,27

6   Conclusion and Comments

In this paper we proposed a method for automatic facial expression classification. The system is able to detect a human face from still image, extract feature vectors (differences of the coordinates of specific important facial key-points), applying PCA and then classify expression presented in the face using trained SVM. From the conducted experiments on CK+ database, the classification rate vary between 76% and 98,8% (recognition rate is 86,27%). The system is capable to distinguish "surprised", "happy", "disgusted", "angry" and "sad" expressions at maximum rate (more than 82%). The other two expressions – "contempt" and "fear" are recognized at lower rates – 77,8% and 76% respectively. In comparison to some state-of-the-art facial expression recognition techniques [3], [6] and [7] our method reaches reasonable improvement of performances over the different classes (Table 3).

It can be concluded that key-points location information is very efficient for facial expression recognition provided that details of coordinates' changes are determined precisely. It can be observed that different emotion expressions cause changes in the texture of the skin from the formation of wrinkles for some specific regions (between eyebrows, cheeks, forehead, etc.). Thereby the current system can be extended by texture based algorithms to improve performance.

Acknowledgment. This work was sponsored by the Ministry of Education and Science of Bulgaria, National Foundation "Science and Research", Slovenian-Bulgarian R&D joint project, NSF Grant DNTS/Slovenia 01/08 – "Fast and Reliable 3D Face Recognition".

References

1. Tian, Y., Kanade, T., Cohn, J.F.: Facial expression analysis. In: Li, S.Z., Jain, A.K., (Eds.): Handbook of Face Recognition, pp. 247–275. Springer (2005)
2. Viola, P., Jones, J.M.: Robust real-time object detection. In: Second International Workshop on Statistical and Computational Theories of Vision-Modeling Learning, Computing, and Sampling (2001)
3. Lucey, P., Cohn, J.F., Kanade, T., Saragih, J., Ambadar, Z., Matthews, I.: The Extended Cohn-Kanade Dataset (CK+): A complete expression dataset for action unit and emotion-specified expression. In: Proceedings of the Third International Workshop on CVPR for Human Communicative Behavior Analysis (CVPR4HB 2010), San Francisco, USA, pp. 94–101 (2010)
4. Xuehan-Xiong, De la Torre, F.: Supervised descent method and its application to face alignment, in CVPR (2013)
5. Chang, C.-C., Lin, C.-J.: LibSVM: a library for support vector machines
6. Chew, S.W., Lucey, P.J., Lucey, S., Saragih, J., Cohn, J.F., Sridharan, S.: Person-independent facial expression detection using constrained local models. In: Proceedings of FG 2011 Facial Expression Recognition and Analysis Challenge, Santa Barbara, CA (2011)
7. Taheri, S., Turaga, P., Chellappa, R.: Towards View-Invariant Expression Analysis Using Analytic Shape Manifolds. Int. Conf, Automatic Face and Gesture Recognition (2011)
8. Li, S., Jain, A.: Handbook of Face Recognition 2nd ed. Springer (2011)
9. Tian, Y.-L., Kanade, T., Cohn, J.: Recognizing action units for facial expression analysis. IEEE Trans. Pattern Anal. Mach. Intell. 23(2), 1–19 (2001)
10. Donato, G., Bartlett, M., Hager, J., Ekman, P., Sejnowski, T.: Classifying facial actions. IEEETrans. Pattern Anal. Mach. Intell. 21(10), 974–989 (1999)
11. Susskind, J.M., Littlewort, G., Bartlett, M.S., Movellan, J., Anderson, A.K.: Human and computer recognition of facial expressions of emotion. Neuropsychologia 45, 152–162 (2007)
12. Littlewort, G., Stewart, M.: Bartlett, I. Fasel, J. Susskind, J. Movellan, Dynamics of facial expression extracted automatically from video. Image and Vision Computing 24, 615–625 (2006)

13. Sebe, N., Lew, M.S., Sun, Y., Cohen, I., Gevers, T., Huang, T.S.: Authentic facial expression analysis. Image and Vision Computing **25**, 1856–1863 (2007)
14. Shana, C., Gong, S., McOwanb, P.W.: Facial expression recognition based on Local Binary Patterns: A comprehensive study. Image and Vision Computing **27**, 803–816 (2009)
15. Tong, Y., Liao, W., Ji, Q.: Automatic Facial Action Unit Recognition by Modeling Their Semantic And Dynamic Relationships, Springer (2009)
16. Zhi, R., Flierl, M., Ruan, Q., Kleijn, W.: Graph-preserving sparse nonnegative matrix factorization with application to facial expression recognition. IEEE, Transactions on Systems, Man, and Cybernetics, Part B: Cybernetics **41**(1), 38–52 (2011)
17. Zafeiriou, S., Petrou, M.: Nonlinear non-negative component analysis algorithms. Image Processing, IEEE Transactions on **19**(4), 1050–1066 (2010)
18. Jiang, B., Valstary, M.F., Pantic, M.: Facial Action Detection using Block-based Pyramid Appearance Descriptors. In: Proceedings of the ASE/IEEE International Conference on Social Computing (SocialCom 2012). Amsterdam, The Netherlands (September 2012)
19. Jiang, B., Valstar, M.F., Martinez, B., Pantic, M.: A Dynamic Appearance Descriptor Approach to Facial Actions Temporal Modelling. IEEE Transactions of Systems, Man and Cybernetics, Part B. **44**(2), 161–174 (2014)
20. Fellenz, W., Taylor, J., Tsapatsoulis, N., Kollias, S.: Comparing template-based, feature-based and supervised classification of facial expressions from static images. In: Proceedings of Circuits, Systems, Communications and Computers (CSCC 1999), Nugata, Japan, pp. 5331–5336 (1999)
21. Lanitis, A., Taylor, C., Cootes, T.: Automatic interpretation and coding of face images using 2exible models. IEEE Trans. Pattern Anal. Mach. Intell. **19**(7), 743–756 (1997)
22. Cootes, T., Edwards, G., Taylor, C.: Active appearance models. IEEE PAMI **23**(6), 681–685 (2001)
23. Cootes, T.F., Edwards, G.J., Taylor, C.J.: Active Appearance Models. In: Burkhardt, H., Neumann, B. (eds.) ECCV 1998. LNCS, vol. 1407, pp. 581–695. Springer, Heidelberg (1998)
24. Huang, C., Huang, Y.: Facial expression recognition using model-based feature extraction and action parameters classification. J. Visual Commun. Image Representation **8**(3), 278–290 (1997)
25. Wechsler, H.: Reliable Face Recognition Methods: System Design, Implementation and Evaluation, International Series on Biometrics, v. 7, Springer Science & Business Media (2009)
26. El Ayadi, M., Kamel, M.S., Karray, F.: Survey on speech emotion recognition: Features, classification schemes, and databases. Pattern Recognition **44**(3), 572–587 (2011)
27. Chen, L., Mao, X., Xue, Y., Lung, L.: Cheng. Speech emotion recognition: Features and classification models, Digital Signal Processing **22**(6), 1154–1160 (2012)
28. Ververidis, D., Kotropoulos, C.: Emotional speech recognition: Resources, features, and methods. Speech Communication **48**(9), 1162–1181 (2006)
29. Sandbach, G., Zafeiriou, S., Pantic, M., Yin, L.: Static and dynamic 3D facial expression recognition: A comprehensive survey. Image and Vision Computing **30**(10), 683–697 (2012)
30. Castellano, G., Kessous, L., Caridakis, G.: Multimodal Emotion Recognition from Expressive Faces, Body Gestures and Speech. Proc Doctoral Consortium Second Int'l Conf, Affective Computing and Intelligent Interaction (2007)
31. Vinay, K.B., Shreyas, B.S.: Face Recognition Using Gabor Wavelets. In: Fortieth Asilomar Conference on Signals, Systems and Computers, ACSSC 2006. pp. 593–597 (2006)

Human Gaze Tracking
with an Active Multi-camera System

Agata Manolova[✉], Stanislav Panev, and Krasimir Tonchev

Faculty of Telecommunications, Technical University of Sofia,
8 Kliment Ohridski Blvd., 1000 Sofia, Bulgaria
{amanolova,s_panev,k_tonchev}@tu-sofia.bg

Abstract. This paper presents a framework for determining the direction of human gaze with an active multi-camera system. A fixed camera is employed in order to estimate the position of the human face and its features, like the eyes. By means of the Supervised Descent Method (SDM) for minimizing a Non-linear Least Squares (NLS) function we can compute correctly the position of the two eyes using 6 landmarks for each of them and the pose of the head. Then an active pan-tilt camera is oriented to one of the users eyes. This way a high precision gaze direction determination is accomplished.

Keywords: Eye tracking · Gaze tracking · Face tracking · Active camera · Pan-tilt camera

1 Introduction

The eyes are one of the most important ways for gathering information about the world around us in our everyday live. A users gaze is suggested to be the best proxy for attention or intention. Using the information from the gaze as a form of input can enable a computer system to gain more contextual information about the users task at hand, which in turn can help to design interfaces which are more interactive and intelligent. Gaze tracking is a promising research area with application that goes from advanced human machine interaction systems, to human attention processes studying, modeling and use in cognitive vision fields, multimedia and gaming systems, marketing and commercial statistical studies, security systems and etc. At the beginning the eye tracking as a form of input was primarily developed for impaired users who were unable to use the keyboard and the mouse as standard input devices. However, with the increasing accuracy and decreasing cost of eye gaze tracking systems the everyday users are able to use gaze as a form of input in addition to keyboard and mouse to augment or facilitate the human-computer interaction experience. In [13] the authors have developed gaze-enhanced interaction techniques for pointing and selection, scrolling [14], password entry [12] and typing [6].

The existing gaze tracking techniques are broadly classified into intrusive and non-intrusive. The intrusive techniques require attachments around the eye

© Springer International Publishing Switzerland 2014
V. Cantoni et al. (Eds.): BIOMET 2014, LNCS 8897, pp. 176–188, 2014.
DOI: 10.1007/978-3-319-13386-7_14

to determine the gaze. These include search coils, electrooculography [4], contact lens and head mounted devices. Non-intrusive techniques use video cameras under infrared or natural light sources.

The non-intrusive or video based techniques are classified into two categories appearance-based and model-based. Appearance-based approaches directly treat an eye image as a high dimensional feature. In [7] the authors use the image contents as to map directly to the screen coordinates. These methods require several significant calibration points to infer the gaze direction from the images. The analysis of the images at calibration points is important for gaze estimation. Baluja and Pomerleau use a neural network to learn a mapping function between eye images and gaze points (display coordinates) using 2,000 training samples [2]. Tan et al. take a local interpolation approach to estimate unknown gaze point from 252 relatively sparse samples [16]. Recently, Williams et al. proposed a novel regression method called S^3GP (Sparse, Semi-Supervised Gaussian Process), and applied it to the gaze estimation task with partially labeled (16 of 80) training samples [18]. Appearance-based approaches can make the system less restrictive, and can also be very robust even when used with relatively low-resolution cameras. The appearance models are used for tracking smaller eye movements compared to the size of the object.

Model-based approaches use an explicit geometric model of the eye, and estimate its gaze direction using geometric eye features. For example one typical feature is the pupil glint vector ([8], [10]), the relative position of the pupil center and the specular reflection of a light source, pupil corneal reflection. Model-based approaches typically need to precisely locate small features on the eye using a high-resolution image and often require additional light sources but can be very accurate. The local gaze features include pupil and limbus position, iris center, eye corner, inner eye boundary and sclera region. The global gaze features are face skin color, inter pupil distance, ratio between average intensity, shapes, sizes of both the pupil and orientation of pupil ellipse with respect to face pose [11].

In this paper we present an improved framework for determining the direction of human gaze with an active multi-camera system. We employ a fixed camera in order to determine the position of the human face and its features most importantly the eyes. By means of the Supervised Descent Method (SDM) for minimizing a Non-linear Least Squares (NLS) function we can compute correctly the position of the two eyes using 6 landmarks for each eye and the position of the head. Then an active pan-tilt camera is oriented to one of the users eyes and this way a high precision gaze direction determination is accomplished. In Section 2 a detailed system overview will be presented with the components of the eye tracking system. Section 3 will introduce the systems geometrical model and the calibration method. Sections 4 and 6 will illustrate the facial feature extraction and tracking and the gaze direction estimation algorithms. The experimental results are described in Section 7.

2   System Overview

The components which the gaze tracking system consists of are shown on Fig. 1.

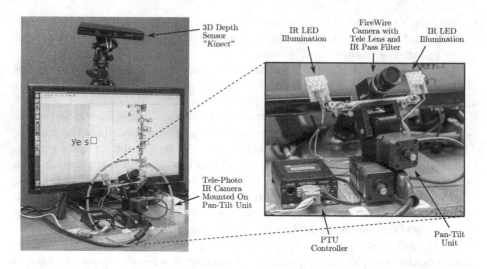

Fig. 1. System overview

The purpose of the system described in this paper is to estimate the gaze direction of a user which is standing in front of a computer screen. To accomplish that task with a video camera, as precise as possible, a larger scale image of the user's eye(s) is needed. This can be achieved by mounting a telephoto lens on the camera, but such an action will narrow the camera's field of view and respectively will constrain the user's movements in order to keep the image of its eye(s) inside the camera frame. To overcome this problem a multi camera gaze tracking system is constructed which consists mainly of two parts - a fixed 3D wide angle depth sensor and a movable telephoto camera which is mounted on an active pan-tilt unit (PTU). The wide angle 3D sensor is used to detect the 3D position of the user's face and eyes in a global coordinate frame. This information is needed by the PTU control system to estimate the angles of rotation of the telephoto camera so it will be pointed towards the user's eye(s). Then the gaze direction can be estimated by extracting eye's features from the large scale image and applying them to a human eye geometrical model.

The 3D depth sensor *"Kinect"* is equipped with two imaging devices - a color RGB camera and a grayscale camera which works in the IR spectrum and in combination with a IR laser projector they construct a 3D range sensor. The disparity map and the pixels registration between it and the image from the RGB camera are automatically calculated. As an output from *"Kinect"* we get a depth map and by employing the *"Kinect"* intrinsic camera parameters, like lens focal length and principal point coordinates, the so called 3D point cloud is estimated. This information will be used later on for 3D face and eye tracking as mentioned above.

The block diagram shown on Fig. 2 describes the main stages and their consistency for processing the information of the two data sources (marked in

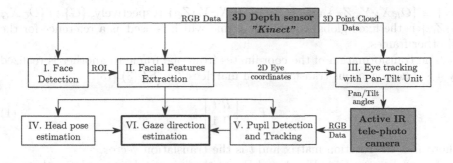

Fig. 2. System block diagram

blue) until the final aim is achieved. All of them are described in the rest of this article.

3   System Geometrical Model and Calibration

The interpretation of the data retrieved from the *"Kinect"*, in order to control the active camera, requires an employment of a 3D system geometrical model which will be the backbone of all the calculations concerning the user's face and eye tracking.

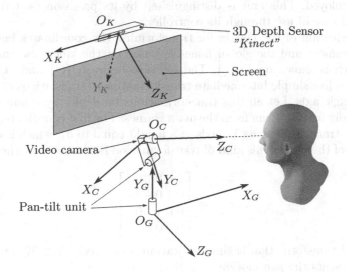

Fig. 3. System geometrical model

On Fig. 3 is depicted the common system geometrical model. The depth sensor and the video camera have their own coordinate frames denoted as

$\{K\} \equiv \{O_K X_K Y_K Z_K\}$ and $\{C\} \equiv \{O_C X_C Y_C Z_C\}$ respectively. $\{G\} \equiv \{O_G X_G Y_G Z_G\}$ is the fixed global coordinate frame which is used as a reference for the all other frames.

The transformation of the coordinates from one frame to another is realized by 4×4 homogeneous transformation matrices $T \in SE(3)$ [15]:

$$T = \begin{bmatrix} R & t \\ 0 & 1 \end{bmatrix}, \tag{1}$$

where R is the rotation matrix and t is the translation vector.

As can be seen from Fig. 1 and Fig. 3 there is no obvious relation between the global and the *"Kinect"*'s coordinate frames ($\{G\}$ and $\{K\}$) which can be expressed analytically as a transformation matrix. That's why a template based calibration procedure is performed to determine the transformation of the coordinates between these two coordinate frames and it is described below in Section 3.2. In contrast the relation between the frames of the telephoto camera $\{C\}$ and global frame $\{G\}$ is clear and it depends only on the pan and tilt angles (θ and ϕ respectively (Fig. 4)) and some physical dimensions. The derivation of this transformation is detailed in the following section.

3.1 Modeling Pan-Tilt Unit

For the aims of the project a pan tilt unit model PTU-D46-17 produced by the company Directed Perception (now known as FLIR Motion Control Systems, Inc.) is employed. This unit is distinguished by its precision ($\approx 0.01°$), build quality and ease of use through its controller.

The derivation of the matrix for transforming the coordinates between the telephoto camera and the global fames is based on the kinematic chain of the PTU, which is shown on Fig. 4. The relation between $\{C\}$ and $\{G\}$ can be expressed as five simple intermediate transformations - translations or rotations about a single axis. Let all this transformations be depict by a numeric index which will distinguish them from the main frames. The first coordinates transformation is a translation along Y_G axis at a height equal to h_1, which is a physical parameter of the PTU. This kind of transformation is expressed by the following matrix

$$T_{G \to 1} = \begin{bmatrix} 1 & 0 & 0 & 0 \\ 0 & 1 & 0 & -h_1 \\ 0 & 0 & 1 & 0 \\ 0 & 0 & 0 & 1 \end{bmatrix}. \tag{2}$$

The second transformation is simple rotation about axis $Y_1 \equiv Y_G$ by angle θ - which represents the *pan* motion

$$T_{1 \to 2} = \begin{bmatrix} cos(\theta) & 0 & sin(\theta) & 0 \\ 0 & 1 & 0 & 0 \\ -sin(\theta) & 0 & cos(\theta) & 0 \\ 0 & 0 & 0 & 1 \end{bmatrix}. \tag{3}$$

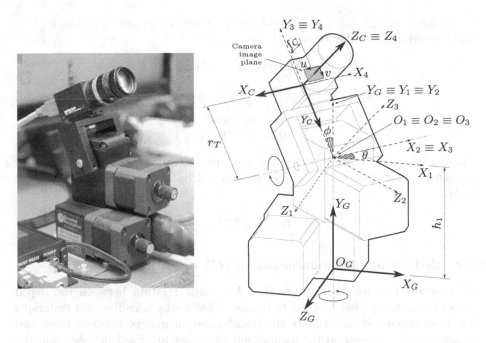

Fig. 4. Pan-tilt unit geometrical model

The third transformation is simple rotation about $X_2 \equiv X_3$ by angle ϕ - which represents the tilt motion of the PTU

$$T_{2 \to 3} = \begin{bmatrix} 1 & 0 & 0 & 0 \\ 0 & cos(\phi) & -sin(\phi) & 0 \\ 0 & sin(\phi) & cos(\phi) & 0 \\ 0 & 0 & 0 & 1 \end{bmatrix}. \tag{4}$$

The transformation from frame {3} and frame {4} is a translation along axis $Y_3 \equiv Y_4$ by the PTU eccentricity radius r_T

$$T_{3 \to 4} = \begin{bmatrix} 1 & 0 & 0 & 0 \\ 0 & 1 & 0 & -r_T \\ 0 & 0 & 1 & 0 \\ 0 & 0 & 0 & 1 \end{bmatrix}. \tag{5}$$

The final simple transformation consists of rotation about axis $Z_4 \equiv Z_G$ by π radians. This rotation is done to align the camera coordinate frame to the image coordinate frame - (u, v)

$$T_{4 \to C} = \begin{bmatrix} cos(\pi) & -sin(\pi) & 0 & 0 \\ sin(\pi) & cos(\pi) & 0 & 0 \\ 0 & 0 & 1 & 0 \\ 0 & 0 & 0 & 1 \end{bmatrix}. \tag{6}$$

By multiplying (2), (3), (4), (5) and (6) the geometrical model of the PTU is constructed and has the following form

$$T_{G \to C} = T_{4 \to C}.T_{3 \to 4}.T_{2 \to 3}.T_{1 \to 2}.T_{G \to 1} =$$

$$= \begin{bmatrix} -c_\theta & 0 & -s_\theta & 0 \\ -s_\theta s_\phi & -c_\phi & c_\theta s_\phi & r_T + h_1 c_\phi \\ -s_\theta c_\phi & s_\phi & c_\theta c_\phi & -h_1 s_\phi \\ 0 & 0 & 0 & 1 \end{bmatrix}, \tag{7}$$

where with s and c are depicted the sin and cos functions respectively. The reverse transformation $\{C\} \to \{G\}$ is achieved by inverting the shown above matrix

$$T_{C \to G} = T_{G \to C}^{-1}. \tag{8}$$

3.2 Estimating the Transformation $\{G\} \leftrightarrow \{K\}$

As mentioned above, there is no clear kinematic relation between the depth sensor's and the global coordinate frames. That's why a calibration technique has been developed to estimate the transformation matrix between these two frames, which is based on the assumption that they are fixed in space and the transformation between them is constant

$$T_{G \to K} = T_{K \to G}^{-1} = const. \tag{9}$$

As a calibration target the simple pattern shown on Fig. 5a was used. The algorithm for detecting such kind of targets is based on the marker detection technique from [1], but it has been modified and the target corner detection accuracy is improved to sub-pixel level. As can be seen from the figure, the calibration target consists of a black square and inscribed in it another white one. The algorithm [1] detects the contours of the squares and tracks them. As the calibration target is planar, its plane defines the XY plane of the 3D coordinate frame attached to it. The origin of this frame is placed in one of the corners of the inner (white) square defined by a little black marker (Fig. 5a).

In order to estimate the transformation matrix $T_{K \to G}$ the calibration target will be used as a reference coordinate frame which will give the relation between the two imaging devices. This means that the target should be present in the images of the two input devices during the calibration procedure. But this is a problem because their FOVs are completely different. That's why a combination of two calibration patterns with different sizes corresponding to the FOVs of the cameras are used. Their coordinate frames share common XY plane (Fig. 5b), thus the transformation between them is described as translation only

$$T_{t_K \to t_C} = \begin{bmatrix} 1 & 0 & 0 & -x_t \\ 0 & 1 & 0 & -y_t \\ 0 & 0 & 1 & 0 \\ 0 & 0 & 0 & 1 \end{bmatrix}, \tag{10}$$

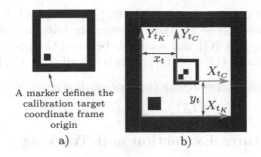

A marker defines the
calibration target
coordinate frame
origin

a)   b)

Fig. 5. Calibration target

where $\{t_K\}$ and $\{t_C\}$ are the coordinate frames of the two calibration target
- for *"Kinect"* and for telephoto video camera, x_t and y_t are the translations
between the two frames along the X and the Y axes (Fig. 5b). As the dimensions of the calibration target are known the pose of the cameras can be estimated with respect to the calibration target by employing an algorithm for
solving the *Perspective-n-Point* (PnP) problem. This will produce the transformation matrices $T_{t_K \to K}$ and $T_{t_C \to C}$. Such kind of algorithms like the iterative
method based on Levenberg-Marquardt optimization or the P3P solution in [5]
are implemented as C/C++ libraries and can be used for real-time applications.

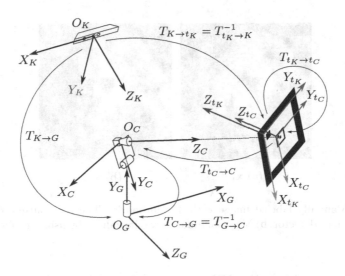

Fig. 6. Estimation of the $T_{G \to K}$ transformation matrix

On Fig. 6 is shown the scheme for estimating the transformation between
the $\{K\}$ and $\{G\}$. From the figure it is obvious that $T_{K \to G}$ can be expressed as
four consequential transformations of the coordinates: 1. between the *"Kinect"*'s

frame to the frame of its calibration pattern ($\{K\} \rightarrow \{t_K\}$), 2. between the two calibration patterns ($\{t_k\} \rightarrow \{t_C\}$), 3. between the telephoto camera calibration and its pattern $\{t_C\} \rightarrow \{C\}$ and finally 4. between the active camera and the global coordinate frame ($\{C\} \rightarrow \{G\}$). This is described by the following product

$$
\begin{aligned}
T_{K \rightarrow G} &= T_{C \rightarrow G}.T_{t_C \rightarrow C}.T_{t_K \rightarrow t_C}.T_{K \rightarrow t_K} = \\
&= T_{G \rightarrow C}^{-1}.T_{t_C \rightarrow C}.T_{t_K \rightarrow t_C}.T_{t_K \rightarrow K}^{-1}.
\end{aligned}
\tag{11}
$$

4   Facial Features Extraction and Tracking

The gaze direction estimations relies on detection of the eye corners positions and the head pose (Section 6). The positions of the eye corners are estimated by employing a modern optimization technique, called SDM (Supervised Decent Method), for aligning a face model, consisting of 48 landmarks, to a face image [19]. The main advantage of the SDM is that during the optimization process none of the Jacobian and Hessian is calculated (in contrast with the Newton's optimization methods), which could be computationally expensive. This is achieved by learning a series of decent directions and re-scaling factors such that a sequence of updates of the optimized function produced starting from the initial face model state ($\mathbf{x}_0$) that converges to the manually aligned face model ($\mathbf{x}_*$) in the training data (Fig. 7). The $\mathbf{x}_0$ are the landmarks positions of the mean face given by a face detector algorithm [17] (Fig. 7b). After aligning the face model to the image of the face, the head pose is estimated.

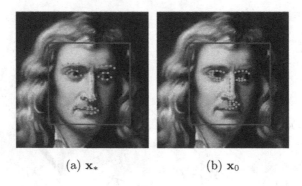

(a) $\mathbf{x}_*$ (b) $\mathbf{x}_0$

Fig. 7. a) Manually labeled image with 48 landmarks. The blue outline depicts the result of the face detector. b) Mean landmarks, $\mathbf{x}_0$, initialized by using the face detector. [19].

Since each pixel from the RGB camera of the *"Kinect"* has a corresponding point from the point-cloud array of the same device, the 2D locations of the eyes, estimated as a mean of the eye landmarks positions, are directly converted into 3D location in the $\{K\}$ coordinate frame. By using (11) they can be transformed into coordinates of the global frame $\{G\}$. Thus the PTU active camera can be navigated to track the location of one of the eye with the help of (7).

5   Pupil Detection and Tracking

Pupil detection and tracking is realized by the means of a Particle Filter (PF). Particularly the pupil's contour is modeled as an ellipse which parameters represent the system (PF) state vector $\mathbf{x}$ (Fig. 8a) [3]

$$\mathbf{x} = [c_x, c_y, \lambda_1, \lambda_2, \theta], \tag{12}$$

where c_x and c_y are the coordinates of the ellipse center, λ_1 and λ_2 are the big and the small ellipse axes and θ is the rotation angle of the contour. The system state evolves according to the following law

$$\mathbf{x}_{t+1} = \mathbf{x}_t + \boldsymbol{\nu}_t, \ \boldsymbol{\nu}_t \sim N(0, \boldsymbol{\Sigma}_t), \tag{13}$$

where $\boldsymbol{\nu}_t$ is a normally distributed random variable and $\boldsymbol{\Sigma}_t$ is a time dependent covariance matrix. The observation is realized with so called Measurement Lines (ML), depicted with blue color on Fig. 8a.

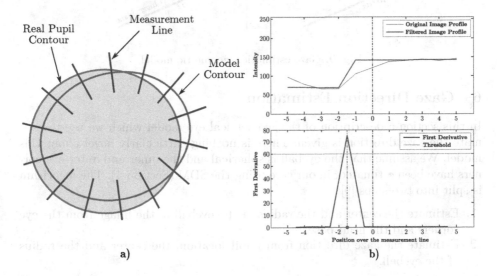

Fig. 8. Pupil detection and tracking with optimized Particle Filter

To decrease the required number of particles and improving the accuracy for contour parameters estimation an optimization stage is implemented as a combination of EM and 1-dimensional MeanShift algorithm (Fig. 8b) [3]. Thus the image intensity profile along a ML is filtered and the pupil contour boundary is underlined, which makes its detection much more robust.

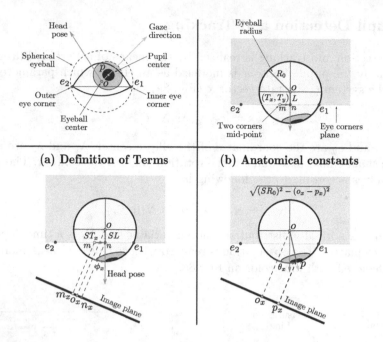

Fig. 9. Gaze estimation geometric model

6   Gaze Direction Estimation

In this section a description of the geometrical eye model which we use to estimate the gaze direction is given. There is nothing particularly novel about this model. We assume that the eyeball is spherical and the inner and outer eye corners have been estimated, in our case using the SDM (Section 4). The algorithm is split into two steps [9]:

1. Estimate the center and the radius of the eyeball in the image from the eye corners and the head pose.
2. Estimate the gaze direction from pupil location, the center and the radius of the eyeball.

The first of these two steps requires the following anatomical constants (Fig. 9):

- R_0 : The radius of the eyeball in the image when the scale of the face is 1.
- (T_x, T_y) : The offset in the image between the mid-point of the two eye corners and the center of the eyeball.
- L : The depth of the center of the eyeball relative to the plane containing the eye corners.

7   Experimental Results

On Fig. 10 is shown an example of aligning a face model to an actual face in the RGB image from *"Kinect"* sensor. By using the information about the eyes

Fig. 10. Demonstration of aligning a model to an image of a face from the RGB camera of *"Kinect"* sensor by the means of the SDM optimization algorithm. Consequentially by taking the information of the locations of the eyes in the image and applying it to the depth map of the *"Kinect"* the 3D coordinates of them are estimated in the $\{K\}$ frame.

locations in the color image their 3D position can be estimated by applying this information to the depth map of the sensor. Thus the PTU is directed to one of the eyes and the gaze direction is estimated by the technique described in Section 6.

The estimated gaze direction estimation accuracy is 1.67°.

Acknowledgments. This work was sponsored by the Ministry of Education and Science of Bulgaria, National Foundation "Science and Research", Slovenian-Bulgarian R&D joint project, NSF Grant DNTS/Slovenia 01/08 – Fast and Reliable 3D Face Recognition.

References

1. Marker detector with opencv (June 2013). https://sites.google.com/site/playwithopencv/home/markerdetect
2. Baluja, S., Pomerleau, D.: Non-intrusive gaze tracking using artificial neural networks. Tech. rep, Pittsburgh, PA, USA (1994)
3. Boumbarov, O., Panev, S., Sokolov, S., Kanchev, V.: Ir based pupil tracking using optimized particle filter. In: IEEE International Workshop on IDAACS 2009 Intelligent Data Acquisition and Advanced Computing Systems: Technology and Applications, pp. 404–408 (September 2009)
4. Bulling, A., Ward, J., Gellersen, H., Troster, G.: Eye movement analysis for activity recognition using electrooculography. Pattern Analysis and Machine Intelligence, IEEE Transactions on 33(4), 741–753 (2011)
5. Gao, sX, Hou, X.R., Tang, J., Cheng, H.F.: Complete solution classification for the perspective-three-point problem. IEEE Transactions on Pattern Analysis and Machine Intelligence 25(8), 930–943 (2003)

6. Hansen, D., Hansen, J., Nielsen, M., Johansen, A., Stegmann, M.: Eye typing using markov and active appearance models. In: Proceedings on Sixth IEEE Workshop on Applications of Computer Vision (WACV 2002). pp. 132–136 (2002)
7. Hansen, D., Ji, Q.: In the eye of the beholder: A survey of models for eyes and gaze. Pattern Analysis and Machine Intelligence, IEEE Transactions on 32(3), 478–500 (2010)
8. Hutchinson, T., White, Jr., K.P., Martin, W.N., Reichert, K., Frey, L.: Human-computer interaction using eye-gaze input. IEEE Transactions on Systems, Man and Cybernetics 19(6), 1527–1534 (1989)
9. Ishikawa, T., Baker, S., Matthews, I., Kanade, T.: Passive driver gaze tracking with active appearance models. Tech. Rep. CMU-RI-TR-04-08, Robotics Institute, Pittsburgh, PA (February 2004)
10. Jacob, R.J.K.: What you look at is what you get: Eye movement-based interaction techniques. In: Proceedings of the SIGCHI Conference on Human Factors in Computing Systems, pp. 11–18. ACM, New York (1990)
11. Khosravi, M.H., Safabakhsh, R.: Human eye sclera detection and tracking using a modified time-adaptive self-organizing map. Pattern Recognition 41(8), 2571–2593 (2008)
12. Kumar, M., Garfinkel, T., Boneh, D., Winograd, T.: Reducing shoulder-surfing by using gaze-based password entry. In: Proceedings of the 3rd Symposium on Usable Privacy and Security, pp. 13–19. ACM, New York (2007)
13. Kumar, M., Paepcke, A., Winograd, T.: Eyepoint: Practical pointing and selection using gaze and keyboard. In: Proceedings of the SIGCHI Conference on Human Factors in Computing Systems, pp. 421–430. CHI '07, ACM, New York, NY (2007)
14. Kumar, M., Winograd, T.: Gaze-enhanced scrolling techniques. In: Proceedings of the 20th Annual ACM Symposium on User Interface Software and Technology, pp. 213–216. UIST 2007, ACM, New York, NY, USA (2007)
15. Spong, M., Hutchinson, S., Vidyasagar, M.: Robot Modeling and Control. Wiley (2006)
16. Tan, K.H., Kriegman, D., Ahuja, N.: Appearance-based eye gaze estimation. In: Proceedings of Sixth IEEE Workshop on Applications of Computer Vision (WACV 2002), pp. 191–195 (2002)
17. Viola, P., Jones, M.J.: Robust real-time face detection. Int. J. Comput. Vision 57(2), 137–154 (2004)
18. Williams, O., Blake, A., Cipolla, R.: Sparse and semi-supervised visual mapping with the s³gp. In: Proceedings of the 2006 IEEE Computer Society Conference on Computer Vision and Pattern Recognition CVPR 2006, vol. 1, pp. 230–237. IEEE Computer Society, Washington, DC (2006)
19. Xiong, X., de la Torre, F.: Supervised descent method and its applications to face alignment. In: 2013 IEEE Conference on Computer Vision and Pattern Recognition (CVPR), pp. 532–539 (June 2013)

Handwriting and Signature Recognition

Effect of Handwriting Changes on the Possibilities for Computerized Handwriting Examination

Dobrin Nestorov[✉] and Detelina Georgieva

Research Institute of Forensic Science and Criminology (RIFSC) – MoI, Sofia, Bulgaria
dobrin_nestorov@abv.bg

Introduction

The long research studies on the use of computer technology to decipher and determine the individual characteristics of handwriting have led to progress in some trends and set limits in others. At present the products for handwriting recognition and its conversion into printed text are widespread and easily accessible. There is a large number of programs which cope with the task to verify the author in a satisfactory way. It is possible to introduce and make use of enough handwriting features which are calculable and may serve as reliable criteria when the author of a particular writing is automatically confirmed or rejected.

However, the use of computer programs in the process of the forensic comparative handwriting analysis with the purpose of identifying the author remains a problem.

In one case when it comes to confirmation, there is a comparison of a specimen and on-line or off-line handwriting made under the same conditions with the help of the author and it is possible to make use of calculable features. In the case of identification the comparison is made between the questioned off-line handwriting and the comparative material. In most cases they are not made under the same conditions and the author tries to prevent the identification, so the calculable features proved to be not insufficient.

Why Identification May Be Impeded in Case of Comparing only Quantitative Handwriting Parameters?

The handwriting characteristics determining its individual nature are formed as a deviation of the handwriting standard. They may be quantitative and qualitative. This depends on the fact whether the author has adopted and acquired as a habit the writing of the handwriting characters with some deviations in calculable parameters as for example the quantity of the movements made (Fig. 1) or in qualitative ones as the sequence of movements (Fig. 2).

There are deviations in both cases. They represent structures which are individual for the particular person. The question however is which are the more stable features regarding the formation of the individual complex of peculiarities rarely displayed.

In order to be able to answer this question we have to start from the fact that unlike the fingerprint, the iris structure, the DNA profile, etc., the handwriting is changeable. The character is not constant and it can vary under the influence of inner factors like the changing environment in which the handwriting character appears (Fig. 3).

© Springer International Publishing Switzerland 2014
V. Cantoni et al. (Eds.): BIOMET 2014, LNCS 8897, pp. 191–197, 2014.
DOI: 10.1007/978-3-319-13386-7_15

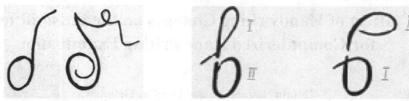

Fig. 1. The models according to the Bulgarian handwriting standards are to the left and the deviations - to the right

Fig. 2. According to the standard for the Bulgarian letter "в" the upper element should be written first and then the lower, but in practice it is possible for the sequence to be changed, which is an example for rare deviation with a strong identification value.

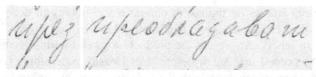

Fig. 3. Different variants of the same Bulgarian letter "р" are found in a particular handwriting depending on the different surrounding characters

There are also external factors influencing the handwriting and they are:

- the conditions of writing;
- the mental status during writing;
- illness or intoxication which influence the nervous and musculoskeletal system participating in the writing process.

The practice shows that under the influence of these factors the quantitative handwriting features are subject to more changes than the qualitative ones. The reason for this is that the latter are related more closely to the subconscious nature of the handwriting process as a type of dynamic stereotype.

This determines also the problems connected with the use of computer and statistical methods in the identification handwriting analysis. No matter whether we work with text-dependent or text-independent methods of extracting features the results [5, 6, 7] show the percentage of faults of acceptance and faults of rejection which, in practice, cannot be used as a ground for drawing a definite conclusion as a court evidence. In fact the given example indicating the sequence of movements in writing a particular character (Fig. 2), illustrates the limitation resulting from the fact that it is very difficult to introduce criteria for determining how to trace and calculate this sequence excluding the observation made by an experienced expert.

Effect of the Handwriting Changes on Its Quantitative and Qualitative Features

The collection and analysis of experimental data is the only way to evaluate the degree and the trend of influence of the changes on the handwriting features which characterize the handwriting as an individual biometrical indicator.

Without claiming for a big representativeness we made experiments which gave us an initial idea about the effect of the changes. We gave 50 students who had relatively high writing practices the following tasks: to write under dictation in Bulgarian Cyrillic alphabet the same text in normal posture – seated and in the non-standard and more inconvenient posture – standing (Fig. 4 and Fig. 5).

Fig. 4.   **Fig. 5.**

The purpose was to determine the effect of the undeliberate changes, which are not isolated phenomena in the writing practices, on the handwriting features.

First, the changes concerning the main handwriting features with quantitative character were reported and analyzed. These features included level of junction, size, slant, stretching, quantity of movements, movement orientation[1]. After comparing the results obtained from writing in the normal seated posture and in the standing posture it was found that the participants in the experiment changed the said features when writing in the standing posture and the number/percentage of the participants making such changes is given in the diagram below (Fig. 6).

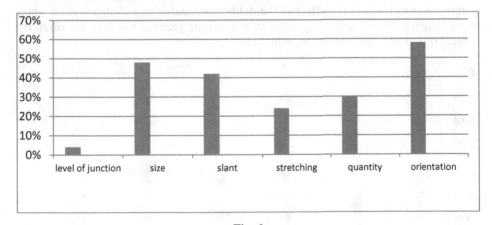

Fig. 6.

---

[1] Calculable by comparing the movement coordinates on the surface area.

It turned out that the most reliable feature is the level of junction. Only 4% of the participants made some changes in this feature. As far as the other features were concerned most of the participants made changes in them. The most significant changes were found in the movement orientation - 58% of the participants and in the size of the writing characters - 48% of the participants.

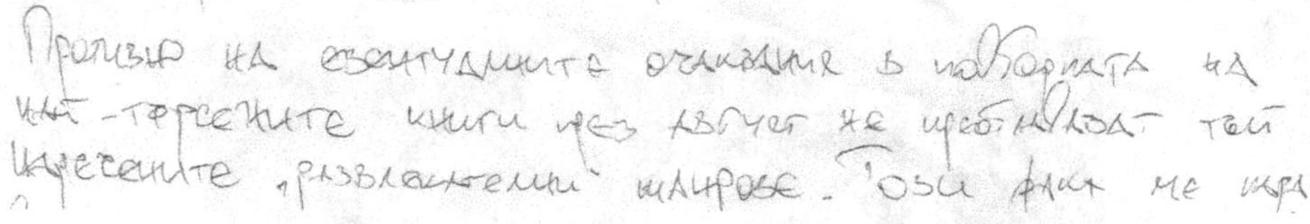

Fig. 7. Handwriting in a seated posture

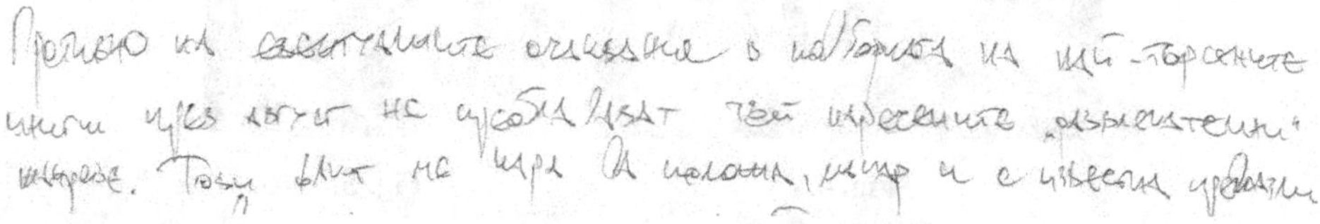

Fig. 8. Handwriting of the same person in a standing posture

As can be seen from the examples above (Fig. 7 and Fig. 8) the quantitative features size and orientation are changed when writing in a standing posture but there are no significant changes in the qualitative ones. All typical ways of writing any particular handwriting character are kept. Thus, for example, the form, the direction, the sequence and the structural complexity of the letter "a" remain unchanged.

In order to make the experiment more extensive the participants were given also another task - to try to change the typical features of their handwriting in such a way that it will prevent their identification as authors of the particular handwriting. The purpose was to find out the effect of the deliberate handwriting changes. As a whole these changes do not occur very often in the writing practice but they are often the subject of forensic handwriting examination.

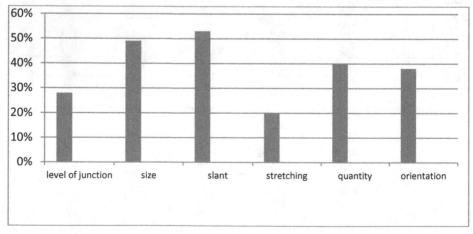

Fig. 9.

The results proved the observations from our expert practice showing that in trying to deliberately change their handwriting the people make changes in all quantitative features and mostly in the slant and the size.

As far as the qualitative features were concerned we got the following results:

    1. Insignificant changes (Fig. 10 and Fig. 11);

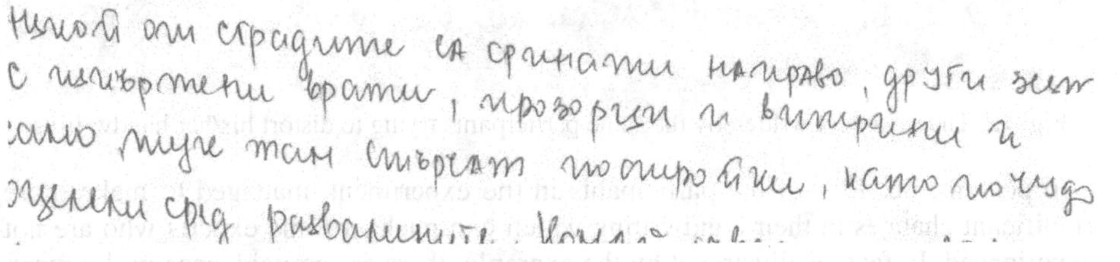

Fig. 10. A text written without trying to distort the handwriting

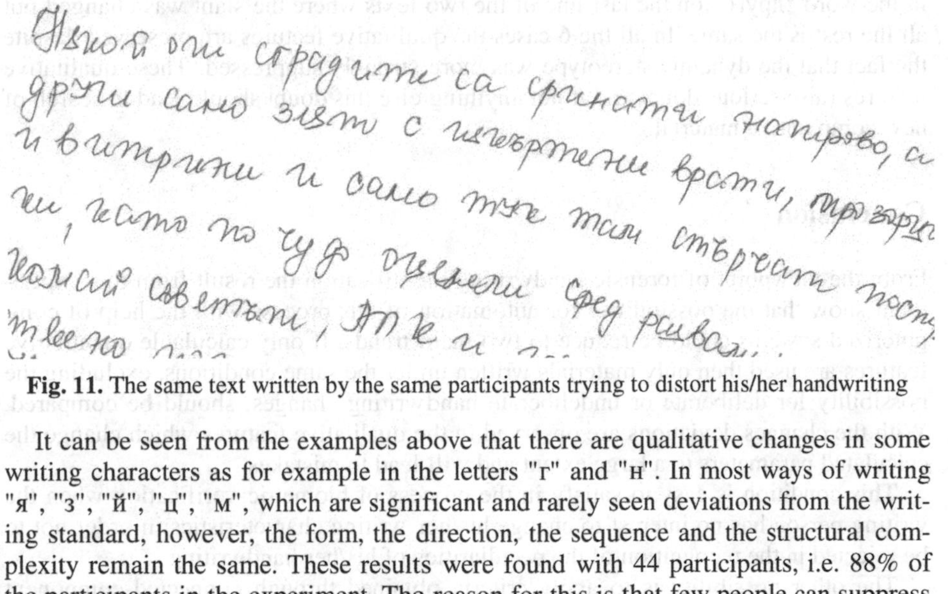

Fig. 11. The same text written by the same participants trying to distort his/her handwriting

It can be seen from the examples above that there are qualitative changes in some writing characters as for example in the letters "г" and "н". In most ways of writing "я", "з", "й", "ц", "м", which are significant and rarely seen deviations from the writing standard, however, the form, the direction, the sequence and the structural complexity remain the same. These results were found with 44 participants, i.e. 88% of the participants in the experiment. The reason for this is that few people can suppress their dynamic stereotype more strongly in order to distort it.

    2. Significant changes (Fig. 12 and Fig. 13).

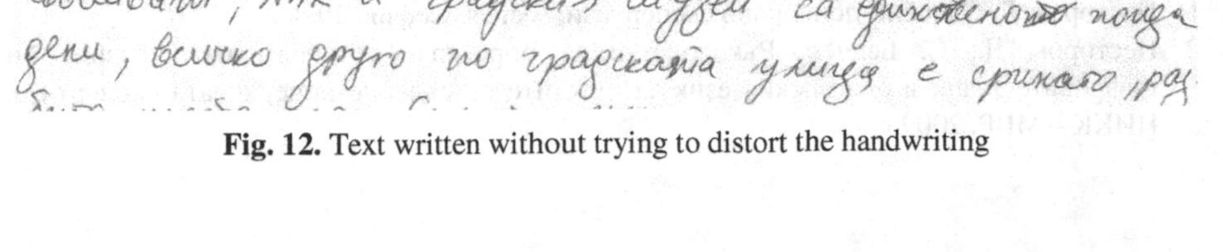

Fig. 12. Text written without trying to distort the handwriting

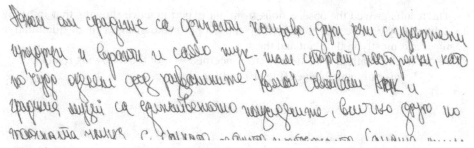

Fig. 13. The same text written by the same participants trying to distort his/her handwriting

6 persons, i.e. 12% of the participants in the experiment, managed to make more significant changes in their handwriting which can mislead some experts who are not experienced. In fact, as illustrated by the example, there are coincidences in the form, the direction, the sequence and the structural complexity despite the good disguise as in the word "друго" on the last line of the two texts where the slant was changed but all the rest is the same. In all the 6 cases the qualitative features are preserved despite the fact that the dynamic stereotype was more strongly suppressed. These qualitative features raise serious doubt and if not anything else this doubt should lead to search of new comparative material.

Conclusion

From the viewpoint of forensic handwriting identification the result from this experiment show that the possibilities for automation of this process with the help of computerized systems could be reduce to two main trends. If only calculable quantitative features are used then only materials written under the same conditions, excluding the possibility for deliberate or undeliberate handwriting changes, should be compared. With the changes deviations are observed in the qualitative features which change the calculated parameters to a large extent and will lead to mistakes.

This condition is easy to satisfy in the process of biometric verification when the writing person has no interest to change his/her writing characteristics in order not to be rejected in the recognition of the peculiarities of his/her handwriting.

The other possibility is to apply criteria obtained through connected-component contours, edge-based features [7] or other similar methods to interpret the qualitative handwriting features which however are more reliable. This concerns mainly the possibility to make use of such automated systems in the process of forensic identification by comparing materials with possible changes because there is a big percentage of fault of acceptance or fault of rejection in such computer guided methods.

References

1. Несторов, Д. Съдебно-почеркови експертизи, Фенея, София, 2014 г
2. Несторов, Д., С. Бенчев, Ръководство за определяне строежа на буквените и цифровите знаци в българския език за нуждите на съдебно-почерковата експертиза, НИКК – МВР, 2009 г

3. Глухчев, Г., В. Шапиро. Автоматизирано изследване на ръкописни символи, сп. Съдебна медицина и криминалистика, бр. 5, 1989 г
4. Несторов, Д., С. Бенчев, С. Бончев, Г. Глухчев. АБВ – Компютърна система за статистическа оценка на частните идентификационни признаци при криминалис тическо изследване на почерка, Кибернетика и информационни технологии, ИИТ – БАН, кн. I, 2008 г
5. Wang, H., Liu, G., Ke, H.: An Improved Direction Index Histogram Handwriting Identification Method. Advanced Materials Research **846–847**, 1230–1233 (2014)
6. Bensefia, A., Paquet, T., Heutte, L.: A Writer Identification and Verification System. Patern Recognition Letters **26**(10), 2080–2092 (2005)
7. Schomaker, L., Bulacu, M.: Automatic Writer Identification Using Connected-component Contours and Edge-based Features of Uppercase Western Script. IEEE Trans on PAM **26**(6), 787–798 (2004)
8. Nestorov, D., Benchev, S., Bonchev, S., Kostashki, R., Gluhchev, G.A.: Computer System for Graphometric Handwriting Analysis, International Conference on Computer Systems and Technologies, Rousse, Bulgaria, 18–19 (June 2009)

Neural Network and kNN Classifiers
for On-line Signature Verification

Desislava Boyadzieva[✉] and Georgi Gluhchev

IICT-BAS, Acad. G. Bonchev St., Block 25A, Sofia, 1113, Bulgaria
d.n.dimitrova@gmail.com, gluhchev@iinf.bas.bg

Abstract. In this paper a method for on-line signature verification is presented. The proposed approach consists of the following consecutive steps: feature selection and classification. Experiments are carried out on SUsig database [5] of genuine and forgery signatures of 89 users. The results obtained by applying two different types of classifiers (NN and k-nearest neighbours) are compared. For each user, several NN and kNN models are evaluated by 10-fold cross validation and LOOCV respectively. The "optimal" models are found together with their parameters: number of hidden neurons for NN, type of signature forgeries for training, input features and value of k. The influence of the signature forgery type (random and skilled) over the feature selection and verification is investigated as well.

Keywords: On-line signature verification · Neural networks (NNs) · Signature features · Feature selection · SUsig database · Mallows Cp · k-nearest neighbours (kNN) · N-fold cross validation · Leave one out cross validation (LOOCV)

1   Introduction

Signature recognition is the process of confirming the identity based on the handwritten signature of the user as a form of behavioral biometrics [1]. From one hand, the signatures are a convenient, widely used and secure mean for authentication, and from the other, their input to biometric systems is fast, easy, natural and non-invasive. For these reasons, the problem of the signature verification is broadly investigated in the past years. Novel methods and algorithms are developed, mostly for on-line signatures, and lots of them are implemented in practice [1, 2, 3, 4, 16, 17].

Signature recognition systems are on-line and off-line depending on the acquisition method. The off- line method uses a captured image of a written signature after the writing process is over while the on-line method uses devices such as graphical tablets to capture signature during signing and thus a lot of writer specific features like pressure, speed, pen tilt, azimuth, etc. are available.

In this paper we propose an approach to signature verification and present the results obtained on SUsig database [5]. The values of 24 global features are evaluated for each user. Since some of the features are interconected, to discard the less informative of them, feature space reduction is achieved applying consecutevely the

© Springer International Publishing Switzerland 2014
V. Cantoni et al. (Eds.): BIOMET 2014, LNCS 8897, pp. 198–206, 2014.
DOI: 10.1007/978-3-319-13386-7_16

method of correlation pleiads [12], and   Mallows Cp criterion [10, 11] for selection of regression variables. Thus, for each user in the database an individual set of features is obtained. Next, several NN and kNN models for verification are constructed and tested. At last, we train, validate and test all the chosen user's models and obtain the average accuracy.

The paper is organized as follows: in Section 2 a brief overview over the proposed methodology is given, the experimental results are presented and discussed in Section 3, and finally Section 4 draws the conclusion and points out directions for further investigation.

2   Methodology

The development of a particular signature recognition system consists of the following steps [6]: signature acquisition, preprocessing, feature extraction, feature selection, verification and accuracy estimation. Below we shall describe our method in the terms of these steps.

Table 1. Global features

A1	Signature length L	A13	Angle of the line between initial and end points
A2	Signature height H	A14	Distance between leftmost and center points
A3	Height to width ratio H/L	A15	Distance between center and rightmost points
A4	Number of points N	A16	Angle of the line between center and leftmost points
A5	Time duration	A17	Angle of the line between center and rightmost points
A6	Number of segments	A18	Distance between leftmost and initial points
A7	Signature density $A4/A1*A2$	A19	Distance between rightmost and end points
A8	Distance between initial and center point	A20	Angle of the line between leftmost and initial points
A9	Distance between end and center point	A21	Angle of the line between end and rightmost points
A10	Distance between initial and end point	A22	Number of strokes
A11	Angle of the line between center and initial points	A23	Average tilt
A12	Angle of the line between center and end points	A24	Average pressure

1. *Signature acquisition*: Signature data is acquired by a graphical tablet (*Wacom Graphire2*). Raw data consist of the following information about each signature point: *x* and *y* coordinates, pressure level, timestamp, stroke indicator.

2. *Signature preprocessing*: To facilitate feature extraction, it is necessary the raw data to be preprocessed. The operations applied depend on the selected features and the acquisition protocol. The coordinates *x* and *y* of the ink coordinate space are called *himetric* units [7] and their values fall in [0, 7999] x [0, 5999]. It is necessary to transform them in the application coordinate system in [0, 1279] x [0,799]. This is performed automatically by a method from *Microsoft Tablet PC SDK*. Since the acquired signatures may be rotated, we have to align them horizontally. The next pre-processing operation is translation of the signatures to a given point of the application coordinate system because it is possible some of the coordinates to obtain negative values after rotation. So the following operations are performed to all the signature data in the databases: coordinate transformation, rotation and translation.

3. *Feature extraction:* There are three groups of signature features: global, local and segmental [8]. Global features are extracted for the whole signature, local features are extracted for each sample point in the signature, and segmental features are extracted for each signature segment. Over 100 features used in signature verification are listed in [9]. The extracted global signature features used are presented in Table 1.

4. *Feature set selection:* Since some features demonstrate higher discriminatory capability than others, feature selection should be performed. This is related to the process of selecting *k* features of most discrimination power out of *p* available ones ($k \leq p$) and it aims to identify and remove as much irrelevant and redundant information as possible. A review of the processes of feature set selection for signatures is done in [8].

We approach feature set selection step in signature verification in two ways (1) by using a common feature subset for all users, and   (2) by using an individual feature subset for each user.

At the beginning we extract all the signature features for all database users and we perform z-score feature normalization. We find all high correlated features at 0.01 confidence level, 99% confidence interval, met in more than 25% of the users. We use Pearson correlation coefficient. By applying the correlation pleiads method [12] we identify all groups (pleiads) of features having high intraclass correlation and low interclass correlation and leave only one random feature in a group. For each pleiad we retain only one feature.   In this way we create the common feature subset.

In order to find individual feature subset for each user we apply the methods of Hocking, Leslie and LaMotte for selection of regression variables based on Mallows Cp criterion for regression [10, 11] on the already found common feature subset. This criterion is used to decide on suitable subset among contending subsets. It is a measure of the standardized total squared error defines as follows:

$$C_p = \frac{RSS_p}{\hat{\sigma}^2} - (n - 2p) \tag{1}$$

Here RSS_p denotes the residual sum of squares for the particular regression with p variables and $\hat{\sigma}^2$ is an estimate of residual mean square σ^2 for full regression.

$$\hat{\sigma}^2 = \frac{1}{n-k}\sum_{j=1}^{n}(y_j - \sum_{i=1}^{k}\beta_i x_{ij})^2 = \frac{RSS_k}{n-k} \qquad (2)$$

If a model is adequate, i.e. does not suffer from lack of fit, then

$$E(C_p) \approx p \qquad (3)$$

This means that we expect Cp value to be about p. A plot of Cp versus p displays the adequate models as points close to the line Cp = p. Subsets with small values of Cp and values of Cp close to p are considered good. Hocking and Leslie [10] further describe a method which allows thus subset to be identified after consideration of only a small fraction of all $\binom{k}{p}$ possible subsets of size p. LaMotte and Hocking [11] modified this algorithm in a way that moderately large problems can be treated with minimum of computation. The algorithm specifies the subset of size r to be deleted. In the following, the terms r-subset and p-subset refer, respectively, to subsets being deleted and subsets being retained. The method for selection of best subset is based on m-variable reductions,i.e. reductions in the regression sum of squares due to eliminating subsets of size m from the k-variable equation. Typically $1 \le m \le 4$ and m = 1 in the original method [10]. These m-variable reductions are used to determine the best r-subset to be removed, for r > m. The reduction in the regression sum of squares due to removing a set of r variables is given by:

$$Red_r = RSS_p - RSS_k \qquad (4)$$

The set of r variables for which this reduction is minimum specifies the subset of size p (p = k - r) variables in the regression to be retained for which residual sum of squares is minimum. It is suggested in [10] that Cp statistic can also be computed by using this reduction in the following way:

$$C_p = \frac{Red_r}{\hat{\sigma}^2} - (2p - k) \qquad (5)$$

The steps of the generalized algorithm can be found in [11].

By applying the methods of Hocking, Leslie and LaMotte we identify best feature subsets of various size for each user on the basis of his/her eight or ten genuine signatures and ten random forgeries. Among these subsets we select the best subset that have Cp value closest to p, but smaller than p, where p is the number of regression coefficients. Thus, for each user we obtain the best feature subset of different size.

5. *Verification*: Neural networks are suitable to be used for signature verification since they are an excellent generalization tool (under normal conditions) and are a useful means of coping with the diversity and variations inherent in handwritten signatures [13]. Usually, a particular NN is built for each user on the basis of his/her genuine and forgery signatures. The number of input neurons is p where p is the number of the features. The single output neuron has a value 1 for genuine

signature and a value 0 for forgery signature. After the training, a score threshold is determined. If the verification result (at the time of testing of a signature) is greater than the corresponding score threshold, the signature is considered genuine, otherwise – forgery. This approach is widespread because it allows fast adding and deleting of signatures for new and existing users [13]. Usually, NN training takes lots of time but in this approach it is done off-line so the users are not forced to wait.

We compare NN classifiers with kNN classifiers with Euclidean distance. Before applying the kNN classifier, we first normalize the features. Since $k_{max} = \sqrt{Ntrn}$, where $Ntrn$ is the number of signatures used for training and it is recommended for the value of k to be an odd number, we choose k= 1 and k = 3.

For each user, several NN and kNN models are evaluated by 10-fold cross validation and LOOCV respectively. The "optimal" models are found together with their parameters: number of hidden neurons for NN, type of signature forgeries for training, input features and value of k.

After finding the "optimal" model of a classifier by cross validation, the corresponding classifier is being trained on all the user's signatures and is ready to be used for verification.

6. *Accuracy estimation:* The performances of classifiers are evaluated by the following well known metrics: FAR (false accept rate), FRR (false reject rate), TAR (true accept rate), TRR (true reject rate), and Accuracy.

3   Experimental Results

Experiments are carried out in MATLAB environment. We use *Neural Network Toolbox*. Tablet PC SDK 1.7 [15] is used to facilitate signature acquisition. Raw and transformed signature data is stored in a database in SQL Server Compact Edition 2008. We experiment with two types of classifiers: NN and kNN with varying parameters values (number of features, forgery signature types, number of hidden neurons H and number of neighbors' k). Since we have small amount of data, we evaluate classifier accuracy with N-fold cross validation [14]. We use 10-fold CV for NN parameters tuning and LOOCV for kNN parameters tuning.

Let us denote by *Var.1* the case in which feature subset is determined by using the genuine and random forgery signatures and denote by *Var.2* the case in which feature subset is determined by using the genuine and skilled forgery signatures. Let us denote by *Case 1* the case in which only random forgeries are used for NN training, and denote by *Case 2* the case in which both random and skilled forgeries are used.

Signature database SUsig [5] consists of genuine signatures, skilled and random forgeries of 89 users. By applying the method of correlation pleiads, the initial number of features - 24, is reduced by around 50% and the remaining features are A1, A2, A4, A6, A10, A12, A13, A16, A17, A21, A22, A23, A24.

The size of the obtained p-subset and the corresponding number of users are specified in Table 2. There is a significant reduction in features number for both Var.1 and

Var.2 since its initial number - 13 is reduced down to 9 for about half of the users, reduced down to 5 or 6 features for 30% of the users.

Table 2. Individual p-subsets

Var.	Size of p-subset	Number of users	Var.	Size of p-subset	Number of users
1	9	42	2	9	48
1	8	5	2	8	9
1	7	7	2	7	4
1	6	12	2	6	10
1	5	14	2	5	15
1	4	5	2	4	3
1	3	4	2	3	0

Table 3. Parameters of the NN models

# of model	Features (input neurons)	Genuine signatures	Forgery signatures		Number of hidden neurons H	Number of neighbors k
1	Common set		15 random	Case 1		
2	Var. 1					
3	Var. 2	8 or 10			1 to 5	1 or 3
4	Var. 2		9 random and 6 skilled	Case 2		
5	*Var. 1*					
6	Common set					

In Table 3, all the NN and kNN models are described together with their parameters. All the 30 NN models are evaluated by 10-fold cross validation for each user and the best performed "optimal" NN model is selected together with its parameters: number of hidden neurons, type of signature forgeries for training and input features. All the 12 kNN models are evaluated by LOOCV and the best performed "optimal" kNN model is selected together with its parameters: value of k, type of signature forgeries for training and input features.

The average estimated accuracy of the "optimal" NN models for all users is equal to 97.95%, and the average estimated accuracy of the "optimal" kNN models for all users is equal to 96.13%. These results demonstrate the advantage of the NN classifier over the kNN classifier. The value of t-statistics is equal to 3.29 and this value is significant for a probability level equal to 0.99 and DF=176. The average estimated accuracy for all the "optimal" models are presented in Table 4 for NN and in Table 5 for kNN.

Table 4. Average estimated accuracy for all the "optimal" models for NN

	Common feature set	Var. 1	Var. 2	Average accuracy	Number of occurances
Case 1	97.36 (Model #1,13 occurances)	98.36 (Model #2, 27 occurances)	97.85 (Model #3, 13 occurances)	97.99	53
Case 2	97.71 (Model #6, 11 occurances)	97.98 (Model #5, 9 occurances)	97.96 (Model #4, 16 occurances)	97.89	36
Average accuracy	97.52	98.27	97.91	-	-
Number of occurances	24	36	29	-	89

The data presented in Table 4 reveals higher NN accuracy if using individual feature subsets (Var. 1 and Var. 2) compared to the accuracy if using a common feature subset. The accuracy is slightly higher if Var. 1 is used. The accuracy of models built on Var. 1, Case 1 (random forgeries for training) suppresses the accuracy of models built on Var. 2, Case 2 (random and skilled forgeries for training).

The data presented in Table 5 reveals higher kNN accuracy if using a common feature subset compared to the accuracy if using individual feature subsets (Var. 1 and Var. 2). The accuracy of models built on Var. 2, Case 1 (random forgeries for training) suppresses the accuracy of models built on Var. 2, Case 2 (random and skilled forgeries for training).

Table 5. Average estimated accuracy for all the "optimal" models for kNN

	Common feature set	Var. 1	Var. 2	Average accuracy	Number of occurances
Case 1	100 (Model #1, 5 occurances)	95.92 (Model #2, 27 occurances)	97.84 (Model #3, 15 occurances)	96.97	[647
Case 2	84 (Model #6, 1 occurances)	95.5 (Model #5, 20 occurances)	95.45 (Model #4, 21 occurances)	95.20	42
Average accuracy	97.33	95.74	96.45	-	-
Number of occurances	6	47	36	-	89

The comparison between the average estimated accuracy of NN and kNN based on common and individual feature subsets demonstrate the advantage of NN.

The number of "optimal" models, trained on random forgeries (Case 1) is met in more than half of the users. It is equal to 53 (for 60% of the users) for NN and it is equal to 47 (for 53% of the users) for kNN. The most frequent "optimal" models are built on Var.1 features: for NN, it is equal to 36, and for kNN it is equal to 47.

NN and kNN classifiers are built for each user. They are evaluated on the same training (~70% of the signatures) and testing sets (~30% of the signatures). The following results are obtained: 1) for NN: average accuracy 98.46 %, 2.70 % FAR и 0 % FRR NN; 2) for kNN: average accuracy 89.47 %, 8.09 % FAR и 14.61 % FRR. These results demonstrate the aadvantage of NN over the kNN classifier. The value of t-statistic is equal to 5.98 and this value is significant for a probability level of 0.99.

For comparison, a classifier of Yanikoglu и Kholmatov [18] has 1.64% FRR и 1.28% FAR on the same signature database.

4 Conclusion

The following conclusions can be drawn from the presented experiments. First, the number of the features is reduced by around two times by consecutive applying of the method of correlation pleiads and Mallows Cp criterion for selection of regression variables. Second, there is not a common feature subset valid for all users; there is a specific feature subset for each user which describes his signature writing style. This subset consists of 3-5 features for some users. Third, the using of random forgeries as negative cases (*Var.1*) in regression model drives to greater reduction in feature number. Initial feature set size is reduced to a higher extend if random forgeries (*Var. 1*) are used for building the regression model for the Hocking, Leslie and LaMotte method instead of skilled forgeries. At last, the classifiers trained on only random forgeries (*Case 1*) gives better verification results than those trained on both random and skilled forgeries (*Case 2*).

Research and investigation in on-line signature recognition are about to continue in the future. They will be towards 1) improvement of the proposed system – its automation and accuracy; 2) testing of the system over different databases and other signature features; 3) forgery detection.

Acknowledgement. This research is (partly) supported by the project AComIn "Advanced Computing for Innovation", grant 316087, funded by the FP7 Capacity Programme (Research Potential of Convergence Regions).

References

1. Nalwa, V.S., Ekeland, I.: Automatic on-line signature verification. Proceedings of the IEEE **85**, 213–239 (1997)
2. Jain, A.: Stan Li. Springer, Encyclopedia of Biometrics (2009)
3. Gluhchev, G., Savov, M., Boumbarov, O., Vassileva, D.: A New Approach to Signature Based Authentication, 2nd Int. Conf. on Biometrics, Seoul, pp. 594–603 (August 26-29, 2007)
4. Savov, M., Gluhchev, G.: Signature verification via Hand-Pen motion investigation. In: Proc. Int. Conf. Recent Advances in Soft Computing, Canterbury, pp. 490–495 (2006)

5. Kholmatov, A., Yanikoglu B.: SUSIG: An on-line signature database, associated protocols and benchmark results. Pattern Analysis & Applications **12**, 227–236 (2009)

6. Plamondon, R., Lorette, G.: Automatic signature verification and writer identification – the state of the art. Pattern Recognition **22**, 107–131 (1989)

7. Ink Data. http://msdn.microsoft.com/en-us/library/ms811395.aspx

8. Richiardi, J., Ketabdar, H., Drygajlo, A.: In: Local and Global Feature Selection for On-line Signature Verification. - Eighth International Conference on Document Analysis and Recognition (ICDAR 2005), pp. 625–629 (2005)

9. Leclerc, F., Plamondon, R.: Automatic signature verification: the state of the art 1989-1993. International Journal of Pattern Recognition and Artificial Intelligence **8**(3), 643–660 (1994)

10. Hocking, R.R., Leslie, R.: Selection of the Best Subset in Regression Analysis. Technometrics **9**, 531–540 (1967)

11. LaMotte, L.R., Hocking, R.R.: Computational Efficiency in the Selection of Regression Variables. Technometrics **12**, 83–93 (1970)

12. Айвазян, С.А., Бежаева, З.И., Староверов, О.В.: Классификация многомерных наблюдений, Москва, Статистика, 240 стр. (1974)

13. McCabe, A., Trevathan, J., Read, W.: Neural network-based handwritten signature verification. Journal of Computers **3**(8), 9–22 (2008)

14. Duda, P.O., Hart, P.E.: Pattern Classification and Scene Analysis. Wiley, New York (1973)

15. Tablet PC SDK 1.7. http://www.microsoft.com/download/en/details.aspx?displaylang=en&id=20039

16. McCabe, A., Trevathan, J., Read, W.: Neural network-based handwritten signature verification. Journal of Computers **3**(8), 9–22 (2008)

17. Berrin, A.: Yanikoglu. Online Signature Verification Using Fourier Descriptors. EURASIP J. Adv. Sig. Proc, Alisher Kholmatov (2009)

18. Kholmatov, A., Yanikoglu, B.: Identity authentication using improved online signature verification method. Pattern Recognition Letters **26**(15), 2400–2408 (2005)

Multimodal and Soft Biometrics

People Identification
and Tracking Through Fusion of Facial
and Gait Features

Yu Guan[1], Xingjie Wei[1], Chang-Tsun Li[1(✉)], and Yosi Keller[2]

[1] Department of Computer Science, University of Warwick,
Coventry, CV4 7AL, UK
{g.yu,x.wei,c-t.li}@warwick.ac.uk

[2] Faculty of Engineering, Bar Ilan University, Ramat Gan 52900, Israel
yosi.keller@gmail.com

Abstract. This paper reviews the contemporary (face, gait, and fusion) computational approaches for automatic human identification at a distance. For remote identification, there may exist large intra-class variations that can affect the performance of face/gait systems substantially. First, we review the face recognition algorithms in light of factors, such as illumination, resolution, blur, occlusion, and pose. Then we introduce several popular gait feature templates, and the algorithms against factors such as shoe, carrying condition, camera view, walking surface, elapsed time, and clothing. The motivation of fusing face and gait, is that, gait is less sensitive to the factors that may affect face (e.g., low resolution, illumination, facial occlusion, etc.), while face is robust to the factors that may affect gait (walking surface, clothing, etc.). We review several most recent face and gait fusion methods with different strategies, and the significant performance gains suggest these two modality are complementary for human identification at a distance.

1 Introduction

Human identity recognition is fundamental to human life, and the technology of human identification and tracking from a distance may play an important role in crime prevention, law enforcement, search for missing people (e.g., missing children or people with dementia), etc. Nowadays, CCTV cameras are widely installed in public places such as airports, government buildings, streets and shopping malls for the afore-mentioned purposes. In 2013, the British Security Industry Authority (BSIA) estimated there are up to 5.9 million CCTV cameras nationwide, and that is around 1 every 11 people [11]. Because of the need for sufficient manpower to supervise such a large number of CCTVs, the need for automatic human identification systems is acute.

Out of various biometric traits (e.g., fingerprint, iris, palmprint, voice, face, gait, etc.), face recognition is deemed as one of the most popular one, which can be performed at a distance without subject's cooperation. CCTV footage or images containing face information are often released to the public for the

© Springer International Publishing Switzerland 2014
V. Cantoni et al. (Eds.): BIOMET 2014, LNCS 8897, pp. 209–221, 2014.
DOI: 10.1007/978-3-319-13386-7_17

(a)   (b)

Fig. 1. (a) CCTV images of the angle-grinder gang, released by BTP [4] (b) CCTV images of the two perpetrators in Boston Marathon bombings, released by FBI [69]

(a)   (b)

Fig. 2. (a) CCTV images for the robbery case in Denmark [57], left: the perpetrator, right: the suspect; (b) CCTV images for the burglary case in UK [34], left: the perpetrator, right: the suspect

identification of the perpetrators. For example, in June 2014, British Transport Police (BTP) released CCTV in hunt for angle-grinder gang, who broke the ticket machines at railway stations in UK, as shown in Fig. 1(a). In April 2013, Federal Bureau of Investigation (FBI) released the face images of the two perpetrators in Boston Marathon bombings [69], as shown in Fig.1(b). However, for automatic systems, factors like illumination, resolution, blur, occlusion (e.g., sunglasses), or pose may make the recognition unreliable.

Recently, a number of reports (e.g.,[57][34]) suggested that behavioral biometrics, gait recognition, can be used for human identification from CCTV footage. In [57], based on a checklist for forensic gait analysis, Larsen et al. managed to identify a bank robber in Denmark by matching surveillance footage, as illustrated in Fig. 2(a). Fig. 2(b) shows a gait recognition scenario in UK where a burglar was identified through gait analysis from a podiatrist [34]. These pieces of gait-based evidences proved their usefulness by providing incriminating evidence, leading to convictions in a court of law. However, similar to automatic face recognition, covariate factors like camera viewpoint, carrying condition, clothing, etc. may limit the performance of the automatic gait recognition systems.

It was shown that combining multiple biometric traits may reduce the error rate effectively[36], [59], [74]. In the context of automatic human identification at a distance, it is natural to fuse gait and face, which can be acquired from the same camera. They may be complementary traits for recognition since gait is less sensitive to the factors that affect face recognition, such as low resolution, illumination, etc. while face is robust to covariates that affect gait recognition, e.g., carrying condition, walking surface, clothing, etc. Although there are various face/gait recognition algorithms, research on gait and face fusion is still at its early stage, which will be reviewed in this paper. The rest of this paper is organized as follows. In section 2 and 3, we introduce automatic remote face/gait recognition and the limitations. In section 4, we review several gait and face fusion strategies and analyze their performance. Summary and further research directions on gait+face fusion will be provided in section 5.

2 Automatic Face Recognition

Automatic face recognition is one of the most active research topics in computer vision and pattern recognition. Over the past decades, major advances occurred in automatic face recognition, yet the recognition accuracy of faces captured at a distance is still unsatisfactory. It is challenging due to the large intra-class variations caused by 1) less controlled environment, e.g., with factors like low resolution, blur, illumination, etc.; 2) non-cooperative subjects, e.g., with factors like pose, occlusion (e.g., sunglasses, scarf, hat, veil), etc.

2.1 Face Recognition Algorithms

A gamut of face recognition algorithms were proposed to tackle the effect of the afore-mentioned factors.

Low Resolution. There are two directions to handle the problem of low resolution. 1) *super-resolution (SR) based methods* [24],[38],[27],[28],[32], which reconstruct high-resolution images from low resolution images for visual enhancement. After applying SR, a higher resolution image can be obtained and used for recognition. One major drawback of SR is that significant reconstruction artifacts may be introduced, thus hampering the recognition accuracy. 2) *Non-SR based methods*, which include support vector data description (SVDD) [46], coupled mappings (CMs) [47], multi-dimensional scaling [8], class specific dictionary learning [63], etc.

Image Blur. There are two classes of blur that affect face images: focus blur and motion blur. A focus is the point where lights originating from a point on the object converge. When the light reflected by an object diverges, a out-of-focus image will be generated by the sensor, resulting in the blur effect. The work in [31] analyzed the impact of out-of-focus blur on face recognition performance. Motion blur, however, occurs when exposure time is not brief enough due to the rapid object moving or camera shaking. There are two main categories of approaches for improving the quality of the blurred face images: 1) *blurred image* *modelling* using methods such as subspace analysis [55] or sparse representation [82], and 2) *blur-tolerant descriptor based methods* which attempt to extract blur insensitive features such as Local Phase Quantization (LPQ) [1],[25].

Illumination Variations. There are three categories of approaches to handle illumination variations: 1) *illumination normalization* [12],[62],[9] which seeks to suppress the illumination variations either by image transformations or by synthesising an unaffected image, 2) *illumination invariant representation* [14],[2],[71] which attempts to extract features invariant to illumination changes, and 3) *illumination variation modelling*[16],[58],[3] which is based on the theoretical principle that the set of images of a convex Lambertian object [45]obtained under a wide variety of illumination conditions, can be approximated by a low-dimensional linear subspace, in which the recognition can be performed [5].

Pose Variations. Early approaches [85] include: 1) *multi-view method* [7] which is an extension of the conventional frontal face recognition where a set of images depicting the object from multiple angles are required, 2) *pose variation modelling* [6] which assumes that the 3D shape of an object can be represented by a linear combination of prototypical objects, and 3) *linear subspace method* [56] which represents each person in the gallery by a parametric linear subspace model. Recently, with the development of novel 3D sensors, 3D-based approaches achieve successful performance when addressing pose variations [84].

Occlusion. There are three main categories of approaches for occlusion handling: 1) *reconstruction-based approaches*, that formulate the recognition of occluded faces as a reconstruction problem [37],[79],[54],[83],[76]. An occluded query face is reconstructed by a linear combination of gallery images before being assigned to the class with the minimal reconstruction error. 2) *local matching based approaches* [52],[67], [66], [48], [77], [78], [75] that extract features from the local areas of a face (e.g., patches), such that the affected and unaffected parts of the face can be analyzed separately. To minimize matching errors of the occluded parts, several strategies can be used such as local space learning [66],[52],[67], multi-task sparse representation learning [48] or voting [75]. 3) *occlusion-insensitive feature based approaches* [10],[70],[88] that utilize features such as line segments [10], image gradient orientation (IGO) difference [70] and the Gabor phase (GP) difference [88] which were shown to be robust to occlusion.

2.2   Open Issues in Face Recognition

As afore-introduced, a plethora of algorithms for handling different types of factors have been proposed. However, in real-world face recognition scenarios, these factors can be coupled. For example, low resolution and blur effects are often coupled with other uncontrolled variations such as pose, illumination or occlusion, making the tasks of automatic face recognition difficult. When a face is fully occluded (e.g., Fig. 2(a)) or at a long distance, most of the afore-mentioned methods would become useless. In this case, the behaviorial biometric trait, such as gait, may be of great aide.

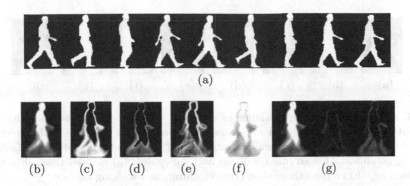

Fig. 3. Gait representations for a subject on the OU-ISIR-LP dataset [35], (a) the original gait silhouettes (b)-(g) the 6 period-based feature templates from left to right: GEI [26], GEnI [39], MGEI [40], CGI [72], GFI [64], and FDF (with 0, 1, and 2 times frequency elements)[51]

3 Automatic Gait Recognition

Existing gait recognition algorithms can be roughly divided into two categories: model-based and appearance-based approaches. Model-based methods (e.g.,[17]) aim to model the human body structure for recognition, while appearance-based approaches can perform classification regardless of the underlying body structure. Although model-based methods may perform well in some challenging cases (e.g., when the view change is large [17]), they generally have lower performance than appearance-based methods. One major reason is that when affected by self-occlusion, low resolution or other factors, it is often difficult to estimate the body structure features precisely, and in this case they only provide limited information for recognition. As such we focus on introducing appearance-based methods in this paper.

3.1 Gait Feature Templates

In early works, researchers formulated gait recognition as a three dimensional video classification problem, based on the preprocessed gait data after background substraction, silhouette binarization and alignment, etc. For example, Sarkar et al. proposed the gait recognition baseline method, which applies spatial-temporal correlation on the gait silhouettes [60]. Wang et al. used spatial-temporal correlation on the gait features extracted through PCA [73]. These algorithms often require significant computational complexity, and tend to be less robust to segmentation errors.

To deal with these dilemmas, period-based gait feature templates were proposed in recent works that encode the information of the frames from a gait cycle into a single image and formulate gait recognition as a two dimensional image classification problem. On the OU-ISIR-LP dataset, consisting of more than 3000 subjects, Iwama et al. [35] conducted a study on six popular period-based feature

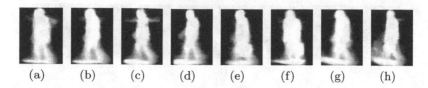

(a)   (b)   (c)   (d)   (e)   (f)   (g)   (h)

Fig. 4. GEIs of one subject walking in different walking conditions from the USF gait dataset [60]. (a) is the GEI in normal condition. (b)-(h) are the GEIs under the influences of (b) viewpoint, (c) walking surface, (d) viewpoint and walking surface, (e) carrying condition, (f) carrying condition and viewpoint, (g) elapsed time, shoe type, and clothing, (h) elapsed time, shoe type, clothing, and walking surface.

templates including gait energy image (GEI)[26], gait entropy image (GEnI) [39], masked GEI based on GEnI (MGEI) [40], chrono-gait image (CGI) [72], gait flow image (GFI)[64], and frequency-domain feature (FDF) [51] (as shown in Fig. 3). The results showed that when there are no covariates, GEI-based template can generally yield the best performance. However, when the walking condition changes, directly applying GEI matching makes the classification prone to errors. Fig. 4 shows some GEIs of one subject in walking conditions with different covariates, from the USF gait dataset [60]. It follows that covariates may significantly change the human appearance, thus giving rise to recognition difficulties. It is important to extract covariate-insensitive features for robust gait recognition.

3.2   Gait Feature Extraction and Classification

Covariates can be roughly divided into three categories: 1) subject-related, e.g., shoe type, carrying condition, speed, clothing, etc., and 2) environmental, e.g., walking surface, elapsed time, etc. 3) camera viewpoint. To reduce such effects, various feature extraction and classification methods have been proposed.

Shoe, (Small Changes in) View, and Carrying Condition. Based on concatenated GEIs, Han and Bhanu utilized PCA and LDA for feature extraction [26]. By using two subspace learning methods, coupled subspaces analysis (CSA) and discriminant analysis with tensor representation (DATER), Xu et al. extract features directly from GEIs[81]. Both methods demonstrate their effectiveness against several simple covariates such as shoe, and (small changes in) camera viewpoint. In [68], Gabor-filtered GEIs were used as the gait feature template, and general tensor discriminant analysis (GTDA) was proposed for feature extraction. The extracted Gabor features demonstrated their robustness in tackling the carrying condition covariate.

Walking Speed. In order to handle variations in walking speed, the feature template head and torso image (HTI) was proposed, which removes the unstable leg parts from silhouettes [65]. Kusakunniran et al. proposed higher-order derivative shape configuration (HSC) to extract speed-invariant gait features from the procrustes shape analysis (PSA) descriptors [42]. Based on the HSC framework, a differential composition model (DCM) was proposed, which can adaptively assign weights to different body parts [43]. Although it was claimed that DCM is insensitive to large speed changes, it requires an additional training data that covers all the possible speeds.

Walking Surface. By using a "cutting and fitting" scheme, Han and Bhanu [26] generated synthetic GEIs to simulate the walking surface effect. By claiming that walking surface may cause spatial misalignment, Image-to-Class distance was utilized in [33] to allow feature matching to be carried out within a spatial neighborhood. By using the techniques of universal background model (UBM) learning and maximum a posteriori (MAP) adaptation, Xu et al. proposed the Gabor-based patch distribution feature (Gabor-PDF) [80]. Significant performance gain can be achieved against walking surface by these methods [26],[33],[80].

Elapsed Time and Clothing. Most existing algorithms perform unsatisfactorily when elapsed time is taken into consideration, as elapsed time potentially also includes the changes of clothing, walking conditions, etc. In [53], by fusing gait features, Matovski et al. studied the effect of elapsed time on a small gait dataset and found that short term elapsed time does not affect the recognition significantly. They claimed that clothing may be the most challenging covariate [53]. Based on a newly constructed gait dataset consisting of 32 different clothes combinations, Hossain et al. proposed an adaptive scheme for weighting different body parts to reduce the effect of clothing [50]. However, this method requires an additional training data that covers all the possible clothes types, which is less practical in real-world applications.

General Covaraite-Invariant Gait Recognition. From the perspective of effect, Guan and Li contended that most of the covariates only affect parts of human silhouettes (with unknown locations)[20]. They proposed an effective framework based on the concept of the random subspace method (RSM) [29]. From the perspective of learning-based methods, they claimed that overfitting the less representative training data is the major problem in gait recognition [21]. They combined a large number of RSM-based weak classifiers to reduce the generalization errors [21]. Experimental results suggest that RSM is robust to a large number of covariates such as shoe, (small changes in) camera viewpoint, carrying condition[21], clothing[22], speed[20], frame-rate[18],[19], etc.

3.3   Open Issues in Gait Recognition

As introduced above, a large number of algorithms have been proposed to tackle different types of covariates. However, gait is a relatively weak trait and the performance can be limited when intra-class variations are extremely large [36]. With gaits taken from the lateral view, the recognition accuracies are still low when facing covariates like elapsed time, walking surface, etc. For cross-view gait recognition, it is challenging when the view difference (between gallery and probe) is large (e.g., greater than $36°$)[44], which can change the gait appearance significantly.

4   Fusing Gait and Face

When performing human identification at a distance without the subject's cooperation, large intra-class variations can affect the performance of gait/face recognition systems substantially. Large intra-class gait variations may be attributed to walking surface, clothing, etc., while face recognition may suffer from low resolution, facial occlusion, etc. Multimodal fusion is a solution to reduce the error rate, and it has been widely applied to the biometrics field [36], e.g., face+fingerprint[59], face+iris[74].

Compared with remote human identification based on gait or face recognition, the technology of fusing gait and face is still at the early stage. We will introduce several recent works on fusing these two modalities. In [61], after applying canonical view rendering technique (CVRT), face and gait information from multiple camera views were fused at the score level. Performance improvement is significant by fusing these two modalities in a multiple camera environment. In [41], Kale et al. showed that even in single camera environment, directly combining the scores of face and gait can boost the overall performance. Based on population hidden Markov model (pHMM), Liu and Sarkar selected gait stances for recognition in the outdoor environment [49]. Extensive experimental results were reported on handling variations in the walking surface and elapsed time covariates, based on different fusion strategies. They found performance is higher when fusing gait and face than intra-model fusion (i.e., face+face or gait+gait) [49]. By claiming that the reliability of face and gait varies with different subject-camera distances, Geng et al. proposed an adaptive score-level fusion scheme [15]. The weights of the face score and gait score are distance-driven. It was experimentally shown to outperform score-level fusion with fixed weights in the multi-view environment. In [87], Zhou and Bhanu performed a score-level fusion of gait and the enhanced side face image(ESFI). Compared with original side face image (OSFI), they found that improving face image quality can further enhance the fusion performance. They further applied feature-level fusion by concatenating the ESFI and gait [86]. In [30], alpha matte preprocessing (AMP) was used by Hofmann et al. to segment gait and face images with improved qualities, before score-level fusion. Recently, Guan et al. proposed the multimodal-RSM framework [23]. In RSM systems, weak classifiers with lower dimensionality tend to have better generalization ability [29]. However, they encounter the underfitting problem if the dimensionality is too low. In [23], face was used as ancillary information to strengthen the gait-based weak classifiers, before the majority voting was carried out among these updated classifiers. Significant performance gains are achieved in tackling the most challenging elapsed time covariate, which also includes the changes of clothing, carrying condition, shoe, etc.

We report the performance of the afore-mentioned fusion algorithms in Table 1. For multiple results based on different fusion rules, only the best ones are reported. As listed in Table 1, fusing gait and face can yield significant performance improvement, given by $\Delta = (Fusion - max(Face, Gait))/max(Face, Gait)$. We find that: 1) Feature-level fusion yields higher Δ than score-level fusion, although more experiments on larger dataset have to be conducted to support the final conclusion.

Table 1. The performance (recognition accuracy) of gait and face fusion algorithms

Algorithm	Condition	Gait	Face	Fusion	Type	Δ	#Subjects
CVRT[61]	Multi-cameras	68%	72%	89%	score-level	23.6%	26
View-invariant[41]	Outdoor+C1	60%	94%	100%	score-level	6.3%	30
Distance-driven[15]	view 0°	82.5%	58.8%	90.0%	score-level	9.1%	20
	view 45°	82.5%	77.5%	95.0%	score-level	15.2%	20
	view 90°	80.0%	70.0%	90.0%	score-level	12.5%	20
pHMM[49]	Outdoor+C2	39%	40%	71%	score-level	77.5%	70
	Outdoor+C3	30%	40%	50%	score-level	25%	70
OSFI+GEI [87]	C4	82.2%	64.4%	82.2%	score-level	0%	45
ESFI+GEI [87]	C4	82.2%	80.0%	88.9%	score-level	8.2%	45
OSFI+GEI [86]	C4	82.2%	64.4%	86.7%	feature-level	5.5%	45
ESFI+GEI [86]	C4	82.2%	80.0%	91.1%	feature-level	10.8%	45
AMP [30]	Outdoor+C5	53.6%	54.6%	65.2%	score-level	19.4%	122
Multimodal-RSM[23]	C6	88.2%	74.0%	95.6%	score-level & decision-level	8.4%	155

Δ denotes the performance improvement. C1-C6: Covariate factors. C1: (small changes in) view; C2: walking surface; C3: elapsed time; C4: clothing; C5: (small changes in) view, shoe, carrying condition, walking surface, elapsed time, and clothing; C6: shoe, carrying condition, elapsed time, and clothing.

2) Fusing gait and face can effectively tackle difficult covariates (e.g.,[49],[30],[23]) like clothing, walking surface, elapsed time, etc. However, to the best of our knowledge, without a multi-view gallery to facilitate in-depth investigations, how (large changes in) camera viewpoint covariate should be handled remains an open question. 3) Generally, Δ is higher when gait and face have similar accuracies (e.g.,23.6% for [61], 77.5% for [49],19.4% for [30]), and vice versa (e.g., 6.3% for [41], 0% for [87], 5.5% for [86]). To improve the overall fusion performance, it is important to improve the performance of relatively weak modality (e.g., [87],[86]), or employ an adaptive mechanism (e.g., [15]).

5   Summary and Further Research Directions

In this paper, we review the contemporary (face, gait, and fusion) algorithms for human identification at a distance. Significant performance gain can be achieved when gait and face modalities are combined to tackle the hard problems in less controlled environments. Research on fusing these two modalities is in its infancy, and we propose the following possible lines of investigation. 1) *Fusion strategy*: Most existing works are based on score-level fusion, and it is desirable to explore the effectiveness of other fusion strategies such as feature-level fusion, decision-level fusion, rank-level fusion, etc. 2) *Adaptive mechanism*: the work in [15] used an adaptive weighting scheme based on different subject-camera distances. In the future, one can extend this scheme to a quality-driven one. For example, gait will have a high weight when face is occluded (e.g., Fig. 2(a)), while face will have a high weight when gait information is unavailable (e.g., Fig. 1(b)). Moreover, before the fusion, different face/gait algorithms should be adaptively chosen for the most suitable scenarios. 3) *Segmentation quality*: the quality for gait or face is important. The works in [86],[87] suggest that the performance of fusion can be improved on higher quality face images. In [30], alpha mattes segmentation is used for higher gait quality. In the future, more advanced segmentation methods (e.g.,the superpixels-based method [13]) will be of great aide.

References

1. Ahonen, T., Rahtu, E., Ojansivu, V., Heikkila, J.: Recognition of blurred faces using local phase quantization. In: ICPR (2008)
2. Ahonen, T., Hadid, A., Pietikainen, M.: Face description with local binary patterns: Application to face recognition. T-PAMI (2006)
3. Basri, R., Jacobs, D.: Lambertian reflectance and linear subspaces. T-PAMI (2003)
4. BBC: Angle grinder gang thefts: Damage put at 109k caused (2014). http://www.bbc.co.uk/news/uk-england-london-27778727
5. Belhumeur, P., Kriegman, D.: What is the set of images of an object under all possible lighting conditions? In: CVPR (1996)
6. Beymer, D., Poggio, T.: Face recognition from one example view. In: ICCV (1995)
7. Beymer, D.: Face recognition under varying pose. In: CVPR (1994)
8. Biswas, S., Bowyer, K., Flynn, P.: Multidimensional scaling for matching low-resolution facial images. In: BTAS (2010)
9. Chen, T., Yin, W., Zhou, X.S., Comaniciu, D., Huang, T.: Total variation models for variable lighting face recognition. T-PAMI (2006)
10. Chen, W., Gao, Y.: Recognizing partially occluded faces from a single sample per class using string-based matching. In: ECCV (2010)
11. David Barrett, D.: One surveillance camera for every 11 people in britain, says cctv survey. http://www.telegraph.co.uk/technology/10172298/One-surveillance-camera-for-e
12. Du, S., Ward, R.: Wavelet-based illumination normalization for face recognition. In: ICIP (2005)
13. Feldman-Haber, S., Keller, Y.: A probabilistic graph-based framework for plug-and-play multi-cue visual tracking. T-IP (2014)
14. Gao, Y., Leung, M.K.H.: Face recognition using line edge map. T-PAMI (2002)
15. Geng, X., Wang, L., Li, M., Wu, Q., Smith-Miles, K.: Distance-driven fusion of gait and face for human identification in video. In: IVCNZ (2007)
16. Georghiades, A., Belhumeur, P., Kriegman, D.: From few to many: illumination cone models for face recognition under variable lighting and pose. T-PAMI (2001)
17. Goffredo, M., Bouchrika, I., Carter, J., Nixon, M.: Self-calibrating view-invariant gait biometrics. T-SMC-B (2010)
18. Guan, Y., Li, C.T., Choudhury., S.D.: Robust gait recognition from extremely low frame-rate videos. In: IWBF (2013)
19. Guan, Y., Sun, Y., Li, C.T., Tistarelli, M.: Human gait identification from extremely low quality videos: an enhanced classifier ensemble method. IET Biometrics (2014)
20. Guan, Y., Li, C.T.: A robust speed-invariant gait recognition system for walker and runner identification. In: ICB (2013)
21. Guan, Y., Li, C.T., Hu, Y.: Random subspace method for gait recognition. In: ICMEW (2012)

22. Guan, Y., Li, C.T., Hu, Y.: Robust clothing-invariant gait recognition. In: IIH-MSP (2012)
23. Guan, Y., Wei, X., Li, C.T., Marcialis, G., Roli, F., Tistarelli, M.: Combining gait and face for tackling the elapsed time challenges. In: BTAS (2013)
24. Gunturk, B., Batur, A., Altunbasak, Y., Hayes, M., Mersereau, R.: Eigenface-domain super-resolution for face recognition. T-IP (2003)
25. Hadid, A., Nishiyama, M., Sato, Y.: Recognition of blurred faces via facial deblurring combined with blur-tolerant descriptors. In: ICPR (2010)
26. Han, J., Bhanu, B.: Individual recognition using gait energy image. T-PAMI (2006)
27. Hennings-Yeomans, P., Baker, S., Kumar, B.: Simultaneous super-resolution and feature extraction for recognition of low-resolution faces. In: CVPR (2008)
28. Hennings-Yeomans, P., Kumar, B., Baker, S.: Robust low-resolution face identification and verification using high-resolution features. In: ICIP (2009)
29. Ho, T.K.: The random subspace method for constructing decision forests. T-PAMI (1998)
30. Hofmann, M., Schmidt, S., Rajagopalan, A.N., Rigoll, G.: Combined face and gait recognition using alpha matte preprocessing. In: ICB (2012)
31. Hua, F., Johnson, P., Sazonova, N., Lopez-Meyer, P., Schuckers, S.: Impact of out-of-focus blur on face recognition performance based on modular transfer function. In: ICB (2012)
32. Huang, H., He, H.: Super-resolution method for face recognition using nonlinear mappings on coherent features. T-NN (2011)
33. Huang, Y., Xu, D., Cham, T.J.: Face and human gait recognition using image-to-class distance. T-CSVT (2010)
34. Bouchrika, I., Goffredo, M., J.C., Nixon, M.S.: On using gait in forensic biometrics. J. Forencics Sci. (2011)
35. Iwama, H., Okumura, M., Makihara, Y., Yagi, Y.: The ou-isir gait database comprising the large population dataset and performance evaluation of gait recognition. T-IFS (2012)
36. Jain, A., Ross, A., Prabhakar, S.: An introduction to biometric recognition. T-CSVT (2004)
37. Jia, H., Martínez, A.M.: Face recognition with occlusions in the training and testing sets. In: FG (2008)
38. Jia, K., Gong, S.: Multi-modal tensor face for simultaneous super-resolution and recognition. In: ICCV (2005)
39. Bashir, K., T.X., Gong, S.: Gait recognition using gait entropy image. In: ICDP (2009)
40. Bashir, K., T.X., Gong, S.: Gait recognition without subject cooperation. PRL (2010)
41. Kale, A., Roychowdhury, A., Chellappa, R.: Fusion of gait and face for human identification. In: ICASSP (2004)
42. Kusakunniran, W., Wu, Q., Zhang, J., Li, H.: Speed-invariant gait recognition based on procrustes shape analysis using higher-order shape configuration. In: ICIP (2011)
43. Kusakunniran, W., Wu, Q., Zhang, J., Li, H.: Gait recognition across various walking speeds using higher order shape configuration based on a differential composition model. T-SMC-B (2012)
44. Kusakunniran, W., Wu, Q., Zhang, J., Li, H., Wang, L.: Recognizing gaits across views through correlated motion co-clustering. T-IP (2014)
45. Lambert, J.: Photometria sive de mensura et gradibus luminus. Colorum et Umbrae", Eberhard Klett (1760)

46. Lambert, J.: Photometria sive de mensura et gradibus luminus. Colorum et Umbrae. Eberhard Klett (1760)
47. Li, B., Chang, H., Shan, S., Chen, X.: Low-resolution face recognition via coupled locality preserving mappings. SPL (2010)
48. Liao, S., Jain, A.K., Li, S.Z.: Partial face recognition: Alignment-free approach. T-PAMI (2013)
49. Liu, Z., Sarkar, S.: Outdoor recognition at a distance by fusing gait and face. IVC (2007)
50. Hossain, M.A., Makihara, Y., J.W., Yagi, Y.: Clothing-invariant gait identification using part-based clothing categorization and adaptive weight control. PR (2010)
51. Makihara, Y., Sagawa, R., Mukaigawa, Y., Echigo, T., Yagi, Y.: Gait recognition using a view transformation model in the frequency domain. In: Leonardis, A., Bischof, H., Pinz, A. (eds.) ECCV 2006. LNCS, vol. 3953, pp. 151–163. Springer, Heidelberg (2006)
52. Martínez, A.M.: Recognizing imprecisely localized, partially occluded, and expression variant faces from a single sample per class. T-PAMI (2002)
53. Matovski, D., Nixon, M., Mahmoodi, S., Carter, J.: The effect of time on gait recognition performance. T-IFS (2012)
54. Naseem, A.I., Togneri, B.R., Bennamoun, C.M.: Linear regression for face recognition. T-PAMI (2010)
55. Nishiyama, M., Hadid, A., Takeshima, H., Shotton, J., Kozakaya, T., Yamaguchi, O.: Facial deblur inference using subspace analysis for recognition of blurred faces. T-PAMI (2011)
56. Okada, K., Von der Malsburg, C.: Pose-invariant face recognition with parametric linear subspaces. In: FG (2002)
57. Larsen, P.K., E.S., Lynnerup, N.: Gait analysis in forensic medicine. J. Forencics Sci. (2008)
58. Ramamoorthi, R.: Analytic pca construction for theoretical analysis of lighting variability in images of a lambertian object. T-PAMI (2002)
59. Rattani, A., Kisku, D., Bicego, M., Tistarelli, M.: Feature level fusion of face and fingerprint biometrics. In: BTAS (2007)
60. Sarkar, S., Phillips, P., Liu, Z., Vega, I., Grother, P., Bowyer, K.: The humanid gait challenge problem: data sets, performance, and analysis. T-PAMI (2005)
61. Shakhnarovich, G., Darrell, T.: On probabilistic combination of face and gait cues for identification. In: FG (2002)
62. Shan, S., Gao, W., Cao, B., Zhao, D.: Illumination normalization for robust face recognition against varying lighting conditions. In: FG (2003)
63. Shekhar, S., Patel, V., Chellappa, R.: Synthesis-based recognition of low resolution faces. In: IJCB (2011)
64. T. H. W. Lam, K.H.C., Liu, J.N.K.: Gait flow image: A silhouette-based gait representation for human identification. PR (2011)
65. Tan, D., Huang, K., Yu, S., Tan, T.: Efficient night gait recognition based on template matching. In: ICPR (2006)
66. Tan, X., Chen, S., Zhou, Z.H., Liu, J.: Face recognition under occlusions and variant expressions with partial similarity. T-IFS (2009)
67. Tan, X., Chen, S., Zhou, Z.H., Zhang, F.: Recognizing partially occluded, expression variant faces from single training image per person with SOM and soft k-NN ensemble. T-NN (2005)
68. Tao, D., Li, X., Wu, X., Maybank, S.: General tensor discriminant analysis and gabor features for gait recognition. T-PAMI (2007)

69. Tara McKelvey, a.K.D.: Boston marathon bombings: How notorious bombers got caught, bbc news magazine (2013). http://www.bbc.co.uk/news/magazine-22191033
70. Tzimiropoulos, G., Zafeiriou, S., Pantic, M.: Subspace learning from image gradient orientations. T-PAMI (2012)
71. Wang, B., Li, W., Yang, W., Liao, Q.: Illumination normalization based on weber's law with application to face recognition. SPL (2011)
72. Wang, C., Zhang, J., Wang, L., Pu, J., Yuan, X.: Human identification using temporal information preserving gait template. T-PAMI (2012)
73. Wang, L., Tan, T., Ning, H., Hu, W.: Silhouette analysis-based gait recognition for human identification. T-PAMI (2003)
74. Wang, Y., Tan, T., Jain, A.K.: Combining face and iris biometrics for identity verification. In: AVBPA (2003)
75. Wei, X., Li, C.T.: Fixation and saccade based face recognition from single image per person with various occlusions and expressions. In: CVPRW (2013)
76. Wei, X., Li, C.T., Hu, Y.: Robust face recognition under varying illumination and occlusion considering structured sparsity. In: DICTA (2012)
77. Wei, X., Li, C.T., Hu, Y.: Face recognition with occlusion using dynamic image-to-class warping (DICW). In: FG (2013)
78. Wei, X., Li, C.T., Hu, Y.: Robust face recognition with occlusions in both reference and query images. In: IWBF (2013)
79. Wright, J., Yang, A.Y., Ganesh, A., Sastry, S.S., Ma, Y.: Robust face recognition via sparse representation. T-PAMI (2009)
80. Xu, D., Huang, Y., Zeng, Z., Xu, X.: Human gait recognition using patch distribution feature and locality-constrained group sparse representation. T-IP (2012)
81. Xu, D., Yan, S., Tao, D., Zhang, L., Li, X., Zhang, H.J.: Human gait recognition with matrix representation. T-CSVT (2006)
82. Zhang, H., Yang, J., Zhang, Y., Nasrabadi, N., Huang, T.: Close the loop: Joint blind image restoration and recognition with sparse representation prior. In: ICCV (2011)
83. Zhang, L., Yang, M., Feng, X.: Sparse representation or collaborative representation: Which helps face recognition? In: ICCV (2011)
84. Zhang, X., Gao, Y.: Face recognition across pose: A review. PR (2009)
85. Zhao, W., Chellappa, R., Phillips, P.J., Rosenfeld, A.: Face recognition: A literature survey. ACM Computing Surveys (2003)
86. Zhou, X., Bhanu, B.: Feature fusion of side face and gait for video-based human identification. PR (2008)
87. Zhou, X., Bhanu, B.: Integrating face and gait for human recognition at a distance in video. T-SMC-B (2007)
88. Zhu, J., Cao, D., Liu, S., Lei, Z., Li, S.Z.: Discriminant analysis with gabor phase for robust face recognition. In: ICB (2012)

Pupil Size as a Biometric Trait

Nahumi Nugrahaningsih and Marco Porta[✉]

Dip. di Ingegneria Industriale e dell'Informazione,
Università di Pavia, Via Ferrata 5, 27100, Pavia, Italy
nahumi.nugrahaningsih01@universitadipavia.it,
marco.porta@unipv.it

Abstract. We investigate the possibility of using pupil size as a discriminating feature for eye-based soft biometrics. In experiments carried out in different sessions in two consecutive years, 25 subjects were asked to simply watch the center of a plus sign displayed in the middle of a blank screen. Four primary attributes were exploited, namely left and right pupil sizes and ratio and difference of left and right pupil sizes. Fifteen descriptive statistics were used for each primary attribute, plus two further measures, which produced a total of 62 features. Bayes, Neural Network, Support Vector Machine and Random Forest classifiers were employed to analyze both all the features and selected subsets. The Identification task showed higher classification accuracies (0.6194 ÷ 0.7187) with the selected features, while the Verification task exhibited almost comparable performances (~ 0.97) in the two cases for accuracy, and an increase in sensitivity and a decrease in specificity with the selected features.

Keywords: Eye tracking · Gaze analysis · Eye-based biometrics · Pupil size · Soft biometrics

1 Introduction

Eye features and behaviors are increasingly being considered as biometric traits. While the cost of *eye trackers* is still rather high, it is likely that relatively cheap devices will become available in a not too distant future, thus opening the door to a wide range of applications. The majority of eye-based approaches are employed for *soft* biometric classification. Therefore, they usually provide a probability that specific features are associated to a certain person rather than finding a one-to-one matching between certain eye characteristics and a subject. Used in conjunction with common authentication solutions, such as those exploiting PINs or passwords, soft biometrics can increase security with limited effort on the part of the user.

Essentially, eye movements occur as very fast *saccades* (< 100 ms) followed by *fixations* (~ 100-600 ms), during which the eye can be considered almost still. Several approaches to gaze-based identification and verification have been developed to date, most of which are based, to a lesser or greater extent, on fixation and saccadic characteristics.

Depending on the specific activity being carried out, the vision process occurs either overtly or covertly, with this last modality capable of capturing the essence of a

V. Cantoni et al. (Eds.): BIOMET 2014, LNCS 8897, pp. 222–233, 2014.
DOI: 10.1007/978-3-319-13386-7_18

person's cognitive and psychological processes [1]. Eye parameters can therefore be employed for emotion and cognitive stress detection, as well as for visual attention studies. In these contexts, pupil size is an important source of information, and has been exploited in several investigations (e.g., in [2]).

In this paper, we explore the possibility of using pupil size also as a biometric trait. In particular, we examine eye data acquired during the very basic task of watching a single static graphical element (a plus sign) displayed on a screen. Through several descriptive statistics, we analyze the performance of different classifiers used for both identification and verification purposes.

The paper is structured as follows. Section 2 presents a short survey of eye-based biometric solutions developed to date. Section 3 describes the data acquisition procedure and the pre-processing stage. Section 4 explains the adopted feature selection criteria and illustrates the results obtained. Lastly, Section 5 draws some conclusions and provides hints for future work.

2   Related Works

In the last decade, several studies have been carried out in the scope of eye-based biometrics. In the following, we propose a short summary of the most relevant works.

Kasprowski and Ober [3] considered gaze coordinates of subjects while watching a point jumping on the screen. Eye features were examined through different classifying algorithms, using the inverse Fourier transform of the logarithm of the power spectrum of a signal. Bednarik at al. [4] exploited eye features such as pupil size and gaze speed in three kinds of tests, involving reading, fixating a static cross (similarly to our experiments) and watching a gray level picture. Deravi and Guness [5] measured gaze duration, pupil position, pupil diameter and the observed point of testers while watching a few images for five seconds. Holland and Komogortsev [6] studied the effects of various stimuli and different spatial accuracies and temporal resolutions. Komogortsev et al. [7] combined eye behaviors and iris structure to obtain better recognition rates, exploiting both eye anatomical properties and visual attention strategies. Cuong et al. [8] proposed Mel-frequency cepstral coefficients (MFCCs) as a technique to code different features (such as eye position, eye difference, and eye velocity) and train various classifiers. Rigas et al. [9] compared the distributions of saccadic velocities and accelerations obtained from the observation of a moving spot on a screen. Also Juhola et al. [10] focused on saccades to develop a computational verification method, involving in their experiments both healthy subjects and otoneurological patients. Darwish and Pasquier [11] exploited eye movement features and iris constriction and dilation parameters, examining changes in pupil diameter during fixations and saccades.

Some works focused on the free observation of specific kinds of pictures, such as faces (e.g., Rigas et al. [12] and Cantoni et al. [13]). Video stimuli were used by Kinnunen et al. [14] in experiments in which eye movements were described in terms of angles traveled by the eyes in certain time spans. Liang et al. [15] devised a video-based identification method which exploited visual attention features such as acceleration, geometric and muscle properties.

With the purpose to detect potentially unusual user behaviors, Holland and Komogortsev [16] analyzed several biometric characteristics based on eye movement and their potential to identify specific persons, especially when reading. With the same goal, Biedert et al. [17] developed an intrusion detection system based on "learning effects", presuming that people become gradually used to certain tasks (e.g., checking for emails and reading messages) as they are repeated over time. Silver and Biggs [18] considered both keystroke and eye-tracking as distinctive characteristics, thus implementing a multimodal biometric approach.

In the context of explicit authentication systems, like ATMs, Kumar et al. [19] discussed different design solutions to allow gaze-based PIN input. De Luca et al. [20] proposed a verification method based on eye gestures, performed by moving the eyes so as to "draw" certain patterns on the screen. Dunphy et al. [21] implemented an approach in which the user has to watch specific faces within a sequence of 3x3 grids. Symbols displayed in a virtual keyboard were instead exploited by Weaver et al. [22] as targets to be watched according to a specific succession. Maeder et al. [23] analyzed gaze sequences of subjects while looking at specific spots of a previously seen picture. Rozado [24], lastly, compared the speed and error rates of different gaze-based password methods.

3   Data Acquisition

3.1   Participants and Experiments

The experiments were conducted in two sessions in 2012 and 2013 (about one year follow-up), with 25 volunteer subjects taken from students and the research staff of our department. Participants were composed of 18 males and 7 females, with ages ranging from 21 to 70. Ten testers attended the experiments in both 2012 and 2013, while 15 of them were involved solely in one year (8 in 2012 and 7 in 2013). In any case, all subjects attended at least three tests, at intervals between two days and one week in the same year. In total, 98 tests were carried out (52 in 2012 and 46 in 2013).

3.2   Apparatus

Eye data were recorded using a *Tobii 1750* eye-tracker, with a 50 Hz sampling rate (which means that 50 data samples were acquired per second). Two different gaze recording software tools were used in 2012 and 2013, namely *ClearView* and *Tobii Studio*. Apart from some negligible differences in terms of numbers' decimal precision, the two programs provided fully comparable outputs.

3.3   Procedure

Experiments were conducted in a quiet laboratory environment. The task of participants was simply to fixate the center of a plus sign (78x78 pixels) displayed in the middle of a blank white screen (1280x1024 resolution), as shown in Fig. 1. This stimulus was in fact part of another experiment, in which the tester was asked to freely watch a sequence of 18 photographs containing mostly faces and shown for ten seconds each. The blank screen with the plus sign (simply "plus screen" in the following) was displayed before each photo, for five seconds the first time and for three seconds afterward.

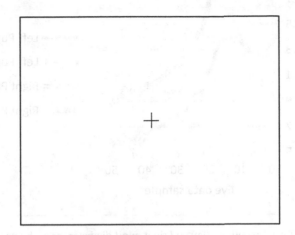

Fig. 1. Experiment stimulus

3.4   Data Pre-Processing

In the pre-processing phase, only valid raw data were selected, thus excluding those samples which missed correct eye information for either the left or right eye (for example because of blinks). From these valid data, only the first 50 samples were extracted. This guaranteed the same number of raw values for all the 18 "plus screens" in each test of each session (except for a few cases, which were excluded from the analysis because less than 50 valid samples could be found). In total, 1,754 "plus screens" were considered for all sessions.

After pre-processing, derivative raw features were calculated, namely the ratio and the difference between the left and right pupil sizes. Pupils' sizes and the derivative data were then smoothed by means of a single-iteration median filter with window size equal to 5 (Fig. 2).

3.5   Features

For each one of the four primary features (left and right pupil size, ratio and difference between left and right pupil sizes), the following 15 descriptive statistics were used to summarize data: minimum, maximum, mean, standard deviation, variance, median, median deviation, geometric mean, harmonic mean, inter-quartile range (IQR), first quartile, third quartile, kurtosis, range and skewness. In addition, two other statistical measures were considered, namely the sum of squares of differences between left and right pupil sizes and the correlation between left and right pupil sizes. Globally, 62 (i.e., $15 \cdot 4 + 2$) features were therefore calculated for each "plus screen". These features were provided as input to four different classifiers.

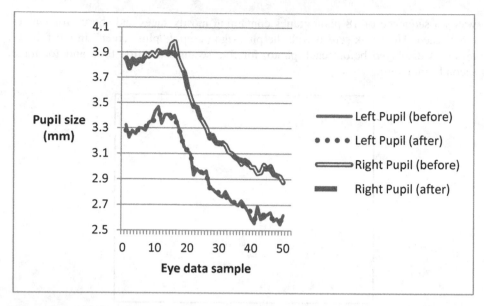

Fig. 2. Example of data smoothing (left and right pupil diameter for each one of the 50 samples considered)

3.6   Classifiers

Both identification (i.e., searching for an individual matching a biometric sample) and verification (i.e., confirming an individual's claimed identity) analyses were conducted. The classifying tasks were carried out using Bayes, Neural Network (NN), Support Vector Machine (SVM), and Random Forest (RF) classifiers. The composition of training and testing data was 70% and 30%, respectively. The classification result was the average value of 10-time repetitions with stratified random data.

4   Results

4.1   Feature Selection

For both identification and verification, we performed two trials: one with all the 62 features and one with a selected subset. In the identification case, the selection was accomplished by sorting features according to their ranking, adding one feature at a time (through an iterative process) and calculating the Classification Accuracy (CA): if the inclusion of a feature increased CA, then that feature was added to the subset; otherwise, if CA was the same or decreased, the feature was omitted. Feature ranking was calculated using an SVM weight approach, and the features obtained were applied separately for each classifier. In preliminary trials, some other feature ranking approaches were also considered, such as ReliefF, Information Gain, Gain Ratio and Gini, but the SVM weight solution produced the best outcomes. The same subset of features selected for identification was also used for the verification case.

As shown in Fig. 3 and Fig. 4, at each iteration (as many as the number of features, i.e., 62) a new feature was introduced (according to the ranking), and the average accuracy of 10-time trials was calculated. In the end, 18, 23, 29, and 27 features were selected for Bayes, NN, SVM, and RF classifiers, respectively (Table 1).

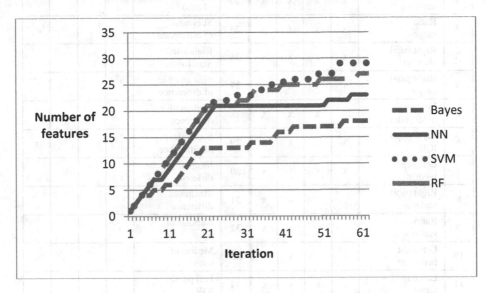

Fig. 3. Number of features used by the four classifiers at each iteration of the selection process

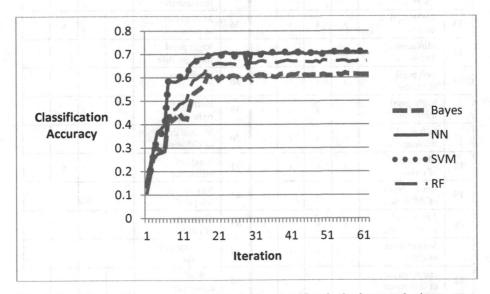

Fig. 4. Classification Accuracy achieved by the four classifiers in the feature selection process

Table 1. Features selected for Bayes (BA), Neural Networks (NN), Support Vector Machine (SV) and Random Forest (RF) classifiers, ordered according to their ranking (R)

R	Feature	BA	NN	SV	RF	R	Feature	BA	NN	SV	RF
1	Left pupil variance	x	x	x	x	24	Stand. dev. of ratio				
2	Ratio range	x	x	x	x	25	Skewness of difference				
3	Right pupil skewness	x	x	x	x	26	Right pupil Stand. dev.				
4	Right pupil range	x	x	x	x	27	First quartile of difference				
5	Left pupil median dev.		x	x	x	28	Median of difference			x	
6	Right pupil IQR		x	x	x	29	Stand. dev. of difference				x
7	Left pupil median	x	x	x	x	30	Mean of difference				
8	Right pupil variance			x	x	31	Maximum difference				
9	Ratio variance			x	x	32	Kurtosis of ratio	x			x
10	Left/right pupil corr.	x	x	x	x	33	Median of ratio			x	x
11	Left pupil range		x	x	x	34	Left pupil IQR				
12	Left pupil stand. dev.		x	x	x	35	Left pupil first quartile				
13	Right pupil median	x	x	x	x	36	Median dev. of ratio			x	
14	Minimum of difference	x	x	x	x	37	Right pupil third quartile				
15	Left pupil skewness	x	x	x	x	38	Minimum ratio	x			
16	Right pupil minimum	x	x	x	x	39	Kurtosis of right pupil	x			
17	Left pupil minimum	x	x	x	x	40	Median dev. of difference				x
18	Maximum of ratio	x	x	x	x	41	Range of difference			x	
19	Geom. mean of differences		x	x	x	42	Kurtosis of left pupil				
20	Third quart. of difference	x	x	x	x	43	Skewness of ratio	x			
21	Sum of squar. of diff.		x	x	x	44	Third quartile of ratio				
22	Harm. mean of difference		x			45	IQR of difference				
23	Right pupil median dev.		x	x		46	Left pupil third quartile				

Table 1. (*continued*)

R	Feature	BA	NN	SV	RF	R	Feature	BA	NN	SV	RF
47	Right pupil first quartile					55	First quartile of ratio			x	
48	Maximum of left pupil					56	IQR of ratio	x			
49	Variance of difference			x		57	Left pupil harm. mean				
50	Kurtosis of difference				x	58	Left pupil geom. mean		x		
51	Mean of ratio					59	Left pupil mean				
52	Geom. mean of ratio		x			60	Right pupil harm. mean				x
53	Harm. mean of ratio					61	Right pupil geom. mean				
54	Maximum of right pupil			x		62	Right pupil mean				

4.2 Identification

The NN classifier produced the best Classification Accuracy (0.708) using all the 62 features, while the SVM classifier had the best performance (0.7187) with the selected 29 features (Table 2). As can be seen, the selection process increased the classification accuracy for all classifiers. In particular, the Bayes classifier had the largest gain of accuracy (12.5%) with the smallest number of features (18).

Table 2. Identification results

Features	Classifier	Num. of features	CA
All features	Bayes	62	0.5508
	NN	62	0.7080
	SVM	62	0.6998
	RF	62	0.6376
Selected features	Bayes	18	0.6194
	NN	23	0.7097
	SVM	29	0.7187
	RF	27	0.6757

4.3 Verification

Using all the 62 features, the best results were produced by the NN classifier for accuracy (0.9773) and AUC (area under ROC curve, 0.9727), by the SVM classifier for Sensitivity (0.9977) and by the Bayes classifier for Specificity (0.8223). As shown in

Table 3, in the verification case the selected features showed a different trend compared to identification. The reduction of the number of features tended to increase Sensitivity (0.07% ÷ 7.8%) but decreased Specificity (2.7% ÷ 24.7%). This tendency made the overall classification accuracy gain vary from -0.19% to 6.75%.

Table 3. Verification results

Features	Classifier	Num. of features	CA	Sensitivity	Specificity	AUC
All features	Bayes	62	0.8964	0.8997	0.8223	0.9438
	NN	62	0.9773	0.9948	0.5208	0.9727
	SVM	62	0.9672	0.9977	0.1482	0.6123
	RF	62	0.9731	0.9955	0.4078	0.9500
Selected features	Bayes	18	0.9569	0.9702	0.6190	0.9604
	NN	23	0.9754	0.9960	0.4445	0.9710
	SVM	29	0.9668	0.9978	0.1421	0.6114
	RF	27	0.9734	0.9962	0.3968	0.9556

As examples, Fig. 5 and Fig. 6 show the ROC curves for the testers with the best and worst classification performance.

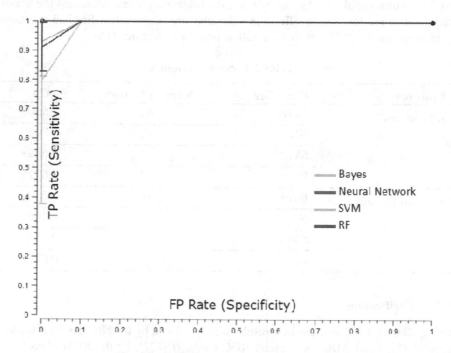

Fig. 5. ROC curve (the best case)

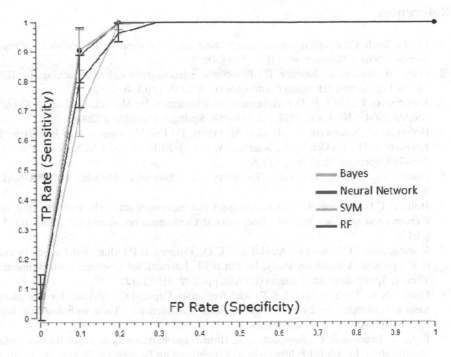

Fig. 6. ROC curve (the worst case)

5   Conclusions

In this paper we have explored the possibility of using pupil size as a soft biometric trait. Apart from very few previous studies (e.g., the work of Bednarik at al. [3], which, however, exploited also additional features), to date pupil size has been little considered for biometric purposes.

Although the number of testers involved in our experiments was relatively low, the obtained results are encouraging, and suggest that pupil diameter can provide reliable information for both identification and verification tasks. In particular, it is interesting to note that a reasonably limited group of features (from 18 to 29, depending on the classifier) can produce results almost comparable with those that can be obtained using the whole set of 62 features.

Future experiments will allow us to further investigate the potential of pupil size as a biometric characteristic. Besides involving more testers, we will also consider dynamic features (such as the evolution of pupil size and related statistics with time). More complex stimuli will be considered too, in order to obtain more variegated and potentially more meaningful data.

References

1. Itti, L., Koch, C.: A saliency-based search mechanism for overt and covert shifts of visual attention. Vision Research **40**, 1489–1506 (2000)
2. Porta, M., Ricotti, S., Jimenez, C.: Emotional e-learning through eye tracking. In: IEEE Global Engineering Education Conference (EDUCON), pp.1–6 (2012)
3. Kasprowski, P., Ober, J.: Eye Movements in Biometrics. In: Maltoni, D., Jain, A.K. (eds.) BioAW 2004. LNCS, vol. 3087, pp. 248–258. Springer, Heidelberg (2004)
4. Bednarik, R., Kinnunen, T., Mihaila, A., Fränti, P.: Eye-Movements as a Biometric. In: Kalviainen, H., Parkkinen, J., Kaarna, A. (eds.) SCIA 2005. LNCS, vol. 3540, pp. 780–789. Springer, Heidelberg (2005)
5. Deravi, F., Guness, S.P.: Gaze Trajectory as a Biometric Modality. BIOSIGNALS, 335–341 (2011)
6. Holland, C.D., Komogortsev, O.V.: Complex eye movement pattern biometrics: Analyzing fixations and saccades. In: 2013 International Conference on Biometrics (ICB), pp. 1–8 (2013)
7. Komogortsev, O.V., Karpov, A., Holland, C.D., Proenca, H.P.: Multimodal ocular biometrics approach: A feasibility study. In: 5th IEEE International Conference on Biometrics: Theory, Applications and Systems (BTAS), pp. 209–216 (2012)
8. Cuong, N.V., Dinh, V., Ho, L.S.T.: Mel-frequency Cepstral Coefficients for Eye Movement Identification. In: 24th IEEE International Conference on Tools with Artificial Intelligence (ICTAI), pp. 253–260 (2012)
9. Rigas, I., Economou, G., Fotopoulos, S.: Human eye movements as a trait for biometrical identification. In: 5th IEEE International Conference on Biometrics: Theory, Applications and Systems (BTAS), pp. 217–222 (2012)
10. Juhola, M., Zhang, Y., Rasku, J.: Biometric verification of a subject through eye movements. Computers in Biology and Medicine **43**, 42–50 (2013)
11. Darwish, A., Pasquier, M.: Biometric identification using the dynamic features of the eyes. In: 6th IEEE International Conference on Biometrics: Theory, Applications and Systems (BTAS), pp. 1–6 (2013)
12. Rigas, I., Economou, G., Fotopoulos, S.: Biometric identification based on the eye movements and graph matching techniques. Pattern Recognition Letters **33**, 786–792 (2012)
13. Cantoni, V., Galdi, C., Nappi, M., Porta, M., Riccio, D.: GANT: Gaze analysis technique for human identification. Pattern Recognition (March 13, 2014). http://www.sciencedirect.com/science/article/pii/S0031320314000697
14. Kinnunen, T., Sedlak, F., Bednarik, R.: Towards task-independent person authentication using eye movement signals. In: 2010 Symposium on Eye-Tracking Research & Applications (ETRA), pp. 187–190, ACM (2010)
15. Liang, Z., Tan, F., Chi, Z.: Video-based biometric identification using eye tracking technique. In: 2012 IEEE International Conference on Signal Processing, Communication and Computing (ICSPCC), pp. 728–733 (2012)
16. Holland, C., Komogortsev, O.V.: Biometric identification via eye movement scanpaths in reading. In: 2011 International Joint Conference on Biometrics (IJCB), pp. 1–8 (2011)
17. Biedert, R., Frank, M., Martinovic, I., Song, D.: Stimuli for gaze based intrusion detection. In: J. (Jong Hyuk) Park, James and Leung, Victor, C.M., Wang, Cho-Li and Shon, Taeshik (eds.): Future Information Technology, Application, and Service, pp. 757–763. Springer (2012)
18. Silver, D.L., Biggs, A.: Keystroke and Eye-Tracking Biometrics for User Identification. In: 2006 International Conference on Artificial Intelligence (IC-AI), pp. 344–348 (2006)

19. Kumar, M., Garfinkel, T., Boneh, D., Winograd, T.: Reducing Shoulder-surfing by Using Gaze-based Password Entry. In: 3rd Symposium on Usable Privacy and Security, pp. 13–19. ACM (2007)
20. Luca, A.D., Weiss, R., Hußmann, H., An, X.: Eyepass - Eye-stroke Authentication for Public Terminals. In: CHI 2008 Extended Abstracts on Human Factors in Computing Systems, pp. 3003–3008. ACM (2008)
21. Dunphy, P., Fitch, A., Olivier, P.: Gaze-contingent passwords at the ATM. In: 4th Conference on Communication by Gaze Interaction (COGAIN), pp. 59–62 (2008)
22. Weaver, J., Mock, K., Hoanca, B.: Gaze-based password authentication through automatic clustering of gaze points. In: 2011 IEEE International Conference on Systems, Man, and Cybernetics (SMC), pp. 2749–2754 (2011)
23. Maeder, A., Fookes, C., Sridharan, S.: Gaze based user authentication for personal computer applications. In: 2004 International Symposium on Intelligent Multimedia, Video and Speech Processing, pp. 727–730 (2004)
24. Rozado, D.: Using gaze based passwords as an authentication mechanism for password input. In: 3rd International Workshop on Pervasive Eye Tracking and Mobile Eye-Based Interaction (2013)

Analysing Soft Clothing Biometrics for Retrieval

Emad Sami Jaha[1,2(✉)] and Mark S. Nixon[2]

[1] Faculty of Computing and Information Technology, King Abdulaziz University,
Jeddah, Saudi Arabia
ejaha@kau.edu.sa
[2] School of Electronics and Computer Science, University of Southampton,
Southampton, United Kingdom
msn@ecs.soton.ac.uk

Abstract. Soft biometrics continues to attract research interest. Traditional body and face soft biometrics have been the main research focus and have been proven, by many researchers, to be usable for identification and retrieval. Also, soft biometrics have been shown to provide several advantages over classic biometrics, such as invariance to illumination and contrast. Other than body and face, little attention has focussed on semantic descriptions of an individual, including clothing attributes. Research has yet to concern clothing characteristics as a major or complementary set of biometric traits. In this paper, we analyse the reliability and significance of clothing information for retrieval purposes. We investigate and rate the viability of semantic clothing descriptions to retrieve a subject correctly, given a verbal description of their clothing.

Keywords: Soft Biometrics · Human Descriptions · Retrieval · Semantic Clothing Attributes · Relative Attributes

1   Introduction

In recent years, there has been an increasing interest in soft biometrics. Traditional soft biometrics such as age, gender, and ethnicity in addition to body and face traits like height, and arm length, have been the most considered traits for different objectives and in a variety of applications.

Subject retrieval is a useful and challenging biometric application. Bodily human features can be described using human understandable labels and measurements, which in turn, allow for recognition and retrieval using only verbal descriptions as the sole query [1, 2]. The features also allow prediction of other measurements as they have been observed to be correlated [3]. Indeed, soft traits are not unique to an individual but a discriminative biometric signature can be designed from their aggregation. Verbal identification can be used to retrieve subjects who have been previously enrolled in database [4] and it could be extended, in a more challenging application, for retrieval from video footage [1]. The capability of verbal retrieval from images and videos can pave the way for applications that can search surveillance data of a crime scene to match people to potential suspects described verbally by eyewitnesses. Soft biometric databases based on categorical labels can be

© Springer International Publishing Switzerland 2014
V. Cantoni et al. (Eds.): BIOMET 2014, LNCS 8897, pp. 234–245, 2014.
DOI: 10.1007/978-3-319-13386-7_19

incorporated with other biometrics to enhance recognition, such as integrating soft body traits with a gait signature [4], and using soft facial traits along with other (hard) facial traits [5]. Nevertheless, soft comparative labels have been demonstrated to be more successful in representing the slight differences between people in bodily descriptions [1]. Facial marks, for instance, can be automatically detected and ascribed to be used as micro soft traits to supplement primary facial features for improved face recognition and fast retrieval, besides they may enable matching with low resolution or partial images [6, 7]. For surveillance purposes, different forms of soft biometrics take place in various means of applications and scenarios [1, 8, 9].

Human clothes are a predominant visible characteristic of the person's appearance. However, clothing has rarely been adopted for representing soft biometric traits for an individual and has been considered unlikely to be a clue to identity [10]. Clothing can reflect some cues regarding social status, lifestyle and cultural affiliation. In addition, clothing encodes more information about an individual, beyond just their visual appearance [10]. There are few research studies associated with using clothing for biometric purposes [2, 5, 9, 11, 12]. The majority of existing research employs computer vision algorithms and machine learning techniques to extract and use visual clothing descriptions in applications including: online person recognition [5, 11]; semantic attributes for re-identification [13]; detecting and analysing semantic descriptions (labels) of clothing colours and types to supplement other bodily and facial soft attributes in automatic search and retrieval [9]; and utilizing some clothing attributes like colour [14] and style to improve the observation and retrieval at a distance in surveillance environments [2]. Even with images captured on different days, there remains sufficient information to compare and establish identity, since clothes are often re-worn or a particular individual may prefers a specific clothing style or colour [15]. Clothing descriptions like indicative colours and decorations could be utilized to supplement other behavioural biometrics like human motion pattern, hence they can form a biometric fingerprint that serves as a person's identifier [11].

This research aims to investigate the capability of soft clothing traits towards reinforcing biometric signatures. We have previously studied the identification capability of these new measures [16]. This paper focusses on using clothing to enable accurate subject retrieval, and the efficacy of the clothing labels. Furthermore, a set of experiments validates and evaluates the retrieval performance of clothing-based techniques and the new sets of clothing labels. We outline and discuss their retrieval performance, measured by a set of evaluation metrics. The main contributions of this paper comprise:

- extended analysis and investigation of reliability and significance of proposed categorical and comparative soft clothing traits;
- new soft clothing-based biometrics techniques for subject retrieval; and
- detailed retrieval assessment and comparison of soft clothing approaches.

Section 2 outlines the proposed semantic attributes and their labels. Section 3 explains the mechanism used for data collection and clothing database design. Section 4 introduces soft clothing biometrics. Section 5 demonstrates clothing information analysis. Section 6 describes subject retrieval using soft clothing biometrics. Finally, Section 7 concludes the paper and discusses future work.

Table 1. Semantic clothing attributes and corresponding categorical and comparative labels

Body zone	Semantic Attribute	Categorical Labels	Comparative Labels
Head	1. Head clothing category	[None, Hat, Scarf, Mask, Cap]	
	2. **Head coverage**	[None, Slight, Fair, Most, All]	[Much Less, Less, Same, More, Much more]
	3. **Face covered**	[Yes, No, Don't know]	[Much Less, Less, Same, More, Much more]
	4. Hat	[Yes, No, Don't know]	
Upper body	5. Upper body clothing category	[Jacket, Jumper, T-shirt, Shirt, Blouse, Sweater, Coat, Other]	
	6. Neckline shape	[Strapless, V-shape, Round, Shirt collar, Don't know]	
	7. **Neckline size**	[Very Small, Small, Medium, Large, Very Large]	[Much Smaller, Smaller, Same, Larger, Much Larger]
	8. **Sleeve length**	[Very Short, Short, Medium, Long, Very Long]	[Much Shorter, Shorter, Same, Longer, Much Longer]
Lower body	9. Lower body clothing category	[Trouser, Skirt, Dress]	
	10. Shape	[Straight, Skinny, Wide, Tight, Loose]	
	11. **Leg length** (of lower clothing)	[Very Short, Short, Medium, Long, Very Long]	[Much Shorter, Shorter, Same, Longer, Much Longer]
	12. Belt presence	[Yes, No, Don't know]	
Foot	13. Shoes category	[Heels, Flip flops, Boot, Trainer, Shoe]	
	14. **Heel level**	[Flat/low, Medium, High, Very high]	[Much Lower, Lower, Same, Higher, Much higher]
Attached to body	15. Attached object category	[None, Bag, Gun, Object in hand, gloves]	
	16. **Bag** (size)	[None, Side-bag, Cross-bag, Handbag, Backpack, Satchel]	[Much Smaller, Smaller, Same, Larger, Much Larger]
	17. Gun	[Yes, No, Don't know]	
	18. Object in hand	[Yes, No, Don't know]	
	19. Gloves	[Yes, No, Don't know]	
General style	20. Style category	[Well-dressed, Business, Sporty, Fashionable, Casual, Nerd, Bibes, Hippy, Religious, Gangsta, Tramp, Other]	
Permanent	21. Tattoos	[Yes, No, Don't know]	

2   Semantic Clothing Attributes

A subject's clothing can be described using different semantic attributes. For the purpose of this research, amongst several possible clothing attributes and labels, an initial set of attributes is considered (see Table 1, as described elsewhere [16]). A group of *categorical* and *comparative* labels are used to describe these attributes.

Categorical labels can be defined as nameable descriptions used to describe semantic attributes of an individual's clothing, usually associated with multiple clothing categories or styles such as (*Upper body clothing category*: 'Jacket', 'Jumper', 'T-shirt' etc.) or can be labels describing the degree of presence of relative attributes such as (*Sleeve length*: 'Very short', 'Short', 'Medium' etc.). *Comparative* labels are nameable descriptions used to describe only relative attributes of an individual's clothing compared with another individual's clothing. In other words, these labels describe the degree of comparisons of relative attributes, such as (*Neckline size*: 'Much smaller', 'Smaller', 'Same', 'Larger' and 'Much larger').

A list of 21 semantic attributes is proposed and each attribute is described by a specified group of suitable categorical labels. Furthermore, seven of the 21 attributes are both categorical and relative enabling comparison, whereas the remaining 14 are unsuited for comparison because they are binary or multi-class attributes that can be described using only categorical (absolute) labels. In Table 1 the seven relative comparable attributes are in bold. We utilise an early analysis [17] used bipolar scales to define traits for whole-body descriptions. For all binary-label clothing attributes, such as 'Belt presence', a label 'Don't know' was included as a choice.

3 Data Acquisition

The Soton Gait Database [18] is a standard database and comprises a subset of full-body fronta and side view still images. The front view images are used to collect clothing descriptions. This subset consists of 115 individuals with a total of 128 front view samples. Here, each sample is handled as an independent individual; multiple samples of a single individual are considered as different and independent entities by which each entity represents that individual only if wearing exactly the same clothing. Otherwise, it is considered as another entity, even though it belongs to the same individual. Here, each entity (i.e. sample in this dataset) is referred to as a *subject*. Note that 90% of the subjects in the database are university students and wear largely similar (summer) clothing (jeans, T-shirt, etc.) and the data appears sufficiently challenging for this initial study.

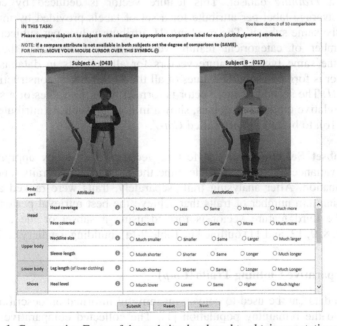

Fig. 1. Comparative Form of the website developed to obtain annotation data

A website, shown in Fig. 1, was designed and developed to obtain clothing labels and comparisons, through two tasks. The first task required a user to annotate ten subjects. Each subject was described by selecting 21 appropriate categorical labels.

The second task required a user to compare one subject, selected randomly from the ten already annotated, with other ten new subjects. A comparison, between two subjects was performed by selecting seven appropriate comparative labels. In this way 27 labellers provided a total of 12747 categorical and comparative labels on 128 subjects. Clothing attributes were grouped based on their zones and relevance as: Head, Upper body, Lower body, Foot, Attached to body, General style and Permanent as shown in Table 1 and Fig. 1.

6636 categorical and 2219 comparative labels were collected from the 27 users via the website. All 128 samples were labelled by multiple users, with one or more separate user annotations per subject describing the 21 categorical attributes such that, each subject's annotation provided by a single annotator. All subjects were compared using the seven relative attributes by multiple users. To enrich the comparison data from the available number of collected comparisons, 3892 additional comparisons were inferred when two subjects were both compared with another same subject.

4 Soft Clothing Biometrics

4.1 Categorical Clothing Traits (*Cat-N*)

Categorical annotations are used to form a categorical-based feature vector for each subject in a *Training* dataset. This feature vector is deduced by computing a normalized average-label per attribute for a set of labels provided by multiple users describing the same subject. The resulting 21 attribute values per subject are used to form a number of categorical feature vectors and to construct their galleries, containing the same type of feature vectors for all subjects in database. The first feature vector is formed using the values of all the 21 attributes, constructing a gallery called *Cat-21*. The second feature vector is formed from the values of a subset of the only seven relative clothing attributes, shown in bold in Table 1 (attributes 2, 3, 7, 8, 11, 14, and 16), to build a gallery called *Cat-7*.

Feature Subset Selection. A third feature vector is formed by applying one-way analysis of variance (ANOVA) to determine the most effective traits (and attributes) for discrimination. After analysing traits separately, traits were ranked as shown in Fig. 2. A minimum number of traits that achieve the best retrieval performance were selected. The third feature vector is formed using a subset of the top five traits (attributes 2, 8, 9, 12, and 11) outlined in Table 2-(a), building a gallery called (*Cat-5*).

4.2 Comparative Clothing Traits (*Cmp*)

Comparison data can be used to convey meaningful information describing a subject in relation to the remaining population [1]. The collected comparative annotations need to be anchored, per attribute, to define invariant relative measurements for each subject. To derive these measurements, a ranking method needs to be applied to arrange a list of ordered subjects with respect to a single attribute. In the ranking process, the comparisons between subjects are used as rules to enforce ordering for subjects, and to adjust a relative measurement per attribute for each.

Ranking SVM. To achieve ordering and to derive the desired relative measurements to represent comparative soft clothing traits, a soft-margin Ranking SVM method [19] is used, along with a supporting formulation of similarity constraints [20]. This applies a pairwise technique based on learning a ranking function per attribute, which can be used not only to determine the relative strength of attributes in a training sample, but also to predict the relative strength in a new test sample. Thus, for a set of attributes A, a ranking linear function r_a is learned for each attribute a such that:

$$r_a(x_i) = w_a^T x_i \tag{1}$$

where w_a is the coefficient of the ranking function r_a and x_i is a feature vector of attributes of a subject being ranked. A set of comparisons is rearranged into two groups to represent the pairwise relative constraints required to learn a ranking function. The first group consists of a set of dissimilarity comparisons D_a of ordered pairs so that $(i, j) \in D_a \Rightarrow i > j$ whereas the second group comprises a set of similarity comparisons S_a of non-ordered pairs so that $(i, j) \in S_a \Rightarrow i = j$. D_a and S_a sets are then utilized to derive the w_a coefficients of r_a according to the following formulation:

$$\text{minimise} \left(\frac{1}{2} \| w_a^T \|^2 + C \sum \xi_{ij}^2 \right)$$

$$\text{subject to } w_a^T(x_i - x_j) \geq 1 - \xi_{ij}; \quad \forall (i,j) \in D_a \tag{2}$$

$$| w_a^T(x_i - x_j) | \leq \xi_{ij}; \quad \forall (i,j) \in S_a$$

$$\xi_{ij} \geq 0$$

The degree of misclassification is measured by ξ_{ij} and the trade-off between maximizing the margin and minimizing the error (i.e. satisfying constraints) is denoted as C. The resulting optimal function w_a can enforce (explicitly) a desirable ordering for all training samples, in respect to a. A feature vector x_i is mapped using Eqn. (1) to a corresponding feature vector comprising a number of real-value relative measurements. Each measurement represents the relative strength of a single attribute.

All subjects in the *Cat-7* gallery are used as a training dataset to learn seven optimal ranking functions for the seven relative attributes. The weighting of each function is derived using the formulation in Eqn. (2). The desirable per attribute ordering of all subjects is deduced from w. Then by Eqn. (1), each value of w is used to map each feature vector in *Cat-7* to a corresponding vector of seven relative measurements (i.e. comparative traits) describing a single subject. All the obtained relative measurement vectors are gathered to compose a fourth gallery called (*Cmp*).

5   Data Analysis

5.1   Analysis of Variance (ANOVA)

Table 2 provides the ordered lists of resulting ANOVA test values for categorical and comparative clothing traits. Accordingly, Fig. 2 shows ordered p-values scaled positively by computing the absolute logarithm of the p-value, which emphasises smaller p-values. Scaling is used to magnify small differences between p-values and to be visually observable. Head coverage is highly discriminative since few subjects had covered heads. It is perhaps surprising that sleeve length is so discriminative, especially compared with the length of the trousers, but that is what this analysis reveals, and no summary analysis is possible by human vision.

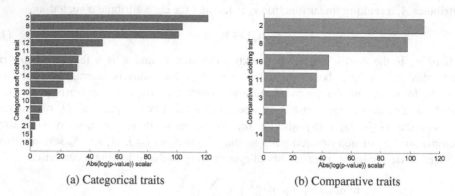

(a) Categorical traits   (b) Comparative traits

Fig. 2. Attributes ordered according to p-values

Table 2. Ordered list of clothing traits by their F-ratios

(a) Categorical trait

Soft clothing biometrics	F-ratio ($df = 315$)	P-value ($p \leq 0.05$)
2. Head coverage	13.239	8.45E-53
8. Sleeve length	10.549	3.07E-45
9. Lower body clothing category	10.189	4.07E-44
12. Belt presence	4.600	2.46E-21
11. Leg length (of lower clothing)	3.478	5.07E-15
5. Upper body clothing category	3.324	4.25E-14
13. Shoes category	3.265	9.66E-14
14. Heel level	3.057	1.80E-12
6. Neckline shape	2.608	1.16E-09
20. Style category	2.326	6.96E-08
10. Shape (of lower clothing)	1.618	0.0013
7. Neckline size	1.608	0.0015
4. Hat	1.471	0.0081
21. Tattoos	1.214	0.1129
15. Attached object category	0.874	0.7910
18. Object in hand	0.874	0.7910

(b) Comparative trait

Soft clothing biometrics	F-ratio ($df = 315$)	P-value ($p \leq 0.05$)
2. Head coverage	11.369	1.08E-47
8. Sleeve length	9.790	7.79E-43
16. Bag (size)	4.258	1.73E-19
11. Leg length (of lower clothing)	3.622	7.16E-16
3. Face covered	2.186	5.30E-07
7. Neckline size	2.140	1.03E-06
14. Heel level	1.852	6.07E-05

5.2   Correlations and Significance

The exploration of clothing traits' significance and correlations, is deemed to be an important analysis resulting in a better comprehension of which of traits contribute most to identification and leading to wider potential predictability of other traits [3]. The proposed clothing traits were assessed to investigate their correlation and effectiveness for subject description. For the sake of this investigation, we used the correlation matrix computed using (Pearson's r) correlation coefficient to highlight the significance of an attribute and the mutual relations between traits. Note that, when one or both of correlated labels are binary or multi-class describing pure (nominal) categorical traits, this indicates that they are simultaneously present in a single annotation. That is because the assigned numeral values of such labels are unlike (ordinal) labels of relative measurements, so they can be assigned values in any order or their values can be exchanged.

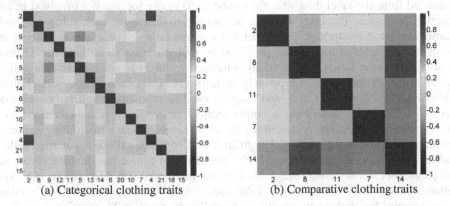

(a) Categorical clothing traits   (b) Comparative clothing traits

Fig. 3. Correlation matrix between the soft clothing traits

Fig. 3 demonstrates the correlation between the most significant categorical traits and comparative traits (see Table 2); traits without correlation are not shown. High correlation is symbolized by orange, and low by blue/green. In the categorical matrix, traits relating to head coverage (2) and (4) are highly correlated, as are the traits (15) and (18) relating to the description of items attached to the body. Clothing categories are well correlated for upper (5) and lower (9) body, as expected. In the comparative matrix, sleeve length (8) and heel level (14) are highly correlated. Heel level is also well correlated with leg length (11) and neckline size (7). The structures of both correlation matrices suggest that the desired uniqueness has indeed been achieved.

6   Retrieval Using Soft Clothing Traits

The main objective of this experimental work is to validate and evaluate the proposed soft clothing approaches, described in Section 4, in retrieval and to explore their viability to supplement the performance of soft body biometrics. The distinction between retrieval and recognition concerns the ability to generalise to unseen data. We use the previously collected soft body descriptions from the Soton database [11] where each of 115 individuals was labelled by multiple users' describing 23 soft bodily traits. These traits were grouped into three categories: *Body shape*, *Global*, and *Head*. Our clothing analysis is used to enhance the retrieval in two different respects. Firstly, to enhance the performance of only the traditional soft traits (Age, Ethnicity, Sex, and Skin Colour) which were grouped as *Global* attributes as in [4]. Secondly, to enhance all the mentioned 23 soft body traits including the four traditional traits.

Biometric based retrieval can be described as a task that aims to identify an unknown subject by comparing and matching their biometric signature with those signatures enrolled in a database [1]. For the sake of retrieval, the collected clothing annotations were divided into two sets: a *Query* set comprising one annotation per subject for each of the 128 subjects, which is used (as unseen data) to examine retrieval; and a *Training* set containing all the remaining annotations, which is used for training and feature selection processes. All annotations in the *Query* set are excluded from the label data, and not reused in *Training* set and not involved in any training processes. The body *Training* set is used to derive for each subject a single feature vector consisting of 23 normalized average-labels. These average-labels are computed for a set of annotations provided by multiple users describing the 23 body traits of the same subject. A set of all computed feature vectors comprises a gallery called *softBody* to be tested separately in retrieval. Then each of the soft clothing galleries (*Cat-21, Cat-7, Cat-5,* and *Cmp*) is used to supplement *softBody* such that, each feature vector describing a single subject in *softBody* is concatenated to a corresponding feature vector describing the same subject in each of clothing galleries, resulting in: *softCat-21, softCat-7, softCat-5* and *softCmp* galleries. Another gallery called *tradSoft* is derived from *softBody,* consisting of a four-trait feature vector per subject subset of only comprising only the four traditional soft descriptions (i.e. Age, Ethnicity, Sex, and Skin Colour). Likewise, *tradSoft* is extended to four versions supplemented by clothing to construct new galleries: *tradCat-21, tradCat-7, tradCat-5* and *tradCmp*. Query-vectors are normalised and reshaped according to the feature-vectors in a tested gallery to enable comparison and matching.

The likelihood between every single query-vector and all subject-vectors in a gallery is estimated and retrieved, resulting in an ordered list of all subjects based on likelihood evaluated by the sum of Euclidean distance between query and gallery vectors. A number of standard performance evaluation methods are used to enable comparison between approaches from different perspectives. The Cumulative Match Characteristic (CMC) curve is applied to summarize the retrieval accuracy, which scores the existence of the correct subjects within a (likelihood-based) ranked list starting from list-length of 1 to 128 the total number of subjects in a tested gallery. Receiver Operator Characteristic (ROC) analysis is used to assess and compare the approaches performance and their generated errors. A set of further performance metrics are deduced from the ROC analysis comprising the Area Under the Curve (AUC) as in our consideration a smaller are under the ROC curve reflecting a less error and a better performance, and the Equal Error Rate (EER). Also the Decidability Index (d') metric is computed form the normalized distance between the two means of *Genuine* (*G*) and *Imposter* (*I*) distributions such that $d' = |\mu_G - \mu_I|/\sqrt{(\sigma_G^2 + \sigma_I^2)/2}$. The overall performance, with respect to all evaluation metrics, is deduced for all approaches to rank them by overall score.

6.1   Retrieval Using Clothing and Traditional Soft Biometrics

The ROC performance of the examined approaches is compared in Fig. 4, where all clothing approaches but *tradCat-21* provide better retrieval accuracy and less error. Table 3 reports the CMC scores and the average-sum scores along different ranks, besides the ROC analysis results for the traditional soft traits (Age, Ethnicity, Sex, and Skin Colour) and when adding soft clothing traits to them; all the best values are shown in bold. In all the retrieval match score, all clothing approaches enhance the retrieval performance of the traditional soft biometrics up to 9% in average at rank 128 achieved by *tradCat-5*. The best overall performance achieved by *tradCat-5* followed by *tradCmp* with slightly low performance and very close scores across all assessment metrics. However, *tradCmp* receives the best scores in the average score up to rank 10 and reaching, and *tradCat-7* attains the highest score at rank 1, then is exceeded by *tradCat-5* and *tradCmp* with the rank increase.

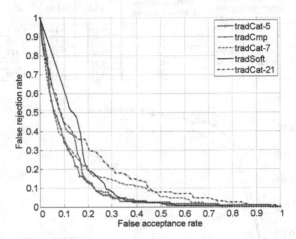

Fig. 4. ROC performance of traditional soft biometrics and when supplemented by clothing

Table 3. Performance metrics of traditional soft biometrics and when supplemented by clothing

Approach	Top rank =1	AVG sum match scores up to rank =10	AVG sum match scores up to rank =128	100% accuracy achieved at rank	EER	AUC	d'	Performance overall rank
tradSoft	0.14	0.27	0.838	106	0.094	0.039	2.379	4
tradCat-21	0.23	0.41	0.866	108	0.107	0.050	1.829	5
tradCat-7	**0.25**	0.47	0.900	95	0.116	0.039	2.292	3
tradCat-5	0.24	0.49	**0.925**	70	**0.086**	**0.032**	**2.436**	1
tradCmp	0.24	**0.50**	0.919	**67**	0.094	0.037	2.416	2

6.2 Retrieval Using Clothing and Soft Body Biometrics

Fig. 5 presents the CMC curves of the retrieval performance of soft body traits and compare the performance the clothing approaches. The figure shows the CMC curves up to rank 25 where the differences between compared approaches are more significant and can be appreciated. Table 4 provides all the produced metric results of CMC and ROC of body soft biometrics and the clothing approaches. The approaches *softCat-5*, *softCmp*, and *softCat-7* respectively gain a highest performance that improves retrieval performance of using soft body biometrics alone, *softCat-21* starts with a higher accuracy than *softBody* but provides a lower performance between rank 2 and 23, and then increase rapidly over all approaches.

The best overall performance is achieved by *softCat-5* as it yields the best scores in all evaluation measurements but two as can be observed in Table 4. All clothing approaches started with better retrieval accuracy at rank 1 than the soft body traits, while *softCat-5* considerably increase the retrieval from only 67% to 82%. Although the inferiority of the *softCat-21* in all used evaluation criteria compared with its clothing-based counterparts, it is the first to reach the reach 100% at a minimum rank of 32. *softCmp* receives the best score in terms of decidability metric d'.

Table 4. Performance metrics of body soft biometrics and when supplementd by clothing

Approach	Top rank =1	AVG sum match scores up to rank =10	=128	100% accuracy achieved at rank	EER	AUC	d'	Performance overall rank
softBody	0.668	0.900	0.988	56	0.196	0.146	1.611	4
softCat-21	0.695	0.882	0.987	**32**	0.259	0.177	0.942	5
softCat-7	0.742	0.923	0.990	49	0.209	0.133	1.417	3
softCat-5	**0.820**	**0.946**	**0.992**	47	**0.167**	**0.105**	1.552	1
softCmp	0.742	0.927	0.990	40	0.170	0.113	**1.770**	2

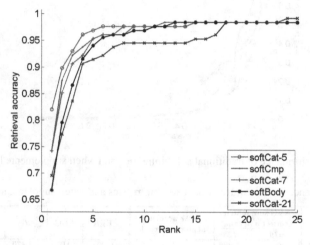

Fig. 5. CMC performance (up to rank 25) of the soft body biometrics and when supplementd by clothing

7   Conclusions and Future Work

This paper explores the viability of using soft clothing attributes to achieve enhanced subject retrieval. The results of this exploration using clothing traits highlights a potentially valuable addition to the field of soft biometrics. This can lead to new and useful enhanced biometric applications and systems, using soft clothing biometrics for various purposes including subject search, retrieval, identification, and re-identification. Our analysis of soft clothing traits indicates that such clothing characteristics can be associated in biometric signatures and achieve successful subject retrieval.

Future work will continue to investigate the ability and significance of the new soft clothing biometrics for retrieval in more challenging scenarios. One possible scenario could be the retrieval using newly collected query annotations describing unseen subjects' images derived from different viewpoints in which some clothing attributes can be occluded or difficult to observe. Therefore, such an analysis appears more vulnerable to subjectivity and missing information. Another future work could be to focus on learning a fully automated clothing labelling for data images and query images for retrieval purposes.

References

1. Reid, D., Nixon, M., Stevenage, S.: Soft Biometrics, Human Identification using Comparative Descriptions. IEEE Trans. PAMI (2014)
2. Thornton, J., Baran-Gale, J., Butler, D., et al.: Person attribute search for large-area video surveillance. In: IEEE Int. Conf. on Technologies for Homeland Security (HST) (2011)
3. Adjeroh, D., Deng, C., Piccirilli, M., et al.: Predictability and correlation in human metrology. In: IEEE Int. Workshop on Information Forensics and Security (WIFS) (2010)
4. Samangooei, S., Nixon, M.S.: Performing content-based retrieval of humans using gait biometrics. Multimedia Tools and Applications 49, 195–212 (2010)
5. Niinuma, K., Park, U., Jain, A.K.: Soft biometric traits for continuous user authentication. IEEE Trans. on Information Forensics and Security (IFS) 5, 771–780 (2010)
6. Jain, A.K., Park, U.: Facial marks: Soft biometric for face recognition. In: Proc. 16th IEEE International Conference on Image Processing (ICIP) (2009)
7. Park, U., Jain, A.K.: Face matching and retrieval using soft biometrics. IEEE Trans. on IFS 5, 406–415 (2010)
8. Tome, P., Fierrez, J., Vera-Rodriguez, R., et al.: Soft Biometrics and Their Application in Person Recognition at a Distance. IEEE Trans. on IFS (2014)
9. Vaquero, D.A., Feris, R.S., Tran, D., et al.: Attribute-based people search in surveillance environments. In: Workshop on Applications of Computer Vision (WACV). IEEE (2009)
10. Bossard, L., Dantone, M., Leistner, C., Wengert, C., Quack, T., Van Gool, L.: Apparel Classification with Style. In: Lee, K.M., Matsushita, Y., Rehg, J.M., Hu, Z. (eds.) ACCV 2012, Part IV. LNCS, vol. 7727, pp. 321–335. Springer, Heidelberg (2013)
11. Wang, H., Bao, X., Choudhury, R.R., et al.: InSight: recognizing humans without face recognition. In: Proc. 14th Workshop on Mobile Computing Systems and Apps (2013)
12. Zhu, J., Liao, S., Lei, Z., et al.: Pedestrian Attribute Classification in Surveillance: Database and Evaluation. In: IEEE International Conference on Computer Vision (ICCV) (2013)
13. Layne, R., Hospedales, T.M., Gong, S.: Person Re-identification by Attributes. In: BMVC (2012)
14. Wang, Y.-F., Chang, E.Y., Cheng, K.P.: A video analysis framework for soft biometry security surveillance. In: Proc. 3rd ACM Int. Workshop on Video Surv. & Sensor Networks (2005)
15. Gallagher, A.C., Chen, T: Clothing cosegmentation for recognizing people. In: IEEE Conference on Computer Vision and Pattern Recognition (CVPR) (2008)
16. Jaha, E.S., Nixon, M.S.: Soft Biometrics for Subject Identification using Clothing Attributes. In: IEEE International Joint Conference on Biometrics (IJCB) (2014)
17. Macleod, M.D., Frowley, J.N., Shepherd, J.W.: Whole body information: Its relevance to eyewitnesses. In: Adult eyewitness testimony: Current trends and developments (1994)
18. Shutler, J., Grant, M., Nixon, M.S., et al.: On a large sequence-based human gait database. In: RASC (2002)
19. Joachims, T.: Optimizing search engines using clickthrough data. In: Proc. 8th ACM SIGKDD Int. Conf. on Knowledge discovery and data mining (2002)
20. Parikh, D., Grauman, K.: Relative attributes. In: IEEE ICCV (2011)

On the Application of Biometric Techniques
for Locating Damaged Artworks

Andreas Lanitis[1(✉)], Nicolas Tsapatsoulis[2], and Anastasios Maronidis[1]

[1] Visual Media Computing Lab,
Department of Multimedia and Graphic Arts, Cyprus University of Technology,
Limassol, Cyprus
{andreas.lanitis,anastasios.maronidis}@cut.ac.cy
[2] Department of Communication and Internet Studies,
Cyprus University of Technology, Limassol, Cyprus
nicolas.tsapatsoulis@cut.ac.cy

Abstract. The continuously increasing art market activity and international art transactions lead the market for stolen and fraudulent art to extreme levels. According to US officials, art crime is the third-highest grossing criminal enterprise worldwide. As a result, art forensics is a rising research field dealing with the identification of stolen or looted art and their collection and repatriation. Photographs of artwork provide, in several cases, the only way to locate stolen and looted items. However, it is quite common these items to be damaged as a result of excavation and illegal movement. Digital processing of photographs of damaged artwork is therefore of high importance in art forensics. This processing emphasizes on "object restoration" and although techniques from the field of image restoration can be applied it is of high importance to take into account the semantics of the artwork scene and especially the structure of objects appeared therein. In this paper, we assess the application of face image restoration techniques, applied on damaged faces appearing in Byzantine icons, in an attempt to identify the actual icons. Several biometric measurements and facial features along with a set of rules related to the design of Byzantine faces are utilized for this purpose. Preliminary investigation, applied on 25 icons, shows promising results.

Keywords: Biometrics · Forensics · Looted Damaged Art · Icon Restoration · Icon Identification

1   Introduction

Looted art has been a consequence of looting during war, natural disaster and riot for centuries. Looting of art, archaeology and other cultural property may be an opportunistic criminal act or may be a more organized case of unlawful or unethical pillage by the victor of a conflict [2]. As the demand for artifacts increases, criminal groups respond promptly with an unfailing supply of illegally obtained or excavated objects by plundering cultural sites, destroying their context and significance [5]. Renfrew [19] noted: "the single largest source of destruction of the archaeological heritage

© Springer International Publishing Switzerland 2014
V. Cantoni et al. (Eds.): BIOMET 2014, LNCS 8897, pp. 246–257, 2014.
DOI: 10.1007/978-3-319-13386-7_20

today is through looting – the illicit, unrecorded and unpublished excavation to provide antiquities for commercial profit".

According to FBI and UNESCO records, looting and trade of antiquities has grown into a multi-billion dollar industry and constitutes the third most profitable illegal traffic after narcotics and arms [5]. As a result, art forensics is a rising research field dealing with the identification of stolen or looted art and their collection and repatriation. Art crime lawyers, forensic experts, computer scientists, and other major players working on legal, forensic, governmental, and political join their efforts to address the enormity of this phenomenon.

Insufficient standardized procedures, the lack of reliable data and the pressing need for improvement of methods employed in forensic practice, have been recognized by the National Academic of Sciences with the publication in 2009 of a scientific report stating: "It is clear that change and advancements, both systematic and scientific, are needed in a number of forensic disciplines to ensure the reliability of work, establish enforceable standards, and promote best practices with consistent application" [17]. This is also true in the case of looting and illicit trade of antiquities. As the origin of looted artifacts is primarily unknown, typological and stylistic studies do not always provide strong support in criminal justice cases for the artifacts' attribution and repatriation.

Scientific investigations of incidents involving stolen or looted art pose many technological difficulties. Methods providing proof beyond reasonable doubt are therefore required to help assign the precise location of origin / provenance through: chemical composition analyses; isotopic fingerprinting; or through other types of analysis that can identify diagnostic markers for an accurate attribution.

This paper deals with a very early stage of art forensics, that of locating artwork which might be stolen or looted, with the aid of simple digital photographs. Since stolen or looted artwork is in many cases damaged (i.e., cutting a larger artwork into small pieces for easy carrying) digital processing of artwork photographs is necessary. This processing is in some cases similar to the classical image restoration. However, the aim here is to digitally restore the "objects" that appear in the artwork scene. Therefore, it is important to take into account the semantics of the artwork scene and especially the structure of objects appeared therein. In this paper, we assess the application of face image restoration techniques, applied on damaged faces appearing in Byzantine icons, in an attempt to identify the actual icons. Several biometric measurements and facial features along with a set of rules related to the design of Byzantine faces are utilized for this purpose.

In the remainder of the paper we present a brief literature review followed by the description of the case study considered in this paper. In Section 4 we describe the experimental set up and present results. Conclusions and plans for future work are presented in Section 5.

2   Literature Review

The art forensics is a new research field. Application of image processing techniques in this field is limited. However, there is a quite extensive literature concerning applications of digital image processing in cultural heritage. This paper borrows several ideas from these techniques and especially from the area of digital restoration of artwork.

A variety of digital image processing techniques have been used in cultural heritage applications for guiding the actual restoration process (e.g. cleaning dirty paintings) or for providing virtual restoration. Morphological techniques and Radial Basis Function (RBF) Neural Networks (NN) have been utilized for crack detection, while order statistics and anisotropic diffusion have been used for crack filling in paintings [11, 20]. In a similar perspective, a methodology based on the Retinex theory of human vision for chromatic restoration of paintings has been proposed by Drago & Chiba [10]. Watermarking techniques have also been applied for protecting the digital reproduction of artworks as well as for simulating the actual restoration process [9]. A "from local to whole" approach methodology to remove cracks from old paintings and frescoes is presented in [3].

The Byzantine icon restoration methodology adopted in this paper combines established statistical methods for occlusion detection and texture restoration on human faces. For instance, in [24], the eyeglasses of a face are removed by learning the joint distribution between pairs of face images with and without eyeglasses from a database. Moreover, in [12, 18, 23] methods for removing facial occlusion based on recursive PCA reconstruction are described. The occluded regions are restored by iteratively processing the difference between the PCA-reconstructed and the original image.

3 Case Study

3.1 Byzantine Icons

Byzantine art refers to the artistic style associated with Byzantine Empire. A large number of Byzantine icons and frescoes showing different Saints, dating back to the 5th century, can be found in churches and monasteries mainly in Eastern Europe. Like numerous other forms of artwork, a number of Byzantine icons of archeological value have been stolen and traded illegally [8]. Especially in the case of frescoes the process of extracting artworks from walls usually causes damages on the original artifacts. Similarly in the case of stolen icons the illegal transportation coupled with non-careful handling, often inflicts damages.

3.2 Byzantine Icon Restoration

In [13, 16] an integrated methodology that can be used for detecting and restoring damages on digitized Byzantine icons is described. The icon restoration method was influenced by the work of professional Byzantine icon conservators. It relies on the use of rules that describe the geometric and chromatic structure of faces appearing in Byzantine icons [22]. The restoration framework was also influenced by previous research efforts in the area of biometrics and in particular in the area of detecting and eliminating occlusions on human face images [12, 18, 24]. However, because faces in Byzantine icons are governed by unique geometrical and chromatic rules, face image processing algorithms were customized for dealing with the unique case of Byzantine style. The final application consists of several modules that include landmark annotation, shape restoration, damage detection and texture restoration.

Given a damaged face appearing in a Byzantine icon, its shape, as this is defined by a set of 68 landmarks, is recovered through a 3D reconstruction process [4], using a Byzantine specific shape model that has been trained by imposing a set of Byzantine geometric rules on a generic human face model [13]. Detection of damaged areas on the shape-restored face involves the estimation of the residuals obtained after the coding and reconstruction of the face image regions using trained Principal Component Analysis (PCA) texture models. Extracted residuals can be used as the basis for obtaining information about the amount of damage and the positions of damaged regions [15].

The texture of damage-detected regions is, then, restored by utilizing the Recursive PCA algorithm. This is an iterative scheme based on data-driven statistical information [18]. Given a dataset consisting of non-damaged Byzantine faces, a texture model is trained. Changing the parameters of the model results in several synthetic face instances. In a partially damaged face image, the occluded regions are firstly located using the aforementioned automatic occlusion detection method and replaced by the corresponding regions of the nearest face, in terms of intensity distance, from the dataset. The resulting face is coded in model parameters and back reconstructed in the initial face space. Pixel residuals that correspond to the damaged areas between the initial and the reconstructed face are calculated. The above code-reconstruction process is repeated until the total residual is minimized.

As a result of the restoration process, an overall 3D instance of the restored face is created. The final step of the restoration phase involves the projection of the 3D instance onto the original 2D face, so that the restored model instance overlaps with the damaged face, completing in that way the process of digital restoration.

The developed algorithms have been incorporated within an integrated user-friendly software application that can be used for digital restoration of faces appearing in Byzantine icons. The application performs all of the above functionalities, i.e. damage detection, shape restoration and texture restoration. A quantitative experimental process proved the effectiveness of this Byzantine icon restoration framework [16].

3.3   Identifying Damaged Stolen Icons

Assuming that digital records of stolen Byzantine icons are available, we wish to have an automated system that indicates possible matches between a digital icon found in different archives (i.e. internet sites) and the stored dataset of digital icons. Towards this end it is sufficient to use standard image similarity metrics that enable the identification of stolen artifacts. However, in the case that a stolen icon appears damaged, either as a result of normal condition degradation or as a result of human actions, the possible identification of such artwork may be inhibited. For example, Figures 1 and 2 show images of icons that were deliberately corrupted with damages and/or noise. The key question is whether it is still possible to obtain positive identifications between the distorted and original icons, despite the appearance transformations caused by damages and noise. Towards this end we propose to use the Byzantine icon restoration method described in section 3.2, in an attempt to minimize the effects of damages assisting in that way the positive identification of stolen icons.

Figure 1 shows, also, examples of digitally restored images (right column), when the restoration method is applied to damaged images (Figure 1, center column). The question that arises concerns the possibility of improving the chances of locating stolen artwork based on the restored versions of the icons rather than utilizing damaged icons.

4   Experimental Evaluation

A preliminary investigation that aims to assess the viability of using icon restoration for enhancing the chances of locating stolen icons is described in the following section. In our approach we only utilize data from the facial region because faces constitute a central part of Byzantine icons and as a result in digitized versions of (possibly stolen) icons the facial region is always shown, unlike other parts of an icon, such as labels, that may not be shown in order to impede the icon identification.

4.1   Experimental Set Up

During the preliminary investigation 25 Byzantine icons were used. On each of the 25 icons, parts of the face were artificially damaged. For each face a set of 68 landmarks is located in order to enable the accurate derivation of facial features of the face shown in the image. Further to artificial damages imposed on the icons in the test set, noise, of three different types and increasing intensity, was also added. In particular the images were blurred using a Gaussian filter with standard deviations ranging from 0 to 50, salt and pepper noise covering 0% to 50% of the image and the correct positions of the landmarks were displaced by a random amount of 0 up to ±10 pixels. It should be noted that the displacement of the landmarks, although it does not affect the image itself, it affects the overall process of feature extraction. Furthermore in real applications it is expected to encounter non-accurate landmark localization, hence it is crucial to assess the effects of shape-displacement on the identification process. Examples of damaged and noise corrupted icons used in the experiments are shown in Figures 1 and 2. The feasibility of using restored icons was assessed through two main experiments.

Experiment 1: This experiment involves the comparison of the difference between image features derived from the original and damaged icons against the difference of image features between the original and restored icons.

Experiment 2: In this experiment image features derived from either damaged or restored icons are used for identifying the actual icon against the original set of 25 icons used in the experiment. For the classification experiment a closest distance classifier was used because the primarily aim of this experiment was to assess the goodness of different features rather than the classifier itself. In addition the relatively small number of samples involved in this pilot study does not allow the training of more statistically rigorous classifiers.

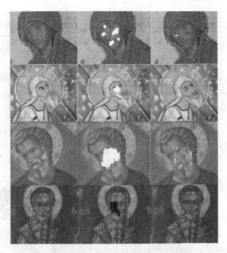

Fig. 1. Examples of original (left), artificially damaged (center) and restored icons (right)

4.2   Image Features

For the two experiments described in section 4.1 six different types of features were used as the means of assessing the image similarity and/or identifying the damaged icon. The actual features used are:

Shape Free Texture (SFT): The textures from the internal facial region are warped to a common shape and the intensities within the shape-normalized facial region are used as the feature vector.

Active Shape Model (AAM) Parameters: The facial region is coded into a number of Active Appearance Model [6] parameters, using an AAM trained on 100 training Byzantine faces. AAM parameters describe in a compact way both the texture of a face and its facial shape as described by a set of 68 landmarks.

Local Binary Patterns (LBP): The shape normalized internal facial region from an icon is divided into 33 patches and from each patch the LBP [1] is estimated. By concatenating the individual LBP vectors an overall feature vector is created.

Histogram of Oriented Gradients (MHOG): A bounding box of the facial area is divided in four windows (2x2) and a 36-dimension Histogram of Oriented Gradients [7] feature is computed in each window leading to a 144x1 vector representation (by concatenating the HOGs in the four windows).

Local Histograms of Oriented Gradients (PHOG): Histogram of Oriented Gradients [7] derived at windows located on 68 key points of each face under consideration. These features highlight the local texture intensity fluctuations at the selected key points.

Spatial Histogram of Key-points (SHIK): Based on an 8x8 fractal grid and SIFT [14] descriptors of 128 elements, each image is represented by a 64x128 element vector made of the concatenation of the accumulated SIFT descriptors ordered according to the order of fractal points so that the final descriptor does not depend on the number of SIFT key-points detected [21].

Fig. 2. Examples of noise corrupted icons. The top row shows blurred damaged icons (with sd=20), the middle row shows icons corrupted with 20% salt and pepper noise and the bottom row shows damaged icons with points displaced (red marks show the correct landmark positions and blue marks show landmark positions after a random displacement of ±6 pixels is applied)

4.3   Experimental Results

Experiment 1 (comparison of the difference between image features derived from the original and damaged icons): Figures 3, 4 and 5 show plots of the mean distance between feature vectors derived from damaged and original icons (blue lines) and the mean distance between feature vectors derived from restored and original icons (pink lines) among all samples in the test set, against the amount of noise added.

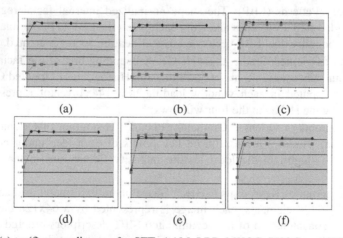

Fig. 3. From (a) to (f) mean distance for SFT, AAM, LBP, MHOG, PHOG and SHIK features when damaged icons are blurred with a Gaussian filter with sds ranging from 0 to 50

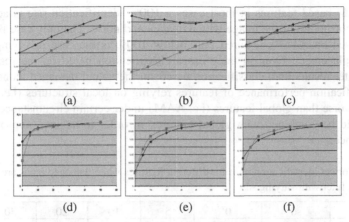

Fig. 4. From (a) to (f) mean distance for SFT, AAM, LBP, MHOG, PHOG and SHIK features when a percentage from 0-50 of damaged icons are corrupted with salt and pepper noise

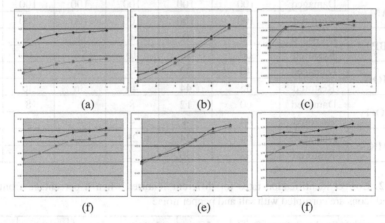

Fig. 5. From (a) to (f) mean distance for SFT, AAM, LBP, MHOG, PHOG and SHIK features when landmarks on damaged images are displaced by 0-10 pixels

In the case of the raw shape-free texture (SFT), AAM and SHIK features and despite the different types and amount of noise added on the damaged icons, the similarity between the restored faces and the original image remains always higher than in the case of the similarity between damaged and original icons. These findings indicate that the restoration process can play an important role in identifying damaged and/or noise corrupted icons. In general the performance of methods relying on local information (i.e. LPB, PHOG) is not as high as the introduction of noise effects distorts the local structure.

Experiment 2 (icon identification based on a damaged or restored icon): Tables 1, 2 and 3 show the correct classification rates when features derived from damaged and restored icons, against the amount of noise added. According to the results, AAM features seem to be the most suitable for identifying damaged icons as in the case of using AAM-based features in most cases a 100% identification rate is achieved despite the corruption of the image with damages and noise. The only case that identification based on AAM's featured falls below 100% is the case involving increased shape displacement. Even in these cases classification based on the restored faces yields better results than classification based on the actual damaged icons. Although the classification performance of features relying on local structures (i.e. SHIK features) is worse than global features (i.e. AAM) under certain circumstances local features could be combined with global features in order to achieve improved overall performance.

Table 1. Correct identification rates for different features when damaged icons are blurred with a Gaussian filter with varying sds

	sd	0	5	10	20	30	50
SFT	Damaged	100	20	17	14	16	16
	Restored	100	44	44	44	44	44
AAM	Damaged	100	100	100	100	100	100
	Restored	100	100	100	100	100	100
LBP	Damaged	56	0	4	4	4	4
	Restored	60	20	16	16	16	16
MHOG	Damaged	40	32	32	28	28	28
	Restored	56	44	40	36	36	36
PHOG	Damaged	60	12	8	8	8	8
	Restored	44	4	4	4	4	4
SHIK	Damaged	64	24	28	24	24	24
	Restored	92	36	32	32	32	32

Table 2. Correct identification rates for different features when a percentage from 0-50 of damaged icons are corrupted with salt and pepper noise

	Noise level	0%	5%	10%	20%	30%	50%
SFT	Damaged	100	100	90	80	70	70
	Restored	100	100	100	100	100	100
AAM	Damaged	100	100	100	100	100	100
	Restored	100	100	100	100	100	100
LBP	Damaged	70	50	30	10	10	0
	Restored	80	70	30	30	20	10
MHOG	Damaged	40	2	8	8	8	8
	Restored	56	8	8	8	8	8
PHOG	Damaged	60	4	4	4	4	4
	Restored	44	8	4	4	4	4
SHIK	Damaged	64	36	24	8	8	8
	Restored	92	32	12	8	8	8

Table 3. Correct identification rates for different features when landmarks on damaged images are displaced by 0-10 pixels

	Displacement	±0	±2	±4	±6	±8	±10
SFT	Damaged	100	76	60	40	36	44
	Restored	100	100	80	68	52	36
AAM	Damaged	100	100	96	96	76	68
	Restored	100	100	96	100	96	72
LBP	Damaged	56	4	4	0	4	0
	Restored	60	12	4	8	0	12
MHOG	Damaged	40	24	24	16	14	12
	Restored	56	40	32	20	24	20
PHOG	Damaged	60	28	20	8	4	4
	Restored	44	32	24	8	8	8
SHIK	Damaged	64	60	48	50	46	41
	Restored	92	84	64	63	61	58

5   Conclusions

A pilot study that aims to assess the feasibility of using digitally restored icons in an attempt to identify damaged icons with respect with a dataset of original icons. Within this context, damaged icons undergo a restoration process that aims to predict the appearance of the missing parts, based on the appearance of the visible parts and a set of rules related to the design of Byzantine faces, incorporated in the restoration system. Preliminary results indicate that the use of the restored instead of the damaged icon, results in reduced differences in different feature spaces, enhancing in that way the chances of positive identifications of the icons involved. In the actual identification experiments for most features a noticeable improvement in identification performance is observed when utilizing digitally restored icons. Apart form few cases involving increased displacement of facial landmarks, AAM features achieve perfect identification performance using either damaged or restored faces. However, it is envisaged that the improved image similarity between a damaged icon and the original icon, observed when using AAM parameters extracted from a restored rather than a damaged icon will lead to improved identification performance when dealing with test sets containing large numbers of icons.

In the future we plan to stage extended experiments that will involve a large number of icons, in order to verify the early findings across a large number of test samples. We also plan to investigate the use of other feature types and metrics that could potentially be used to offer enhanced identification performance between the restored icons and the original. We expect that our preliminary work and findings in this area will be expanded to cater for different types of artworks so that the efforts of preventing stealing, looting and trafficking of artworks are enhanced.

Acknowledgements. This work was partially supported by the Cyprus Research Promotion Foundation and the European Union Structural Funds (project RESTORE: TPE/PLIRO/0609(BIE)/05).

References

1. Ahonen, T., Hadid, A., Pietikainen, M.: Face description with local binary patterns: Application to face recognition. IEEE Transactions on Pattern Analysis and Machine Intelligence **28**(12), 2037–2041 (2006)
2. Atwood, R.: Stealing History, Tomb Raiders, Smugglers and the Looting of the Ancient World. St. Martin's Griffin, New York (2006)
3. Barni, M., Bartolini, F., Cappellini, V.: Image processing for virtual restoration of artworks. IEEE Multimedia **7**, 34–37 (2000)
4. Blanz, V., Vetter, T.: Face recognition based on fitting 3D morphable model. IEEE Transactions on Pattern Analysis and Machine Intelligence **25**, 1063–1074 (2003)
5. Bowman, B.A.: Transnational Crimes Against Culture: Looting at Archaeological Sites and the "Grey" Market in Antiquities. Journal of Contemporary Criminal Justice **24**(3), 225–242 (2008)
6. Cootes, T.F., Edwards, G.J., Taylor, C.J.: Active Appearance Models. IEEE Transactions on Pattern Analysis and Machine Intelligence **23**(6), 681–685 (2001)
7. Dalal, N., Triggs, B.: Histograms of Oriented Gradients for Human Detection. In: Proc. of the 2005 IEEE Conference on Computer Vision and Pattern Recognition, pp. 886–893 (2005)
8. Hadjisavvas, S.: The Destruction of the Archaeological Heritage of Cyprus. Trade in Illicit Antiquities: The Destruction of the World's Archaeological Heritage, 133–139
9. Del Mastio, A., Cappellini, V., Caldelli, R., De Rosa, A., Piva, A.: Virtual restoration and protection of cultural heritage images. In: 15th International Conference on Digital Signal Processing, pp. 471–474 (2007)
10. Drago, F., Chiba, N.: Locally adaptive chromatic restoration of digitally acquired paintings. International Journal of Image and Graphics **5**, 617–637 (2005)
11. Giakoumis, I., Nikolaidis, N., Pitas, I.: Digital image processing techniques for the detection and removal of cracks in digitized paintings. IEEE Transactions on Image Processing **15**, 178–188 (2006)
12. Lanitis, A.: Person Identification From Heavily Occluded Face Images. In: Procs. of the ACM Symposium of Applied Computing, vol 1, pp. 5–9 (2004)
13. Lanitis, A., Stylianou, G., Voutounos, C.: Virtual restoration of faces appearing in Byzantine icons. International Journal of Cultural Heritage **13**(4), 404–412 (2012)
14. Lowe, D.G.: Distinctive image features from scale invariant keypoints. International Journal of Computer Vision **60**(2), 91–110 (2004)
15. Maronidis, A., Lanitis, A.: An Automated Methodology for Assessing the Damage on Byzantine Icons. In: Ioannides, M., Fritsch, D., Leissner, J., Davies, R., Remondino, F., Caffo, R. (eds.) EuroMed 2012. LNCS, vol. 7616, pp. 320–329. Springer, Heidelberg (2012)
16. Maronidis, A., Voutounos, C., Lanitis, A.: Designing and Evaluating an Expert System for Restoring Damaged Byzantine Icons. Multimedia Tools and Applications, 1-24 (2014)
17. National Academy of Sciences. Strengthening Forensic Science in the United States: A Path Forward. Doc. No. 228091, Washington, D.C. (2009)
18. Park, J.S., Oh, Y., Ahn, S., Lee, S.W.: Glasses removal from facial image using recursive PCA reconstruction. In: Kittler, J., Nixon, M.S. (eds.) AVBPA 2003. LNCS, vol. 2688. Springer, Heidelberg (2003)
19. Renfrew, C.: Loot, legitimacy and ownership: the ethical crisis in archaeology. Duckworth, London (2000)

20. Spagnolo, G.S, Somma, F.: Virtual restoration of cracks in digitized image of paintings. Journal of Physics Conference Series 249(1) (2010)
21. Theodosiou, Z. Tsapatsoulis, N.: Spatial Histogram of Keypoints. In: Proc. of the 20th IEEE Intl. Conference on Image Processing, pp. 2924–2928.
22. Vranos, I.C.: H Techniki tis Agiographias. P. S. Pournaras (In Greek), Thessaloniki (2001)
23. Wang, Z.M., Tao, J.H.: Reconstruction of partially occluded face by fast recursive PCA. In: International Conference on Computational Intelligence and Security Workshops, Harbin (December 15-19, 2007)
24. Wu, C., Liu, C., Shum, H.Y., Xy, Y.Q., Zhang, Z.: Automatic eyeglasses removal from face images. IEEE Transactions on Pattern Analysis and Machine Intelligence **26**, 322–336 (2004)

Multifractal Analysis of Posturograms of Young and Elderly Persons

Peter Dojnow[✉]

Institute of Information and Communication Technologies,
Institute of General and Inorganic Chemistry,
Bulgarian Academy of Sciences, Sofia, Bulgaria
Dojnow@bio.bas.bg

Abstract. Multifractality Sw, auto- and crosscorrelations h_2 of medio-lateral and anteroposterior postural sways of healthy young and elderly subjects is studied by the MDFA, WTMM and MDCA methods. MDFA and MDCA reveal a random walk like time series with $h_2 \sim 1.7$. Vibrating soles or aging decreases h_2 of the elderly persons. Sw of the medio-lateral sways is lesser than the anteroposterior sways. The random permutation of the series vanishes the multifractality which is related with the long-range power-low correlations.

Keywords: Multifractality · Crosscorrelations · Posturography

1   Introduction

The vestibular system and motor control as a complex nonlinear system can be studied with a variety of experimental and mathematical analytical methods that can give different, seemingly noncomparable estimates. Posturography is a method which studies the variations (sways) of the standing human body. It is used for clinical and experimental studies. Advantage and convenience of the method is that it is noninvasive and one of the easiest to implement/execute by experienced persons/patients: they usually just stand upright resting 30 seconds. Posturography is used in clinical medicine for studying patients with problems of the vestibular system. As a research method it is used to study the motor control. Recorded sways are called posturograms and they are like other biosignals non-stationary, noisy-like with power law spectrum density. Mathematical methods of the nonlinear dynamics, the theory of chaos and the fractals are appropriate for analysis of such signals [1], using monofractal metods such as DFA [2,3] but the contemporary multifractal metods are more suitable to extract additional information from the complex biosignals.

2   Methods

2.1   Posturographic Experiment

Data used here is obtained from the experiment described in [4] and are published in [5](Noise Enhancement of Sensorimotor Function). 15 healthy young (yng),

© Springer International Publishing Switzerland 2014
V. Cantoni et al. (Eds.): BIOMET 2014, LNCS 8897, pp. 258–264, 2014.
DOI: 10.1007/978-3-319-13386-7_21

mean age 23, and 12 elderly (eh), mean age 73, participants took part in 10 and respectively 5 30-second trials with stimulations (stim) with subsensory vibration in the insoles, and equal number of trials (null) without vibration. The order of the null and the stim trials is random so the participants were not aware about the stimulus. The sampling rate is 60 Hz and the length of the record is 1800 samples. The vibration is low-pass filtered at 100 Hz white noise signal. The posturograms are records of displacements of *Medio/Lateral* (ML) (left-right) and *Antero/Posterior* (AP) (forward-backward) directions.

2.2   Mathematical Methods

The following methods are used: Multifractal Detrended Fluctuation Analysis (MDFA) [6], Wavelet Transform Modulus Maxima Method (WTMM) [7] and Multifractal Detrended Crosscorrelatoin Analysis (MDCA). MDFA in the developed MFA toolbox is modified version of the original one with double sliding windows for smoothing of the fluctuation function and extracting the dynamics of the (multi)fractal parameters in the course of time in case of nonstationarity. MDCA is a method for investigation of crosscorrelations of series, possessing multifractal characteristics. It is appropriate for investigation of interdependence of the sources of the multichannel signals such as sways in ML and AP directions. MDCA is a generalization and further development of MDFA and DCCA [8] therefore in the following subsubsection a brief description of the method will be given. The evaluated parameters are generalized Höledr (Hurst) correlation exponent $h(q)$ (6), scaling exponent $\tau(q)$ (7), multifractal spectrum $f(\alpha)$ (8) and the multifractality - the multifractal spectrum with Sw (10). From the initial posturograms labeled as Si after random shuffling Si_{rp} values are obtained. Amplitude (Am) and phase (Ph) are derived from analytical signal with Hilbert transform from the initial posturograms and thence Am_{rp} and Ph_{rp} components.

Multifractal Detrended Crosscorrelation Analysis. As it was pointed out above MDCA is a combination of MDFA and DCCA. As the real data is often multichannel, let we have an array of time series X with dimension $(M \times N)$, where M is their length (number of points (samples)), N is the number of the time series, for example the channels of EEG or the sways in *Medio/Lateral* (left-right) and *Antero/Posterior* (forward-backward) directions in the posturograms.

Firstly we calculate the integrated series (the columns of the matrix):

$$\widetilde{X}_{ij} = \sum_{i=1}^{i}(X_{ij} - \frac{1}{M}\sum_{i=1}^{M}X_{ij}) ,$$

$$\widetilde{X}_{ik} = \sum_{i=1}^{i}(X_{ik} - \frac{1}{M}\sum_{i=1}^{M}X_{ik}) .$$

$$(1)$$

Next we divide the series (the columns of the matrix) on a $M - s$ overlapping segments, every one with a length $s + 1$. For every segment from i to $i + s$, we define the "local trends" $\widetilde{X}_{\imath j}$ and $\widetilde{X}_{\imath k}$, $i \le \imath \le i + s$, $\imath \in [i, i + s]$ and their linear approximations $\overline{X}_{\imath j}^{(r)}$ and $\overline{X}_{\imath k}^{(r)}$, obtained by the least-square method. For an approximation curve a polynomial of a higher order can be used, like in a DFA$^{(r)}$ and MDFA$^{(r)}$, but in this case it will be limited to the first order: $r = 1$. We define the residuals as the difference between $\widetilde{X}_{\imath j}$ and $\overline{X}_{\imath j}^{(r)}$ and from $\widetilde{X}_{\imath k}$ and $\overline{X}_{\imath k}^{(r)}$. From the residuals, the crossdispersion f_{ijk}^2 is obtained,

$$f_{ijk}^2 = \frac{1}{s - 1} \sum_{\imath=i}^{i+s} (\widetilde{X}_{\imath j} - \overline{X}_{\imath j}^{(r)})(\widetilde{X}_{\imath k} - \overline{X}_{\imath k}^{(r)}) . \tag{2}$$

The fluctuation function $F_{jk}^{(q)}(s)$ is obtained after summation of all segments, raised to the q-th degree,

$$F_{jk}^{(q)}(s) = \left\{ \frac{1}{M - s} \sum_{i=1}^{M-s} [f_{ijk}^2]^{q/2} \right\}^{1/q} . \tag{3}$$

At $q = 0$,

$$F_{jk}^{(0)}(s) = \exp\left\{ \frac{1}{2(M - s)} \sum_{i=1}^{M-s} \ln[f_{ijk}^2] \right\} . \tag{4}$$

If the analyzed series (the columns of the matrix) are power-law, long-range correlated, then the following relation is valid as well,

$$F_{jk}^{(q)}(s) \sim s^{h_{jk}(q)} . \tag{5}$$

From where the generalized crosscorrelation Höledr (Hurst) exponent $h_{jk}(q)$ is derived,

$$h_{jk}(q) \sim \frac{\log F_{jk}^{(q)}(s)}{\log s} , \tag{6}$$

thence the crosscorrelation scale exponent $\tau_{jk}(q)$

$$\tau_{jk}(q) = q h_{jk}(q) - 1 , \tag{7}$$

and the crosscorrelation multifractal (singular) spectrum $f_{jk}(\alpha)$

$$\alpha_{jk} = \frac{d\tau_{jk}(q)}{dq} , \tag{8}$$

$$f_{jk}(\alpha) = q\alpha_{jk} - \tau_{jk}(q) . \tag{9}$$

The multifractality is evaluated form the singular spectrum $f_{jk}(\alpha)$,

$$Sw_{jk} = \alpha_{jk_{min}} - \alpha_{jk_{max}}. \tag{10}$$

3   Results

Figures 1a-3b are boxplots that show lower quartiles, median, upper quartile values of h_2 or Sw of the posturograms (Si), the amplitudes (Am) and the phases (Ph). Comparison of medians is as a visual nonparametric test of hypothesis, analogous to the t-test used in the averages [9]. Medians in contrast to means are resistant (robust) to outliers.

The cases for MDFA and WTMM are:

1 - MLsi,eh,null; 2 - APsi,eh,null; 3 - MLam,eh,null; 4 - APam,eh,null; 5 - MLph,eh,null; 6 - APph,eh,null; 7 - MLsi,eh,stim; 8 - APsi,eh,stim; 9 - MLam,eh,stim; 10 - APam,eh,stim; 11 - MLph,eh,stim; 12 - APph,eh,stim; 13 - MLsi,yng,null; 14 - APsi,yng,null; 15 - MLam,yng,null; 16 - APam,yng,null; 17 - MLph,yng,null; 18 - APph,yng,null; 19 - MLsi,yng,stim; 20 - APsi,yng,stim; 21 - MLam,yng,stim; 22 - APam,yng,stim; 23 - MLph,yng,stim; 24 - APph,yng,stim.

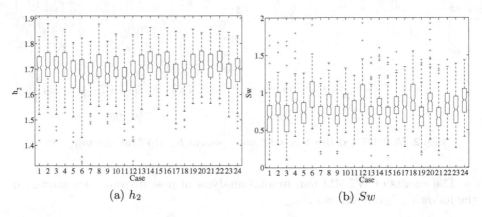

(a) h_2 (b) Sw

Fig. 1. MDFA: (a) Hurst correlation exponent h_2; (b) Multifractality Sw

The values of h_2 shown on Fig. 1a are ~ 1.7, which is a Brownian noise, only the phases are slightly smaller. Stimulation of young people does not change the correlation and aging slightly loweres it. Stimulation of old ones shows slightly decreased correlation. The correlation of the old on stable support is slightly higher compared to the others. Changing h_2 from ~ 1.7 to ~ 0.52 after random permutation of series indicates that multifractality of the posturograms is of the correlation type.

The results for multifractality Sw are presented Fig. 1a. No difference between Si, Am is revealed. Ph have bigger multifractality compared to Si and Am. The AP values are distinctly higher than those of the ML. There is no distinction between unstimulated (null) and stimulated (stim) eh persons. There is no difference between the three components of the AP. Si has multiple outliers. There are no statistically distinguishable differences between individuals and conditions, except a slight increase at eh,null and yng,stim against eh,stim and yng,null. The phase gradually declines from 1 to 0.9 in the following order: eh,null, eh,stim, yng,null, yng,stim. There aren't statistically distinguishable differences between persons and conditions as the medians ML are ~ 0.65, by 0.1 less than that of AP, between Si and Am and between null and stim, as eh medians are ~ 0.75, 0.1 more than those of Si and Am. yng are slightly larger than eh and are the highest at yng,null - over 0.8. The change of Sw from $\sim 0.65.. \sim 1$ to $\sim 0.2.. \sim 0.3$ at Sw_{rp}, shows that the random permutation destroys the multifractality of the posturograms. The multifractality of ML is always $\sim 0.15.. \sim 0.25$ less than the AP, and outliers are mainly above.

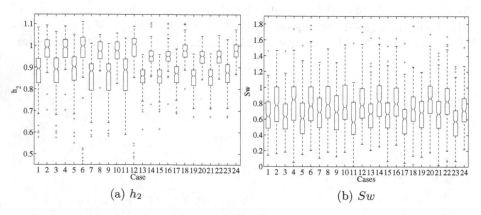

$(a)\ h_2$ $\qquad\qquad\qquad$ $(b)\ Sw$

Fig. 2. WTMM: (a) Hurst correlation exponent h_2; (b) Multifractality Sw

The results of WTMM multifractal analysis of posturograms are shown on the following figures 2a and 2b.

Correlation exponent h_2: At the eh people all ML medians are ~ 0.9, and APs are ~ 1, which is $1/f$, pink noise. Opposite to MDFA, the outliers are underneath. ML values are with greater dispersions, whiskers and outliers. At the yng people all ML medians are ~ 0.86, and APs are ~ 0.95. Outliers at AP are opposed to ML. The distinction between the medians of ML ($\sim 0.85.. \sim 0.9$) and AP ($\sim 0.95.. \sim 1$) is clear. Outliers are mainly underneath. Random permutations decreas h_2 to ~ 0.15, which is unexplained anomaly, as it is expected to be $h_{2rp} \sim 0.5$.

Comparison with the results of MDFA: h_2 from MDFA are ~ 1.7, which is a Brownian noise, only the phases are slightly smaller. Since MDFA is verified with the reference DFA and with an external (foreign) program realizing MDFA, then the differences in results from experimental signals are inexplicable, given that the methods showed similar accuracy, but with synthesized, not real (experimental) signals. Identical results for the two methods are that the ML are always smaller than the AP.

Multifractality Sw: ML is always less than the AP with $\sim 0.15.. \sim 0.25$. Outliers are mainly above. Permutation not only reduces the multifractality, but at ML even increases and equalizes with AP, which is absolutely inexplicable anomaly.

The results of MDCA multifractal crosscorrelation analysis of ML and AP components of the posturograms are shown on the following figures 3a and 3b. The cases for MDCA are:
1 - si,eh,null; 2 - am,eh,null; 3 - ph,eh,null; 4 - si,eh,stim; 5 - am,eh,stim; 6 - ph,eh,stim; 7 - si,yng,null; 8 - am,yng,null; 9 - ph,yng,null; 10 - si,yng,stim; 11 - am,yng,stim; 12 - ph,yng,stim.

The values of h_2 are ~ 1.68, which is a Brownian noise, only the phases are slightly smaller. The crosscorrelation at eh,stim is slightly lower, while yng,stim is slightly higher than the others. Stimulation increases the multifractality of the posturograms and their amplitudes, but decreases their phases. As it should be expected, randomization of the posturograms breaks of crosscorrelations apart of the multifractality as $h_2 \sim 0.49$, $Sw \sim 0.2$.

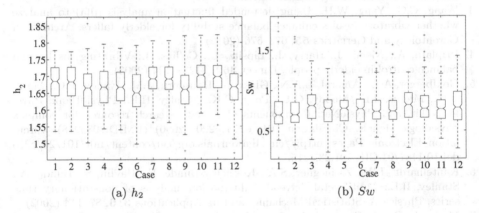

(a) h_2 (b) Sw

Fig. 3. MDCA: (a) Hurst crosscorrelation exponent h_2; (b) Multifractality Sw

4   Conclusion

The posturograms showed that they possess multifractal properties of the second type with nonlinear temporal correlations. The correlations h_2 from MDFA and the crosscorrelation from MDCA, showed Brownian motion type. This was verified by the reference DFA. This significantly differs by ~ 0.7 from those obtained with WTMM, but WTMM has shown that contrary to the ideal deterministic synthesized signal, there is a problem with the real noisy complex data, which in this case are relatively short.

On the other hand the multifractality Sw obtained with MDFA, MDCA and WTMM proved similar - ~ 0.8, so the issue of the discrepancy at h_2 remains open for further study. The fluctuations in the *Antero/Posterior* (AP, back and forth) direction were found to have larger values of h_2 and Sw than those of

Medio/Lateral (ML, left and right) direction, which coincides with their larger amplitudes. The change of $Sw \sim 0.65.. \sim 1$ to $Sw_{rp} \sim 0.2.. \sim 0.3$, shows that the random permutation destroys the multifractality of the posturograms. The multifractality of ML is always $\sim 0.15.. \sim 0.25$ less than AP and extreme deviations are mainly above.

Acknowledgments. The research work reported in the paper is partly supported by the project AComIn "Advanced Computing for Innovation", grant 316087, funded by the FP7 Capacity Programme (Research Potential of Convergence Regions).

References

1. Shelhamer, M.: Nonlinear Dynamics in Physiology: A State-space Approach. World Scientific (2007)
2. Amoud, H., Abadi, M., Hewson, D.J., Michel-Pellegrino, V., Doussot, M., Duchêne, J.: Fractal time series analysis of postural stability in elderly and control subjects. Journal Neuroengineering Rehabilitation 4 (2007)
3. Wang, C.C., Yang, W.H.: Using detrended fluctuation analysis (dfa) to analyze whether vibratory insoles enhance balance stability for elderly fallers. Archives of Gerontology and Geriatrics **55**, 673–676 (2012)
4. Priplata, A., Niemi, J., Harry, J., Lipsitz, L., Collins, J.: Vibrating insoles and balance control in elderly people. Lancet **362**, 1123–1124 (2003)
5. Goldberger, A.L., Amaral, L.A.N., Glass, L., Hausdorff, J.M., Ivanov, P.C., Mark, R.G., Mietus, J.E., Moody, G.B., Peng, C.K., Stanley, H.E.: PhysioBank, PhysioToolkit, and PhysioNet: Components of a new research resource for complex physiologic signals. Circulation 101, e215–e220 (2000) (PMID:1085218). Circulation Electronic Pages: http://circ.ahajournals.org/cgi/content/full/101/23/e215 doi:10.1161/01.CIR.101.23.e215.
6. Kantelhardt, J.W., Zschiegner, S.A., Koscielny-Bunde, E., Havlin, S., Bunde, A., Stanley, H.E.: Multifractal detrended fluctuation analysis of nonstationary time series. Physica A: Statistical Mechanics and its Applications **316**, 87–114 (2002)
7. Muzy, J., Bacry, E., Arneodo, A.: Relative change and difference. International Journal of Bifurcation and Chaos in Applied Sciences and Engineering 04 (1994)
8. Podobnik, B., Stanley, H.E.: Detrended cross-correlation analysis: A new method for analyzing two nonstationary time series. Phys. Rev. Lett. **100**, 084102 (2008)
9. Mathworks: boxplot. (Mathworks)

Author Index

Printed in the United States
By Bookmasters

Author Index

Printed in the United States
By Bookmasters

Printed in the United States
By Bookmasters